SOCIOPATHS
I'VE KNOWN AND LOVED

By K.L. Huntley

© 2017 K.L. Huntley

Author's Disclaimer: I invite you to travel through this fictional family labyrinth of mental illness, forgiveness and love. The characters are imaginary set in real geographical places for credibility. Any resemblance to people, living or dead is coincidental. A good story always has a little myth interwoven with a dash of reality. The reader should not consider this book anything other than a work of literature.

SOCIOPATHS I'VE KNOWN AND LOVED, All rights reserved. No part of this book may be reproduced or transmitted in any form or by any means without the written permission of the Publisher.

Brett Batchelor, Cover Design

Turtle Moon Publishing

Gail Burkett, Publisher
Laura Wahl, Art Director
Janis Monaco Clark, Editor

Printed in the United States of America

ISBN: 978-0-9913590-3-5

Library of Congress Control Number: 2017963620

I COULDN'T TELL THE TRUTH

NO ONE WOULD LISTEN.

SO

I WROTE A FICTION

It is wrong to assume that brainwashing is limited exclusively to governments, exotic cults and ensconced rebels. Brainwashing in fact, takes place frequently within the confines of everyday homes. This seems to have been true in my childhood home where it was done with such efficiency that it took me nearly 50 years to realize what was going on. More insidious yet was that it continued into the successive generations.

The objective, though, has always remained the same...
CONTROL!!!

Dedication

To Carole Ann and John and all the children like them.

I can't thank enough Janis Clark and Tom Newbill for their friendship, non-stop encouragement and help for bringing this manuscript to fruition.
It was love in action and I so appreciate both of them.

Introduction

The scars of childhood can be hidden and sometimes may fade, but they can never be ignored. You may not notice them for years at a time, however, they will unpredictably come roaring, rope red and unexpected to the surface at some point. It happens anytime those areas of the heart are re-invaded or opened again, intentionally, with the efficiency of a sharp scalpel crossing virgin flesh.

I've managed to hide my scars for endless, time-crawling decades. Few people were allowed to briefly see them and fewer still knew they were even there. The ugliness not only embarrassed me it went far beyond that. It was a shame deep inside my soul and I felt stigmatized. If you say you were a battered child eyebrows shoot up and eyes widen. In an instant you are moved from one category to another in the perception of your peers, friends, lovers and most of all your own children. My children never knew, nor my husbands. I have only recently been able to state the fact it even happened. Those who knew the shiny side, the sweet side, the glowing personality of my mother Isobel would never believe it anyway. They would think this is a fictional account. The only people who know the truth are my sister-victims and a few psychiatrists and psychologists I've seen over the years.

This isn't, however, exclusively the story or litany of my mother's battering ram. It is a story of brainwashing and survival, the story of successful escapes from a dim and demeaning environment. It is not the story of those who went on to continue the behavior, the so-called "battered child syndrome," but those who got away to live semi-normal lives. I use the term normal quite loosely because I've never quite figured out what that was.

Chapter 1

THE BEGINNING

Right now I am looking out the south window of my Montana cabin, facing a green lawn that needs mowing, a seven-foot-high wire fence surrounding my vegetable garden, and then a stretch of field reaching into the tree line. There is a hint of mountains beyond that, and the sky is telling me the storm is breaking up with a brilliant, silver streak outlining the dark purple gray clouds. This morning I feel a need to squint my eyes, being slightly assaulted by the light.

Blue sky and the always hopeful hint of sunshine is a pleasure to behold here in western Montana. The weather can change violently within minutes and the stark gray skies of winter can suddenly reappear as the azure blue darkens and the cottonwoods, with their lettuce green leaves, take on shadows. Then, crawling across the tree line will be the fluffiest, whitest clouds possible perched above an ominous gray base.

I see my family somewhat like that when I think about us and how we appeared to others. We were all beautiful white and fluffy on top but the hurt-filled tears, accumulating on the bottom of pain-heavy clouds were always ready, without notice, to explode and release their sorrow to earth.

A warm breeze blows now and all seems well. Then, as the air heats up there is a shattering strike of lightning and a clap of thunder that rattles the ground and reverberates through my very being. I was in a house once that was hit by lightning and only those who have had similar experiences know what I mean when I say the bones in your body actually vibrate from the percussion of the air.

This is the story that has many beginnings and as I write I'm not sure it has ended. I'd like to wake up sometime and know for sure the nightmare is over, but then there is the next generation, also heavily affected whose stories and dreams involved the same characters, the heroes and villains switching roles as rapidly as the weather changes. Yet all of us are connected as threads in the intricate tapestry across our lifetimes. The patterns change, the perceptions change, but nevertheless we are forever tightly wound together.

Are we really punished for the sins of our fathers or in this case our mothers? That concept hardly seems fair, but undeniably their actions do leave marks on us all, both positive and negative. We are formed, molded and remodeled then re-formed by our individual environments. We also have free will and are players in what we allow other people to do to us. As young people we have no such options yet as we mature, grow and move on we can choose which memories to hold onto and which to let go. And we know also those memories are different to each individual even living in the same environment.

That has been my life, a collection of storms and then tranquil blessings of sunshine. I've always managed to come through the thrashing violence of most turbulences to emerge on the other side of them stronger. Except for this time. This time, my very strength, my pier footings were knocked out from under me. I was shaken to the core when the clarity of truth came crashing like a herd of elk through my forest. I literally didn't see the lights of that proverbial oncoming train or the ensuing tragedy about to unfold. I was knocked down and sideways, dismembered by my illusions of happiness and trampled in the spring mud.

This is how it all began — that family storm.

Chapter 2

THE ARRIVAL

As we slowly crawled through the congested Friday evening traffic of southern California, the speed of my mind far outdistanced the speed of the cars. I glanced solemnly out the dusty car windows to the miles of earth-tone, stucco buildings and concrete walls. It all seemed so monochromatic and so homogenized. Yet, here and there, green vines crept to freedom over the confines of their roots. The green almost made me thirsty for vegetation. I barely noticed the vehicles on both our flanks, all seeming like robots in motion. The windows were rolled up on most of them and the drone of the engines was only occasionally broken by the throbbing beat in the younger folks' cars. A drum beat whose monotony escaped their interior and reached out to inflict itself on the other vehicles. The rhythm seemed to match the beating of my heart and the slow creeping throb in my head. For the most part I was ignoring the goings on as we rolled numbly to our destination.

My mind was racing with questions and emotions colliding and contradicting each other. There was no clarity of thought and no focus in my consciousness other than the question of how will she know it is me? My sister's and my voice were so identical that we had spent the last 50 years of our lives announcing who we were on the phone. "Hi Mom, it's me Kat" or "Hi Mom, it's me Noel." We always had to identify who was speaking to her to avoid the inevitable confusion. Even as young girls, sharing the same closet of clothes, if she wasn't paying close attention she would get us mixed up. Were those soft voices we had a blessing or a curse? Whatever, they were confusing to people and right now it was imperative there wouldn't be any confusion.

Noel and I weren't twin sisters by any stretch of the imagination. We were actually born almost three years apart. She was slightly taller than I, but everything else about us was similar. We shared the same room, the same clothes, make-up and occasionally the same hairstyle. One of our favorite tricks as teens was to switch the phone while talking to boyfriends. It was before the mute button and she could run off to the bathroom or get a drink of water while I carried on the conversation. Later we'd giggle and talk about our successful deceptions and adventures as we lay in our beds in the night.

But this time it was very different and much too critical. It was imperative in my heart of hearts that my mother know I was there at her hospital bedside. Mom was slipping in and out of our world with one foot here and the other in the next life. She was sailing unpredictably in and out of consciousness.

The phone call, dreaded by everyone at some point in their lives had come to me. It was almost curt but that is how Noel is in tense situations. Her words can cut clear to the bone; she didn't mince niceties just the simple unedited statement, "Our mother is dying."

Biting my upper lip I had barely, gently set the phone back in the cradle while trying to get my mind around the enormity of the situation when the phone rang again, almost causing me to jump. The next call came from Matthew, my sister Marilyn's husband. He started in immediately making excuses why I was hearing his voice, why he was calling and not Marilyn.

"Poor Marilyn has no money, no phone," and he was calling me to let me know she was back at the hospital with my mother. Mother had been taken in a little after 9:00 a.m. that morning and the neighbor, Brian Carper, had driven both my mother and Marilyn back to Community Hospital.

I thanked Matt for the call and forgot to mention, whether it was important or not, that Noel had already called me. Matt was a nice man but not one I'd call assertive. In my younger days I would have referred to him as a "milquetoast." He was easy to get along with, always affable and friendly. His only vice was his penchant for gambling, yet I immediately began to doubt what he told me. There were nagging questions in my mind. Marilyn didn't have a phone? She didn't have money? That was strange as she had access to all of our mother's money and Matt himself made more than an excellent salary. Then, of course, there was the "house cash." Our mother always had cash at her house. Well, what difference would it make if Matt knew Noel had already called me?

After the initial, but not totally unexpected shock of the news, I sprang into action. Clutching just a quick change of underwear and a black T-shirt, I stuffed a few things into my well-worn olive green backpack. With my hands gripping the steering wheel I drove three hours from my cabin in Montana, across the Idaho panhandle and then south to Spokane, Washington where the only airport existed for miles around. I had called ahead and Alaska Air had an open emergency seat waiting for me. With little money in any bank account I swiped my plastic charge card, not knowing when the balance would be paid. Budgets be damned, I thought. I needed to keep things in perspective. I didn't have time for tears, but there was a cold hand gripping my heart which was painful and the rest of me felt hollow inside. I knew and I felt strongly Mom would be waiting for me. She needed me there as much as I needed to be with her. It was always a given, an unsaid promise, that I would be with her at her at the end.

The plane edged skyward and six long hours later, which felt more like six long strung-out years, I touched down at the Ontario Airport in southern California, and with the intermittent screeching and jolting of the plane, my emotions came into focus.

Noel was waiting for me on the main lower-level floor and as soon as I walked through the gates I saw her behind the glass of the descending escalator. She looked weary, her black mascara was slightly smudged under her eyes and her shoulders were stooped making her appear much older than her sixty-two years. As our eyes made contact through the crowd her pensive expression softened and changed quickly from one of tension to relief. I wanted to jump past a few people or push them out of the way feeling an urgency to ground myself in her embrace.

Nothing else at that point had seemed real but the cacophony of sound after we landed; it seemed like 80% of the people pulled out their cell phones as soon as the airplane touched the ground. Silence went instantly to a montage of directions, greetings and what all considered to be their public breaking news. I reached for Noel and we instinctively touched hands. After a quick, uncomfortable hug we made our way out to the vast parking lot and into her battered, faded yellow, mini pick-up truck. Noel reached under her oversized blouse as we got between the parked cars and I heard the ripping sounds of Velcro. No wonder she looked stooped. She had on not one, but two black back braces double crossed under her shirt with a blue cardigan sweater over it all.

She was readjusting these cumbersome braces with swift expertise, first one side of the stretched elastic and then the other across her midriff.

"Your back is hurting you again?"

She gave an exasperated sigh then took a long, deep breath and simply said, "Still." Noel's lips pulled back in a slight smile yet her eyes betrayed her pain.

We didn't go into more detail of her chronic injuries and Noel hoisted herself into the cab grabbing first the steering wheel then pulling herself up. She dragged out a set of keys from the depth of her purse and preceded to unbolt the metal orange bar latched to her steering wheel, which was supposed to keep people from stealing your car. I couldn't help thinking who in the world would want it? Again with a little quiet groan my sister reached around and put the orange club in her back seat. It seemed so alien to watch this procedure when you come from an area like I do where some people still leave their keys in their cars. Noel then pumped on the gas pedal a few times, twisted the key hard in the ignition and the engine started coughing. She let it idle for a bit while she dug around her purse for a pack of cigarettes and lit one up with a quick apology. "Sorry."

"It's OK," I said. How could I complain?

We rolled almost silently onto the connecting street which took us to the on-ramp of the Riverside Freeway and towards the hospital. I reached into my green backpack and felt the round can of the SlimFast that I had the presence of mind to toss in. I didn't open it. I was afraid I might just throw up.

Still my thoughts raced on. How could I tell Mom it was me in her hospital room? It was me who was by her side. How will she know it is really me and not someone else? I had read that people in comas could hear and understand conversations around them. I wanted so much that my mother would know it was me. I wanted her to feel the love I felt only I could give her. That may or may not have been totally true, but I felt it was my love for her that she needed now. I had forgiven her years ago. I wanted her to know I was here with her on her walk and she wasn't alone — but how?

As these musings flew around my head like buzzards, I heard the melody of the ballad *Mary Hamilton* in the back of my brain. It wasn't unusual for me to think in terms of music and in lyrics, since I had done it from about the age of seven. I heard the high soprano voice of Joan Baez singing somewhere in my skull. I recalled the lyrics and the first day my mother and I really connected on the same plane. I was sweet sixteen and in love with folk music and folk musicians. In all probability, like all teenagers, I was playing the music a little louder than necessary. I fully expected to be in trouble the moment my mother entered my bedroom with her embroidered dish towel hanging loosely in her hand. I glanced nervously at the towel wondering if it was going to snap at me like a whip. However, this day Mom's face told me something quite different. It was childlike, soft and almost in rapture. Her blue-gray eyes were glistening, "Where did you get that music?"

I explained it was my new record album and it was a folk song from Scotland and did she want me to play it again?

My mother sat down quietly on my turquoise bedspread and listened. This in itself was a first, Mom sitting calmly in my room. No one was home but the two of us and it truly was a special occasion. Those same blue-gray eyes misted over again and a bit of sadness crept in. Ever so quietly she told me her grandmother in Aberdeen, Scotland had sung that very song to her frequently when she was a little girl, but not all the verses she was hearing now. She said back then, she didn't know why Mary was to be hung.

I played her the song over and over and from then on, when Mom and I were alone I would sing her the folk songs I was learning and sometimes together we would listen to my latest record. What cherished times these were for both of us. It was the beginning of a new relationship at a time when most teenagers are emotionally distancing themselves from their parents. I'd sing to her in the car when we drove home from our jobs in downtown Los Angeles. Yes, that might seem odd, however, there was a program at my school where I went to class four hours and then worked four hours learning a job skill.

I would sing to Mom at home and my singing was one of the only things she did not criticize or find fault with. We found a common ground and it was the turning point in our relationship. The beatings had stopped, my sisters had married had moved away and slowly the two of us began building a shaky bridge over the troubled waters that previously existed.

The following Christmas my mother gave me a record album collection that I have to this day, *Folk Songs and Minstrelsy* from Vanguard Records. It was an expensive gift for the time and together we often listened to it over and over enjoying the minstrels and the troubadours. I've kept that record for over fifty years. It is tattered and worn now, much like me. Scotch tape holds it together, but it is one of those things that remains a treasure, not of gold but of warm memories that like down, covers the sharp edges of pain.

I remembered one time Mom and I were driving down Denker Avenue in Los Angeles and I was singing *Motherless Child*,

"Sometimes I feel like a motherless child. Sometimes I feel like a motherless child — sometimes I feel like a motherless child a long way from home — a long way from home."

That one must have hit a frayed nerve or perhaps a bit of honesty, because her mouth tightened in a straight line and she asked me not to sing that one anymore.

Suddenly, I had an epiphany on the way to the hospital. That was it! In the drifting of my mind and memories I got the answer to the nagging question in my head. How to get word up to "Madam the Queen" that her youngest daughter was with her now. I made up my mind I would sing to her at the hospital, it had been years, but I would do it! I didn't tell Noel. I was just going to do it and not ask anyone's permission nor hear their negative comments. I wasn't sixteen anymore, I was a much tougher cookie and just a young fifty-nine.

It wasn't easy locating the multi-storied hospital in Riverside. Noel had been there before, but exhaustion, confusion and a different terrain from what we were used to had us driving up and down more than just a few streets. We could see the hugely lit and looming structure from a distance, but locating the Entrance Drive, not the Emergency Drive was a bit of a challenge. In our confusion there was what in Montana we refer to as "visual pollution." The colorful collection of moving neon signs were sparkling all around us and flashing in the dark. Neither Noel nor I were used to that. I was even accustomed to driving for hours without a single stoplight let alone dozens of them within a few blocks. The real challenge looming ahead of us was to find our mother.

It was after 7:00 p.m. by the time we actually got into the hospital. We had eventually parked after circling the lot several times near the entrance so Noel wouldn't have far to walk. The parking lot seemed rather empty and that turned out to be a good thing. Noel's handicapped card had been stolen and distance was a challenge for her. We got out, wove our way through the planters and yellow lights toward the huge, cathedral-like glass door entrance which was void of life.

No one was in the building and the doors gave the automatic swish sound as Noel and I quietly entered into the vast room. An empty receptionist desk sat in the center of the room, sterile like a marble crypt.

Minutes passed as we stood in awe and then, as if on cue, it was broken with the loud "bing" of the elevator doors echoing in a cave. To our amazement, who should walk out but my actress niece Julie carrying a vase with a fresh floral arrangement. Glancing briefly at us and showing little recognition, she walked quickly over to the marble desktop with the sound of her high heels echoing clicks off the marble walls. No greeting or words of affection were uttered towards her mother and me. No reaching out or stepping forward, she just stood looking coldly at us. My mouth wasn't working as I had gone into a state of temporary paralysis with shocked eyes and a locked jaw. I stood transfixed feeling rather stunned by Julie's sudden appearance, as it had been several years since I had seen her. She was still beautiful, brown eyed and less than a size five, but the years of habitual dieting and tanning salons were showing a little on her face and her dyed hair appeared dry and brittle. Nevertheless, Julie continued to remain striking.

Julie's painted red lips started moving. I expected a hello or some kind of greeting, but all we got was a quick and abbreviated explanation of "I can't take flowers in there." She could have been talking to anyone, or even herself. She was, however, addressing the two women who had provided her all the love and nourishment they could in her formative years, one of whom was her mother. With her short statement Julie spun on her stiletto heels and rhythmically disappeared just as rapidly as she had appeared, into the warmly lit elevator. The roar of silence was almost deafening as the door automatically closed and the lights at the top told us she was ascending.

Stunned might be an explanation as to what we were feeling. We also were clueless as to where, "there" was, but figured okay, logically Mom must be upstairs somewhere in this building. We had been so speechless and caught off guard, neither of us noticed to which floor Julie had gone. Maybe we could find a nurse's station? At first we didn't see a directory on the wall next to the elevator, but we both thought there must be somebody to help us with directions.

"Good God, we aren't on the set of the Twilight Zone are we?"

Noel didn't answer me but then spotted a chapel tucked away in the corner of the lobby. It was an unspoken yet mutual decision that we best go there, collect ourselves and say our prayers before facing the rest of the family. Noel and I were the only ones who currently still practiced our respective forms of Christianity. We were the only ones left with any religious philosophies at that time. Our mother was a proclaimed atheist up until last week and my sister Marilyn also openly voiced atheistic philosophies. I was tired of having to defend my faith from condemnation, having been actually attacked by Marilyn over and over again, so I took the subject off the table at every opportunity.

Mom was more polite and curious as to how I could maintain the Christian philosophy and still be "educated," in her words, as if the belief in God was a primitive primordial practice. Noel was simply put down as an "idol-worshiping Catholic with too many kids." Both of us, Noel and I, simply chose not to speak of our beliefs any longer with the family, a decision made almost thirty years prior.

We tried to apply our faith in daily living, but as everyone knows that can be a monumental challenge. I'm sure we were criticized behind our backs frequently, because that was standard operating procedure within the family. Everyone was talked about at one time or another and it would always take the negative road.

No one was off limits to the verbal shredding with the exception of Isobel. Yes, tragically and mistakenly, she viewed herself above all others. She was, in her opinion, the crown jewel and anointed child, the one who knew all, saw all and understood all. In the end, she was the one who judged us all.

Noel and I respected each other's differences and we really had never argued in our adult lives about our different church choices. We knew that each of us was a "believer," not an easy position at all in this particular heathenish and hedonistic family group.

We knew that at this very moment we would rely on prayer to get us through the challenges that lay ahead. She suggested we go into the chapel, sit quietly in meditation and say a prayer. Little did she know we would need all the help we could get, not just for the current dark and looming storm but also for the years ahead. We also would need courage to forgive the wretched and turbulent years behind.

The chapel was quiet with just a few padded pews and a central non-denominational altar on which sat a few lilies in a clear vase. There was a simple unadorned wooden cross and a backlit stained glass window. After sitting and collecting ourselves in the comfort of a spiritual environment, we rose and returned to the lobby slightly refreshed. We said little to each other and what we did say was in hushed tones. We crossed that cold lobby again and approached the same elevator where Julie had disappeared. We pushed the triangular button indicating up. Once inside the elevator we saw a list of floors posted on the wall, intensive care was on the third floor.

Up we went and when the heavy metal doors of the elevator automatically opened on the third floor, Noel and I both peered into another empty hallway. It was void of the expectation of bustling activity and for a hospital it appeared uninhabited. Was everyone asleep, including the personnel? There was a pervasive silence and it felt like a morgue. The hall walls were empty of art or signs and were painted a soft cream color. The floors were over-waxed linoleum reflecting the ceiling lights in wavy lines all down the never ending corridors. We might as well have been deposited in an uninhabited desert the place was so empty.

We walked up and down setting our feet gently down as if walking on cracked eggs. We didn't want to disturb — who? Noel and I were looking for information or signs and repeatedly drew a blank. The heavily shellacked pine doors were unmarked and closed. The entire hall was eerie and cold, again empty. Both of us looked at each other questioningly making frowning motions with our eyes and mouths.

Finally, we came upon a small group of people huddled together in an alcove with sofas and tables. Some were holding each other and there were plates of half eaten food and stale coffee cups spread across their end tables, a testament to the hours of ordeal they had endured. The invisible wall of grief said, "Don't come here. Leave us alone. We are clinging to each other like life preservers. We don't want or need you."

With heads down in respect we walked on, avoiding eye contact with the grieving group of people. Thinking Noel and I had the wrong wing we went back downstairs via the elevator again and looked at the directory for some clue. We needed a map to our mother's destination. Was the sign in the elevator misleading? No, it said, intensive care was on the third floor.

Not being quitters we decided to try again. We were bewildered that this hospital was nothing like we had ever been in before. In my small town, where everyone knew everyone else, there was always a steady stream of helpers. Where was everybody? Where was our own family? Where had Julie gone? Why didn't she wait for us, direct us or at least hug us?

Feeling like Hansel and Gretel making their way through the forest we came to a door marked Isolation Unit. Isolation! The mere word sent shivers down my spine: the state of being isolated, detached, separated or alone. My mother was there? I pressed an intercom button the size of my palm and the wall talked back.

"Who are you?" came the faceless voice. I found myself speaking into a lifeless, stainless steel grid.

"I'm looking for my mother." and then as if an afterthought, said her name, "Isobel Graham."

The voice gave us instructions. "Come in and put on the Hazmat suit in the inter-room, there are signs and directions. She is here waiting. When you are dressed in the jumpsuit, press the red button on the wall next to the double doors."

With that announcement and armed with instructions, the first set of sliding doors opened automatically and Noel and I found ourselves in what only can be described as a portal of pain. Stacks of faded medical green, one-size-fits-all Hazmat suits were on a white enameled shelf to the left of the door. There were old, black and bright yellow signs against the wall. Noel who had been pretty quiet up until now was making "tsk tsk" sounds and mumbling to herself as she shifted into one of the outfits.

Again, the wall grid spoke and I looked up to see a camera pointing in our direction. Funny, I thought, I was feeling hostile toward the camera. This one was obviously friendly and then I chuckled to myself. How could an inanimate object be friendly? Amazing how meandering thoughts zip around your mind.

"You will also need to glove up," the voice said. "There is a box of gloves on the top of the rack and in addition please put on the paper booties." Then the anonymous voice added, "You put them over your shoes."

Thank you, I thought sarcastically. I didn't see the "boot pile" so often found at the doorways where I live in Montana. Noel and my eyes met. We had the same questioning look. It was the look of panic reflecting back at ourselves and mirroring our emotions. What the bloody hell? What is wrong with our mother that they are treating her like a contaminated Petri dish? Good God – What the hell was going on? The chatter in my brain finally stopped as I focused on the problems at hand and the questions formulated into words.

"Did you have any idea she was so bad?" I whispered as I zipped up the baggy cotton overalls. "What is she infected with? Has anyone told you anything?"

Noel whispered in response as if the same speakers could be two-way and someone was listening.

"No. No one has talked to me in two days." Noel's zipper was stuck slightly and she jerked on it. "I called you knowing something was terribly wrong here. I called up to the house to see how she was doing and no one answered. Then I called her neighbor Esther and she told me Mom had been re-admitted to the hospital. No one called me." Well, damn, I thought. Not totally unusual there considering Noel and I had been left out of way too many things over the years. Vilified and trivialized, Noel frequently, and me sometimes, had been set on the back burner of family functions like pieces of discarded pottery. I felt like I was being transported into a Steven King novel. Whoosh – there went reality and welcome to a horror show.

My feet were swimming in the booties and the blue, mediguard gloves felt strange. My hands felt instantly warm but uncomfortable and there was the strong synthetic plastic smell coming from the box. These said loudly that you are about to touch something yucky and that yucky thing is your mother. I stashed my backpack up on the shelf where I had taken the Hazmat suit and pushed the red, but not easy, connection button on the hospital wall. We both looked like green Bobbsey Twins from the planet Mars as the doors opened and we were in the Isolation Unit.

It wasn't much of a walk, just a few feet when our long search for our mother came to an end. At last we were standing with other human beings in a well-staffed nurses station. Across from the dividing counter was another long counter and on the opposite wall above were banks of TV monitors and machines watching each patient carefully. Around the main operation base were three more separate small cubicles all visible in a semi-circle facing the nurses station. Each private cubical was closed off again with sliding doors and privacy curtains. The first held a young woman in her thirties, motionless in her bed, eyes closed with blonde hair circling her pillow. As I glanced at the young lady a nurse came from behind the counter and led us into the middle room.

There, lying very still was my mother, all in alabaster white in a metal hospital bed looking smaller than I ever recalled. Over her head was an additional bank of medical measuring equipment and monitors registering with green lines, bar graphs and numbers I didn't understand. I knew they were life and breath-measuring machines, but to what degree I was ignorant. The pumping sounds were rhythmic. Mom appeared relaxed in a dream world of deep sleep. Crawling out of her arms were a series of worm-like clear tubes with a variety of potions dripping down into her body.

Needless to say it was a shock to see my once so vital and powerful mother lying ill like a helpless child. My stomach lurched and I realized that I actually had never seen her in bed. The only times I had seen my mother sleep was in her older years when she fell asleep in her chair while watching TV. It is always disconcerting to see friends or family injured, but your parent or your child is an unfathomable stress. This illness was unexpected, and in all probability preventable, leaving me bewildered with so many questions. I realized this might be the last time we would be together on earth. I had to set my frightened little girl feelings aside and pull back on the rope. I knew in my heart I needed to be totally linear and unemotional, to dig deep and be professional, but at the same time let her know her youngest daughter, the one she called "little one" was by her side.

I cleared my throat — took a deep breath, set all my apprehensions and shyness into the back pocket of my blue jeans and then stepped, booties and all into her isolated room. It was the performance of my life on a stage not seen, the most important audience, my own flesh and blood. I swallowed hard, moistened my lips by pulling them nervously together and then opened my mouth and began to sing. It was the purest voice that had ever come out of me. I surprised myself by singing on key without faltering. From my soul I was reaching out to my mother with the sweet rose of music. I was singing for my dying mother but the angels gave me voice and strength. There was volume and there was clarity and it was me. The lyrics lilted not in the Joan Baez version but my steady alto voice.

Last night there were four Marys – tonight there'll be but three – There was Mary Beaton and Mary Seaton, Mary Carmichael and me.

Scotland reached across the pond and woke Mom gently from her slumber. As I came to the end of the chorus my mother slowly opened her eyes and a faint smile crept across her face as she recognized the ancient song of her homeland, the one I reintroduced her to some forty years earlier. Mom lifted her parchment-like hand and reached toward me whispering, "Kat, you are here." She knew. She knew I had come and I stood holding her hand, tears silently streaming down my face. My first mission was accomplished. Then breaking all the Hazmat rules I kissed her gently on her cheek.

Mom's smile didn't fade as she lay sunken against her white pillow and I continued singing. The next song I literally had learned at my father's knee as he strummed the guitar. The staff outside her door gathered and stood in silent respect. They hadn't seen her rally in hours and then she started talking.

"How did you get here?" was her first whispered question.

"Well, Mom, I flew down and Noel picked me up at the airport. She is here with me now. We are here together." I stepped aside so Mom could see Noel and motioned for her to join us.

Again, we were met with a weak smile but it obviously was taking most of her strength just to whisper a few words. We both held her hands as she drifted back into that dreamlike state in which we found her, contentment spreading across her face like a comforting quilt.

I thought it was amazing that such strength could be rendered to such fragility. Time, I thought, there is always the reckoning of time. What I see in her I will eventually see in myself. Noel and I had been with our mother less than thirty minutes and she was drained. She couldn't stay awake or conscious in spite of her determination and our efforts. With knowing glances and nods we decided to leave her and slipped quietly outside the cloistered room. Noel, exhausted and shaken, had spoken little to Mom but reached over, pushed back her curly hair and kissed her gently on her forehead.

"Goodbye," she whispered. "God Bless."

Now all of us are made of parts, and different personalities that we rely on for use at different times. We can be children at heart, parents, advisors, lovers and firm professional people. It was my assertive self, the one I save for difficult situations that stepped into me after the tender poignant moments with my mother. The "take charge" personality stepped forward with shoulders back. I wiped my tears with the ever handy tissue on the counter and approached the nursing staff. Mouth straight and with my practiced business mask I spoke, beginning with, "I need some information." Question after question was evaded and I was getting stock, rehearsed answers. I recognized their dodging as I was trained in that myself. Don't give out any real information. Only doctors are allowed to tell them — and then the files are held closely to their chests as they fold their arms. Thirteen years working in criminal law and you get to be an expert at having conversations which say nothing and the listener gets little if any information. It was an even match all of us holding professional and respectful ground. I wasn't taking the "there, there little girl" pats on the head very well.

Noel was silent but I felt her support like a pillar standing alongside me, her arms also crossed and her legs spread in a stance. I was leaning on her figuratively and she was content letting me handle the business end this time. Slowly and in my best legal-trained modulated voice, while also trying not to alienate the hospital staff, I began enunciating each word and gazed softly into the nurse's eyes.

"I need information on my mother straight on," I began. "I handle things best when told the truth. I want percentages here, I want to know what her chances of survival are. I need to speak to the doctor attending my mother." I paused and put on my best non-threatening look.

"The doctor just met with your family," was the reply.

"I'm sorry," I apologized. "I missed the meeting. I just flew in from Montana and I was not with the family when he discussed this and I want to see him NOW! Please page him." I didn't waiver nor raise my voice. I just emphasized a few syllables to let her know I wasn't playing any games. This was my "trump card" — to ask for the doctor and go over their heads. This was one standoff I wasn't backing down from. Then, to alleviate some tension and as if I was reading a well memorized script, I gave her my "courteous, but I do mean business smile."

She nodded and went back to her station leaving Noel and I standing together in solidarity in front of the counter. It wasn't long, maybe just a few minutes, when a kind man also dressed in a Hazmat suit came in and introduced himself. His tag identified him as Dr. so-and-so. And there he was holding the ever-present file against his chest. He began with, "I just met with your family."

I straightened myself again and attempted to appear taller. I deliberately held my shoulders back and took a deep, calming breath. That is when I apologized again, which seemed to be a habit of mine, but continued eye contact.

"I need to know my mother's condition. I haven't seen my

family and I've traveled from Montana non-stop. I came here straight from the airport. I don't know where my family is and I had a devil of a time just finding my mother. I'm not feeling particularly patient." At that point I'm sure I was biting my lip.

We stood eye to eye for a moment; I felt like I was looking into his soul and he was looking into mine. I could see he appreciated the candor and it wasn't necessary to beat around the bush. I continued, "I want statistics and I want percentages, please. I'm better with information head-on."

With that the young doctor informed me that my mother had C-Diff. I thought he said See-Death. I felt light headed and grabbed Noel's hand. She anticipated the move and gave me an encouraging gentle squeeze that said, "Hold steady, Sister. I am here."

"What is that? See-Death? I've never heard of that."

It was his turn to apologize. "No ma'am. It stands for Clostridium Difficile. We shorten it to C-Diff. It is a severe infection of the colon. She has had way too many antibiotics and all her natural fighters are gone. She needs a colostomy right now and we can't wait." He was a gentle man and let the information sink in.

I moved my jaw back and forth and shifted a bit on my tired feet. "I thought she had MRSA. That is what my sister Marilyn told me."

"She did and probably still does. MRSA is a staph infection resistant to antibiotics. She has been given so many antibiotics that they have killed all the normal flora in the colon and now it is severely inflamed."

My linear mind was still in operation and holding, even though I wasn't too sure how much longer my knees would. They felt like Jello rapidly melting in the sun. My mother had an infection in the colon but also a condition resistant to antibiotics. So what were her odds? It sounded as if she was damned if she did and damned if she didn't. "What are the chances of survival? Give me the percentages." It was a cold statement, but not without feeling and the doctor realized he was dealing with a woman who needed facts.

With eyes full of pity he quietly said, "Not good, 15% at best. I already spoke to your family down the hall. They thought it over and felt it best not to do any additional surgery. We have an added problem with her kidneys shutting down."

"Where is the family?" My throat betrayed me and I was aware my voice had moved up an octave and cracked.

"They are in the family hospice room where we allow privacy." He motioned toward the contamination prevention doors. "Just turn right out the door and you can't miss it."

The doctor touched my arm briefly in a sympathetic motion as he left Noel and me in the hall and went out of the unit himself. The swish of the doors broke the silence as they closed behind him. The nurses continued to busy themselves at the station watching all the remote life monitors connecting to the quiet bodies in the dimly lit rooms. Noel and I flapped our hands aimlessly and signaled that we wanted out of the Isolation Unit for now. Me, I wanted to run across the yellow ribbon and spring into a flowered meadow and pretend none of this was happening.

The heavy plate glass doors slid open for us again and Noel and I were permitted into the sally port to remove our Hazmat suits. Simultaneously we both started pulling and tearing away the costumes as quickly as we could, stepping out of them angrily when they hit the floor. We deposited them, more or less, into the forest green disposal bin marked again with the bright, orange biohazard sign. I found myself staring at the three circles meeting a fourth in the center. My mind wandered for a moment thinking of the Trinity. Maybe that is what we needed here, cosmic interventions because things were looking dim for our mother. We are visiting her dressed like aliens. Not at all how we were raised. We pulled the elastic booties off our shoes, wadded them up into balls and also threw them into the bins. I suppose it would all be burned tomorrow. The clothes you wore last to see your mother literally go up in flames. The visual concept made me feel again like vomiting right then and there. We signaled the staff and then we slid out the second group of double doors into the hall where we could breathe easier.

Noel had been standing way too long for her back condition. She was shifting uncomfortably from side to side and placing her hand on the wall for balance. Pain was etched across her beautiful face. As we entered the simulated freedom of the hospital hall, still bereft of people, her face went pale and she automatically reached out to both sides of the back brace and readjusted the Velcro supports. As she did she leaned against the wall and I looked about. The only chairs available were those at the very end of the hall and occupied by the other group of grieving people. I wondered if they were the young curly blonde's family. And I wondered if we could locate our own somewhere in this emotional inferno.

Chapter 3

THE FAM

Even though it was only about 8:00 in the evening in southern California, the hospital corridor on the third floor remained eerily silent and uninhabited. We turned to the right as instructed and headed down the hall as quietly as possible so as not to interrupt the sterile cavern with the sound of life. I asked Noel in whispers who had called her about Mom, having forgotten what she told me earlier. Every sound we made felt as though it had to be conducted in secret, vespers in a convent. I wondered if I was repeating myself again and having trouble focusing on all the details of the day.

"I told you it was her neighbor Esther. I called her because no one was at the house. Then I called Cyndie who had just found out the same thing from the other contingent. I called you next."

"Did anyone tell you it was this bad?" I was furrowing my brow trying to figure out why we hadn't been told the truth or better yet told anything. Nothing was computing at this point. Questions were whirling around my mind, questions without answers. What was the motive for not informing us? This whole thing had been odd from the get-go and logic seemed to be lacking, any logic at all. Was it just a jumble of confusion and everyone thought that someone else had informed us? Marilyn's behavior had been out of character for almost a year. And then there was the call two days ago when Marilyn actually told me she planned on returning to her home, leaving our mother alone.

Noel, always a little psychic, had called me anyway. She may not have had all the facts at the moment, but she knew she had been deceived and she knew our mother wasn't going to recover. This was so similar to what happened eighteen years earlier when our beloved Great Aunt Lillie passed on. It was Noel who called me then.

As we walked down the hall we were aware we were approaching the family in the alcove again. Thinking we missed the door to the hospice room, we turned around and walked back toward the Isolation Unit. Again – nothing! Were we blind? There were no other marked doors nor alcoves to protect a family. I couldn't even find a plastic chair. Did I not hear the directions correctly? I kept saying to myself, repeating in a recorded loop, "focus Kat – focus." I was sure the doctor had said it was just outside the door of the Isolation Unit.

In frustration, with all my muscles tightening, we turned and walked by the elevators for the third time. I then suggested we should go downstairs to the cafeteria and coffee shops in the basement. The thinking was that maybe our family had gathered down there. Maybe they had abandoned their comfort room for a change of scenery. At least I could get a cup of coffee.

But, like everything else in this immense building, the cafeteria was closed, the doors locked and the lights out. The only thing we could see were two large over-lit, plastic vending machines. Neither of us wanted the lukewarm institutional dribble sold from those. What I really wanted now was a cold beer and I knew Noel was getting fidgety and probably needing a cigarette.

"This doesn't make sense Noel. The family knows we are here, where are they?" I was feeling irritated. "Julie saw us. Surely she told them we were here. Why wouldn't she?" Realizing I was getting loud I dropped back into the church whisper. Nothing was making sense and I was trying to figure out why this group wasn't searching for us. Coupled with the pain of Mother's bleak situation, we both were feeling equally abandoned.

It was uncharacteristic for my chatty sister to be so quiet for so long. She was picking at the chipped bright enamel on her nails. I also knew she was fighting to stay on her feet, fighting pain and trying to stay focused on the absolutely insane scenario in front of us.

"I don't know Kat, but we have definitely been abandoned."

I couldn't help thinking that we somehow and for some unknown reason to us, had become personae non gratae in what I always thought was a tight-knit family.

Boy, I thought, that was an understatement. What was plaguing me further was why? Why wasn't someone coming after us or looking for us? Nothing was making sense. We had done nothing to alienate them — no name calling or finger waving. Good Grief! What was going on? Julie would have announced to the rest of the family we were in the building. Why wouldn't she? Yet no one came for Noel and me. They were held up somewhere, but the question was where? We were being ignored and snubbed without a clue. Our opinions dissipated in the wind. Sister Marilyn was the Durable Power for Mom's medical and had been calling all the shots. We really had no power or say in the matter.

Beyond hunger now there was a growing hollow feeling deep in my stomach. My mouth felt dry and I ran my tongue around, swallowed hard for control, cognizant that being in control here was going to be a battle. Once again I was experiencing the feelings of fright and nausea that I had as a little girl when our mother would leave us alone for hours at a time.

Finally, after what seemed another hour of walking in circles, a gentleman came towards us down one of the turns in the corridor. It was nice to see a walking, breathing person. Our first thought was he must be the hospital chaplain. He was a little on the portly side, clean and dressed conservatively, wearing a suit and tie. His professionally manicured haircut was recent, showing a little gray at this temples and his measured speech and controlled manner simply reminded me of the sophisticated clergy I had been around most my life. He walked right up to us.

"Are you looking for your family?" he asked quietly, but above our now accustomed whispers.

The eternal humor, black at best, came sliding out of my mouth. "Yes," I replied "and at this point any family will do, but how did you know we were looking for ours?"

The gentleman's smile spread softly across his face as he gazed into my eyes. "You have Julie's eyes," he said. With that statement Noel turned to face him directly and a bit of embarrassed color came to her cheeks as she instinctively flung her hand up to her mouth. "Oh! I'm so sorry. You are Julie's boyfriend. I didn't recognize you."

There was a gentleness about this man and a deep-seated presence of peace. Yet we could tell that he too felt uncomfortable on the mission for which he was sent. Why would a total stranger be sent out to meet two grieving sisters when there was a whole family in a room somewhere that could have done the same? He had been sent to find women he didn't know, one of whom he had met briefly months before and the other he didn't even have a picture of. How awkward and uncomfortably strange that must have felt to this obviously professional man. This added to our first sense that there were deeper problems aboard. I liked him immediately and it wasn't because he thought I had the same eyes as Julie. He had the manners and more importantly the vibrations of a quality person and I was trusting my instincts.

Julie's gentleman, in the full sense of the word, ushered us back towards the Isolation Unit to a faded pine door with absolutely no markings. We must have passed it a half dozen times in our search. It blended in so well with the plain decor that it easily could have been the custodian's closet. With all the gallantry the man could muster he turned the worn knob and swung it open, then courteously stood aside to let us in to the room filled with familiar faces and the members of our own immediate family.

The room itself was still austere, but some attempts had been made here, to take the edge off dire situations. The walls were muted and two-toned with inexpensive prints on a few of the walls. I didn't need Poussin's cherub painting and all the dark colors, but obviously someone had made attempts to give the room a warmer feeling than the sterile surroundings. Seemingly, because it was in a contaminated area, every surface required that it could be wiped with disinfectant. There were no warm fabrics or carpeting on the floor.

Marilyn was sitting opposite the door as we entered. Her arms were crossed across her chest, her face drawn, and she seemed quite small in between her son Dan and husband Matt.

No attempt was made by anyone in the room to get up or to welcome us even though their heads snapped up and we were met by multiple pairs of look-alike eyes. The aura of the room continued to make us feel as unwelcome usurpers in a foreign land. You might say that Noel and I were "party crashers." Not one welcoming step was made or motion in our direction for way too long. Paralysis seemed to overtake one and all. I couldn't help thinking of the deer-caught-in-the-headlights look so many of us are familiar with in Montana. You could have heard a pin drop. Did we walk into the middle of an intense conversation not meant for us to hear? Were we the subjects of the conversation or was it our mother? Our mere presence seemed surprising to the assembly as if we had just dropped in from another place and time. Talk about "awkward moments," this one was classic.

It was Julie, thankfully, who eventually got up first and glided toward her mother and me. With a quick hug, the rest followed in dutiful, if not enthusiastic, succession. Oh yes, Julie the actress gave the first cue. Was it possible she hadn't told them we were here? Once again I chalked off the strange behavior to stress. I had seen things in the past under similar circumstances that didn't seem appropriate. Well, I thought, maybe there would be an icebreaker. Matt got up from the black leather sofa leaving Marilyn sitting and came to give us both a warm, genuine hug. We had always been great friends or so I thought. I also suffered from the illusion that Marilyn and I were close. It was clear under these circumstances that comfort, both emotional and physical was not coming from this group as a whole, not at this point and time.

The gray awkwardness of the meeting descended into the room like a sky getting ready for a summer thunderstorm. I could feel the hair on the back of my neck raising but I couldn't identify the cause. I had to brush all aside for the moment and think perhaps it was just my exhaustion from the trip. God, was I slipping? I thought. I hadn't spoken to any of these people in months with the exception of Marilyn and Matt. But, it was apparent that all of them had been informed of their grandmother's condition and had gathered at the hospital quite early in the day. Their chain calls of information were working for the lot, however, they excluded Noel and myself. Apparently our appearance registered as a surprise to one and all and they obviously hadn't planned on seeing us. They were probably each wondering which one of them had called us. Which one of them had been the snitch?

Was that some sort of twisted betrayal? Later, in retrospect, I could see that Marilyn probably fed them some story as to why we were unable to be with our mother at her deathbed. I really never saw Marilyn as a liar. That is true, I really never did. However, as I interviewed people from her past, puzzle pieces fit together revealing a different picture of Marilyn's history. Her lies were so convincing that I imagined viable reasons were given for our absence and they were proclaimed and accepted as gospel. Our vilification began early in her planned program and it was our naivety at the time that we didn't see it.

Marilyn eventually rose slowly from the sofa with the assistance of her son Dan. She appeared worn, her hair greasy and her clothes rumpled. She hadn't put on any makeup and her color was pale in the fluorescent lights. Her entire demeanor was that of one encased in grief, the sagging shoulders, sunken sad eyes and trembling mouth. She crossed the small room where Noel and I were still standing by the door. Neither of us were embraced nor really greeted by her. She didn't say she was glad we were there, that my mother's other two daughters had made it. She simply opened her mouth and recited robotically, almost word for word, what the doctor had said about Mother needing an emergency colostomy and that her chances of survival were not good at all. The rest of the group listened respectfully to her explanation, nodding as if they were listening to the rehearsed State of the Union Address.

When she finished her explanation, I told her we already had spoken to the doctor and were given all those facts and information. Her facial expression changed completely. We had caught her off guard. I had the facts already? She didn't need to be the Mother Superior delivering them? How could that be?

In front of the group I thanked Marilyn for giving Noel and me the courtesy to let us know Mom's condition and that Noel and I both agreed with their decision to decline the option of an operation. Again Marilyn looked quite surprised; Noel just stood looking at her own two children, her son not even moving towards her.

Finally, every one began to shift around on the available sofas and chairs so we could both sit. We hadn't sat down since entering the hospital an hour earlier and Noel and I both let escape audible sighs of relief, hers more intense as she lowered her pain-racked body. She reached up under her shirt and the only sound in the room was Noel's Velcro once again ripping as she readjusted the braces holding her body together.

Chapter 4

1957 – THE ACCIDENT

Teenagers around the world are similar in many respects. They all feel invincible and believe that accidents only happen to others and never to themselves. That was the case with Noel in the early winter of 1957. She borrowed Dad's 1938 blue Dodge Coupe and drove the two hours from Los Angeles to the community of Big Bear in the San Bernardino Mountains with two of her friends. They planned to go tobogganing most of the day.

Their day at Big Bear was pure fun, giving the "city girls" a taste of real winter and some playful time in the snow. It was the last run of the day and Noel was on the front of the rental toboggan. They had spent hours flying down the same hill and the snow had hard packed from the action forming an almost hard plastic surface. It was so slick that the sunlight mirrored on it causing them all to grimace and close their eyes when they really shouldn't have. Noel's two girlfriends each had their legs spread out and around Noel as they clung together looking for the last thrill of the day.

As the girls sped and whirled down the slope at now breathtaking speed, the side of the toboggan hit a small bump of ice that had frozen solid. It acted like a big rock and when the toboggan hit, it propelled up and over causing it to tip wildly onto one side. The back two girls let go and flew off into the snow while Noel gripped the front handles attempting to change the erratic direction she was heading. A huge Ponderosa pine loomed dead ahead and it didn't occur to her to roll off in the split seconds it took. She clung on for dear life and it was the wrong decision as the crash was immediate and painful. She lay like a rag doll dazed at the base of the tree well. The toboggan's front was smashed with splinters of wood lying about, the frame was bent, and the braces were cracked and broken. The tree was virtually unscathed except for a slight scrape on the reddish bark. It was Noel who also was broken. How she got up or even moved was miraculous.

Cold, numb and dazed Noel didn't even realize the extent of her injuries. Her girlfriends helped her back to the Dodge in the now emptying parking lot. Noel was the only one who could drive in the group and the only one who could get them home. Her girlfriends helped her into the driver's seat and she made the painful journey back to Los Angeles delivering her friends first and then driving slowly back to our house.

I was home alone when Noel returned that late afternoon walking stiffly yet stoically into our house. It didn't take a rocket scientist to know she was badly hurt, the extent of which I was totally ignorant. I was barely thirteen years old at the time. She limped through the house directly to our bedroom and crawled into her bed moaning. I was scared but I knew my mother would be home from work within the hour. I got Noel some aspirin, water and then put my favorite brown and green afghan over her.

When my mother got home from work she checked Noel and diagnosed her as just having a twisted muscle and that Noel would be better the next day. But Noel wasn't getting better and I was worried. Noel was in bed for three days before I convinced my mother she needed to see a doctor. Being young we honestly thought our mother's medical knowledge was extensive. She was working for orthopedic doctors but in a secretarial position. She had told us she had nurse's training twenty-five years earlier, however, she had been there for only a short time before being kicked out for insubordination. The little white aspirins dutifully delivered by Mom and me to Noel were evidently not helping her nor were the warm washcloths I kept laying on her back. I finally went into the big bathroom and dug out the red rubber hot water bottle with the black stopper and started applying it to her back.

Now there is a story within the story here. I really hated — hated to even touch the hot water bottle. The mere sight of it sent a nauseous feeling that I had to fight down. The damn thing had been used on me again and again in what I consider an undue amount of enemas. We couldn't possibly have been that constipated. Hadn't our mother heard of apple juice or apples? I say that in jest, but that old hot water bottle was filled all too frequently, the faded red tube attached to the black stopper and a grooved tip attached to the other end was routinely shoved up our little butts. Now I know there is a group of people today that feel this is a healthy way to "cleanse" their systems. They can have it! We were forced to lie naked on the cold tile floor of our bathroom, warm water filling our little bodies until we could no longer hold it and then flying to the relief of the porcelain bowl.

One of the most humiliating and demoralizing events in my young life involved just such a scene. My mother was going to "instruct" one of the neighbors on how to give an enema and I was to be the model. Can you imagine? I was somewhere around seven years old. I was marched down to my best friend's house, two doors down. We went into her pink and black ceramic tile bathroom with her and her mother. I was stripped of all my clothing and made to lie down naked on a little towel they put on the floor. I was so embarrassed I wished I could die right then and there. The tile was stone hard on my skinny little body and I could feel my pelvic bones against the cold surface with the chill running right through me. Then, with my girlfriend looking on and my mother casually chatting incessantly about nothing, the black tip was inserted up my butt and the warm water began filling my cavity. I had to close my eyes and pretend to be somewhere else it was so horrifying. Just when I felt like I could stand no more she pulled it out and in front of my girlfriend and her mother I found myself exploding shit all over their toilet.

The embarrassment was too much. I couldn't make contact with my little friend's eyes and was so humiliated I didn't come out of my room for days. In later years I wondered, did my mom walk down the street swinging the hot water bottle back and forth for all to see? The bottle duplicated as her douche bottle so how did that work? Had she put it in a sack or some kind? It made me sick to even think of it.

Now I dug out the hated instrument from the big bathroom and filled it with hot water for Noel who wasn't getting any better. Marilyn was busy at college and didn't seem too concerned and Mom was busy with her job. Dad was working swing shift and between his boat and work wasn't home too often. He always checked us by "peeking in" our bedrooms when he got home at 2:00 a.m. but nothing would have seemed out of the ordinary with both of us sleeping. For all he knew we could have been dead. Poor Dad — always kept in the dark along with so many others.

By this time I'm sure Mom was missing coming home to Noel's warm dinner that she always had ready for her at 5:30 p.m. sharp. On the fourth day with no improvement Mother loaded Noel into her car and drove her downtown to work, with Noel complaining the whole way. Noel was hurting with every bump and twist in the pavement. Mom kept saying it was probably nothing and we were overreacting and where did we think the money was coming from? Who did we think was going to pay for the doctor? She had a regular and routine speech as to why we shouldn't go to the doctor, along with not wanting to "bother" the doctor. We were actually raised thinking that seeking medical help was a "bother" for them. It never occurred to us until later that these people were in the business to help others get well.

My mother continued with her tirade. "Noel just wanted the same attention Marilyn got and what was she thinking? Poor Marilyn had just gone through hell with her back surgery and now there wasn't much wrong with Noel and she was whining when poor Marilyn had slipped discs, etc., etc., etc." What are the odds there could be two in the same family?

I think that particular day the entire speech must have fallen on Noel's deaf ears as she leaned her face against the window of the car during the excruciating journey to downtown Los Angeles and the orthopedic doctors.

Of course, once there the doctor's exam and x-rays showed something quite different from our mother's diagnosis. Noel wasn't faking her pain at all but in fact had three broken vertebrae in her back. The bones were fractured and she was lucky she hadn't damaged her spinal cord. She was tightly laced into a full-body corset that she would wear for the next two months. It wouldn't be her last fracture, but rather the first in a long line. In truth Noel would never fully recover. Back pain became a constant companion and injuries would plague her the rest of her life.

It wasn't like Marilyn's back injury, which was also diagnosed around the same time, yet both had all the earmarks of neglect. I think it is fair to defend my mother's medical negligence as she may have been neglectful out of a mixture of ignorance and arrogance. Isobel continued to chronically suffer from the illusion that she possessed an insurmountable amount of medical knowledge and enough, quite frankly, to be an excellent doctor. She repeatedly told us this and being children, of course we believed her. She brought home all the medical journals from her work and read them cover to cover. There was also the dusty and worn Grey's Anatomy that stood proudly in her bookcase.

I said earlier that she was kicked out of Catholic nursing school for insubordination. She always said it was because she hid some cookies in her Kotex box but that couldn't have possibly been the truth. A good story for young daughters but we will never really know the whole truth.

What was astounding is that my mother was so convinced of her own medical capabilities she was even able to convince others. A great imposter at work.

Marilyn's back injury didn't come on dramatically as Noel's. Marilyn not only had ballet lessons she also simultaneously took gymnastics and acrobatics. Her long limber body provided her the perfect ability to actually do a back bend, grab a small paper cup with water in her teeth and raise back up without spilling it. Marilyn was quite the rave at the grand recitals the ballet school produced twice a year. The studio lights were dimmed and the spotlight set to Marilyn's routines with music. She was as impressive as any Olympic gymnast or at least I thought so. There was no television in our home back then so there wasn't anyone to compare with as she expertly tumbled and did incredible splits. I was always so proud of her as I sat in the audience watching her spine-bending manipulations, the graceful, lithe little fairy dancer.

For several years our household functioned exclusively on ballet and acrobatics. The satin and tulle costumes were all assembled in the back bedroom on the old White sewing machine. We all sewed individual sequins on the tutus and bodice of the acrobatic outfits. The smell of pure lanolin filling her pink satin ballet shoes permeated not only Marilyn's bedroom but the house. I'd watch with awe as my sister practiced both at home and in the studio where I tagged along. I thought she was beautiful and convinced that she, along with my mother, would both be famous.

Watching Marilyn from the sidelines I learned the steps, first position, tour jete and plies. I wasn't, of course, allowed to have lessons; I assumed it was because I was too young. The spotlight remained exclusively on Marilyn. Noel also took some little tap dancing lessons, but was told she was too big, awkward and uncoordinated to continue. She was in only one recital where she was a "Dutch boy." Mom made her a pair of pants from cotton with stiff pellon sewed to the sides so they stood out like wings in the air. Watching my sisters was somewhat like watching performances of a butterfly and a frog. There was quite the contrast there and I was viewing it from the sidelines. I felt sorry for Noel.

By the time Marilyn was in the eighth grade, she started experiencing a great deal of pain her in lower back. Tragically the warning signs of injury were overlooked until it could be ignored no longer. My mother took Marilyn to a chiropractor. Again, something went terribly wrong and I can only tell parts of that story in retrospect. I know that no one suspected Marilyn had slipped a disc in her lower back. No x-rays were taken. I won't blame here, just stick to the facts as well as I remember them. The result of this mishandling was that Marilyn left the chiropractor's treatments with a second and undiscovered slipped disc. She began walking with a decided bent and the ballet and acrobatic lessons ended. She took up art and immediately was given art lessons along with her music. But physically Marilyn didn't stand upright for several years. She slowly deteriorated during her high school years and then somewhere along the line she was given prescription pain pills.

When Marilyn graduated from high school my mother went to work part time for the orthopedic doctors in Los Angeles. The reason for this was to help Marilyn through college. We were all so proud of both of them. Marilyn, however, developed excruciating pain and her boyfriend at the time began carrying her upstairs to some of her classes. Mercifully, a diagnosis was made in her freshman year of college and a surgery was performed. The damage was extensive, the surgery long and she required several pints of blood. We were all so frightened and grateful when she finally came home.

None of us expected then to have to witness her withdrawals from the pain pills prescribed months before. Not much was known about drugs then nor addictions. She sat on a straight chair in our darkened living room for what seemed like hours and days just crying. Crying constantly as her body withdrew and her back began to heal. She was nineteen.

In a few weeks she began to walk upright again and her attentive boyfriend, just about to graduate, spent a lot of time at our house with her.

Within that year Marilyn was married and had her little son Dan in her arms.

Chapter 5

THE HOSPITAL

After the initial conversations about Mother's diagnosis there was an uncomfortable lull. Marilyn cleared her throat several times as we all sat stiffly around the family room at Community Hospital. No one really had anything to say, and after a few false starts there was an ensuing quiet. After about five or ten minutes Marilyn's authoritative voice broke the silence and she proceeded to inform Noel and I in front of everyone that there were to be staff changes in the Isolation Unit now and that no one would be allowed back in to see Mother this evening. She said if things got worse, the hospital staff would call the house and they were all going to meet us up there. I figured at that point it was information she had been given earlier.

It was indeed late and I hadn't eaten all day. That, along with the time difference between Montana and California, made me ravenous. My stomach actually was in pain and felt like it was poking against my backbone. There was a murmuring in the family and everyone seemed to agree that we would caravan back to our parent's home in Yucaipa and eat there. Noel concurred it was a great idea.

Marilyn looked at Noel again with surprise and arched her eyebrows. "You're staying at Mom's?"

"Yes," was all my usually assertive sister replied, "I am staying." She didn't raise her voice or spit the words, she just made a calm statement.

I was thinking that my two sisters were sharpening their claws and that any moment something was going to fly. I had been the liaison between them many times over the years, and to my relief it didn't happen then and there. I thanked God in my mind and picked up my backpack. Noel stood and grabbed her oversized leather purse and everyone made their way down to the ground floor, out to their cars and threaded their way to the family home. At least we thought everyone did as we weren't actually counting the cars or who was in them.

Getting back on the freeway was a breeze compared to the difficulty finding the hospital in the first place. From there we simply headed south to find familiar territory. For almost forty years off and on we drove these roads and the route to the house my father built, a sprawling Spanish style home on a hill overlooking the town. It had been the long held dream of both my parents. Each bedroom was designed so spaciously that all three could hold a king size bed, bookcases and dressers. Each also had wall-to-wall built-in closets with ample storage cupboards overhead. My father, an eclectic man of many talents, actually built it over a five-year period. It was literally his castle and definitely my mother's status symbol. Well, on thinking about it, I would say he built the mansion for her. Dad would have been much more comfortable in my Montana cabin with too many cats and a couple of dogs watching over a few cows and horses. None of his children actually ever lived in this beast of a house. I frequently referred to the house as a "mausoleum" because it was never warm but rather chronically cold and uncomfortable like most castles.

We had all stayed there for short periods of times during a variety of events and adverse circumstances. Several of the grandchildren stayed for years while they went to college and trade schools with my mother generously assisting them. Both my parents were supportive on all fronts of their grandchildren's educations. I don't know when they made that shift, but shift they did and credit must be given where credit is due.

I stayed in the home briefly when my children were tiny and I was gravely ill. Even though the home was capable of entertaining hordes, and occasionally did, we all remained visitors and on visitor status. Nothing but good manners and approved conversations and absolutely no liquor or profanity were allowed.

The formal living room of the house was more than spacious. It held two sofas, two easy chairs, an upright piano and a full flagstone fireplace along one wall. That room, however, was only used for company. Most of the living was done in the family room with its adjoining kitchen. There was also a formal dining room with a carved Spanish antique dinette set and buffet. They weren't antiques when purchased but seventy-five years later they qualified nicely.

Basically, my parents lived in the den and kitchen and after my father died and Mother aged, most of the house was closed off. Everything remained for "show" and all staged for appearances, as were our lives for others to look at.

It was here, the site of so many Kodak moments over the years that we returned, late and in the dark. Our cars, both Noel's and her son's, pulled into the graveled driveway together. Not a light had been left on and out in this area, darkness takes on a whole new meaning. Noel was exhausted as she stepped carefully out of her truck; I could tell by the way she slid one leg out, touched the ground and then dragged the other to follow. We grabbed our bags and with Julie and her brother behind us negotiated our way down the tiered steps to the front door twenty feet beyond.

The carved door from Mexico was firmly locked and so was the window next to it. Everything was bolted tight. Noel's younger children volunteered to go around to the veranda in back and get the house key, hidden always on the top pillar near the back door. A spare key had been there since the pillar was cemented in place thirty or more years earlier. Everyone in the family knew where it was, it wasn't a secret but rather common knowledge. Nothing like the secrets that were going to slowly unravel themselves and then snarl again in the following days and nights to come.

It was really nasty and unpleasant to reach up and get the key, though. You could feel the cobwebs and there were black widow spiders. Bats had adopted the opposite corner for a habitat and it was a great bug eating area. I usually came away with webs on my fingers so was more than delighted that someone else volunteered to do it.

Noel whispered to me, "Did you bring your key?"

"Yes. I just didn't know who knew we had them. Things are really weird here. I don't know…" I thought I'd play dumb on the key issue.

"Mom gave it to me just before the hip surgery, Kat. She had a little piece of red yarn tied to it. She said I might need it and she wanted me to have it, that's when I mailed it to you." The question occurred to me, why would Mom have done that? Did she forget the spare key was on the porch? The locks hadn't been changed. Maybe she was afraid the spare key would go missing.

We heard giggling from the back of the house and didn't know if they found the key or not. They weren't returning very fast to where we stood. "OK," I answered groping my hand around the backpack's bottom and shaking it a bit so I would be guided by the jingling sound. I felt around locating my wallet in the dark, then my makeup bag, and finally the ribbon with the brass key. With a flourish I pulled it out, inserted it in the lock and opened the door. What difference would it make for anyone to know we also had a key? But around the back the "kids," who were all pushing forty, were acting as if they couldn't get in. Interesting. For what purpose? The deceptions were piling up and I added my first to the accumulating pile.

As we entered, Noel started flicking the bank of switches by the side of the entrance door and the property lit up. With a click the cement cherub in the fountain came to life first, then the coach lights on the walkway. Last came the light flooding down the interior hall and illuminating the steps through the glass panels by the door. I grabbed Noel's satchel with my free hand and headed down the series of halls for the back guest bedroom. It was the room Noel and I always got as if by assignment. I put her satchel, bags and backpack on the bed together like we always did and then headed for the family room and the thermostat.

As I said earlier, Noel and I grew up sharing the same bedroom so it wasn't unusual for us to share at Mom's. We had even shared clothes growing up with minimal squabbles. Above the beds at my mom's house were pictures of all her grandchildren and in the center the word *Love*. They were lovely, professionally taken and each one a work of black and white art. It was a comfortable room.

By the time I got back to the den the lights had been turned on along with the heater. Noel's son who had lived there during his high school and college years had started everything going, including a small fire. We all tumbled into the heavy upholstered chairs and Noel stretched out on the sofa at the end of the room.

Once tall and lithe, her body had now compacted two inches shorter than mine. She had thickened in the waistline and the cumbersome brace made her shoulders appear pinched toward her head. She was still beautiful and took the time to put every bit of makeup in place, her tiny jeweled earrings and a new frosted hair color and cut were flattering. She may have been caving in on the inside but not on the outside.

No one's spouse or companions were with them. Everyone was by themselves and it felt good and relaxed, as it had been when the kids were young. It was always Noel and I dragging our combined six children to parks, kite-flying events and just having good old fashioned times. The conversation started out relaxed as I relayed my excursion and flights. I had told the story of the poor lady who had screamed as the airplane hit an air pocket and she grabbed my arm. I told them how everyone at the airport had been so courteous and helpful to me, snippets of this and that conversation with all of us staying away from the topic of Grandma. After about an hour of unwinding, it was apparent that Marilyn, Matt and Dan hadn't followed us as they indicated at the hospital.

I struggled into the kitchen announcing for all to hear that I was starving and would see what I could stir up for all of us. Opening the refrigerator I stood staring into the fluorescent-lit white chamber. Empty! For all intents and purposes, like basic eating, it was empty. Sure, there were butter and the usual collection of condiments on the door shelves, even some eggs, but the usually packed refrigerator was virtually empty. I must have blinked a time or two in total shock before I opened the cross top freezer. Certainly there was something here to eat. There I was met with a dozen or so little packages each wrapped in plastic wrap and stacked like little blocks. Apparently, it was chicken or something because they all looked white and not appetizing in the least. I didn't notice if they were labeled or not — it just looked like toy food to me, some little kid's project.

Now, my mother was an extremely organized person. Her repeated mantra over the years had been "a place for everything and everything in its place." In fact I still hear it in my head now and then — along with a collection of other "gems." Mom always kept on hand enough food to feed a small army of relatives on a moment's notice. Her Scottish nature and fear of famine caused her to be a great shopper and to stockpile food, her pantries were always full.

With this in mind and my grumbling stomach, I then opened the rolling pantry shelves in the corner of the kitchen. You can imagine how I felt to find they too were virtually empty! Drawer after drawer, shelf after empty shelf. No tuna, no bread, no fruit, not even her staple of bananas. Basically there wasn't much to eat — or anything for that matter. I didn't want to panic or even concern the others with the revelation so I just went in and talked to Noel's son. I knew he was doing quite well in his new business.

"Got a credit card sweetie or any money?"

"Why Auntie Kat?"

"Well, there isn't any food here and if we don't get some soon I'm going to have visions of the Donner Party. I feel like Mother Hubbard because these cupboards are more than bare. I'll be barbecuing the cat here shortly."

He laughed and appreciated my humor. "OK – no problem. I'll have Dominos here in minutes."

"Order a big whatever. Marilyn and gang should be here any minute."

I then proceeded to feed my mother's yowling cat assuring him that I wouldn't really eat him. Mom had named him Waylon Jennings because she said he was always singing. I liked the way the real Waylon sounded better than this furry guy, but then I wasn't sure when the last time was he had been fed. The food in his bowl on the floor was gone and what was left in one corner was so hard it could be used as a weapon. Fortunately, there were a few cans of cat food left above the washing machine on the back of the utility porch.

Mom had had Waylon for years and he was her dear friend. He too must wonder where she was. He was a beautifully marked cat, gray with black stripes and piercing green eyes. Marilyn always had hated him because for some reason he frequently attacked and bit her. I hadn't had the same experience and especially right now. I chuckled as he was literally rubbing against my leg and purring in appreciation for the food he was about to receive.

Time is strange isn't it? Sometimes when you are having a grand event it goes by too quickly, all ending in what seems like a moment. On other occasions, time itself seems to drag its feet, spreading the space between seconds at an unbearable pace. This was such a particular evening — or by now, night.

The two hours it took Marilyn and her entourage to return to my mother's house seemed three times as long. The clock slowly ticked and we wondered what the delay was. Had something happened to them? The noise and loud conversation through the front door finally announced their delayed arrival.

We had locked the front doors out of habit after we had entered, so obviously Marilyn also had her own key. They hadn't knocked or rung the bell. As they walked down the hall, tucked underneath Dan's arm was a huge box of Kentucky Fried Chicken and the red and white striped bags of additional food was carried in his other hand.

The three of them, Marilyn, Matt and Dan didn't enter the den where the rest of us were parked or even inquire as to our well-being. Instead, they made a sharp right into the kitchen, pulled the wooden chairs out from the kitchen set and sat down with their bounty. The box of chicken was plopped in the middle of the table and the waft of food filled the room.

"Hi," I said. "We ordered pizza. Would you like some?" I didn't mention that there was nothing to eat in the house and we had few options or where have you been for the last two hours. No sense being picky now, I thought.

"No," Marilyn said opening the chicken and passing out napkins to Dan and Matt. Her back was turned to me and there was no offer to share their great-smelling meal. Also interesting to note was that there wasn't enough to go around. Her two sidekicks were silent and began immediately reaching and munching the food. They pulled the chairs a little closer together and no one made eye contact.

Body language says a lot doesn't it? The backs turned, the mouths being stuffed with no offer to anyone else. The failure to smile or even converse. They were definitely shutting invisible doors in my face and on all four of us in the other room.

Again, the continued plaguing question, why all the extreme rudeness? It was puzzling and I tried to attribute it to grief having seen grief bring out an assortment of emotions. I've seen grown people show anger, children act like adults, and adults act like little children. Grief seems to be one emotion that encompasses many.

I thought to myself that they, in all probability, had to pull into their own hearts and comfort zones at this time and place. Deep down I also knew we had been lied to when Marilyn let slip she had gone back to visit Mom. We all had been deceived that everyone was returning to the house. The announcement the visiting hours were over was a ruse and I, along with everyone else, had innocently believed her. Marilyn had gone in one more time alone to the bedside of our mother. Precious time Noel and I were denied.

I was saddened and very hurt yet excused Marilyn, thinking how much she had been through the previous weeks. She had house-sat while Mom was in the first surgery and then continued when she was at the convalescent hospital. She had returned with Mom to the house for a few days continuing to take care of her and Waylon before this last re-admission.

Dan was stuffing his mouth with both hands and I couldn't help feeling disgusted towards him. He had on a dirty black turtleneck shirt, his hair definitely could have used a wash and the fat from the chicken was running down the sides of his mouth. He still had on his ID tag from the TV station like a badge of honor. I had had these feelings for years as Dan was verbally nasty to me every time I visited. At least he didn't disguise his feelings. At forty-four he still lived at home and was rarely employed. Maybe the dogtags hanging from his neck were a sign saying, "I made good." He could have been parking cars for all I knew, but I could count on the fact he wouldn't hold the position for long. This was a temporary job as they all were with years of unemployment between and my sister supporting him.

Dan had additionally a growing rap sheet of petty crimes, arrests and drug abuse all supposedly a family secret. It was most definitely information kept from my parents. I could forgive all that in his youth twenty years ago, but it continued into the present. To everyone but he and his mother, I referred to him as Slither.

Everyone was exhausted and I'm sure I didn't look all that hot either. Noel's back had given out hours ago and it was only her tenacity that kept her going. After Marilyn finished her dinner she bade Dan goodbye; he had to go to work and drive back to LA that night. Everyone was turning in including the brother and sister team of Noel's.

Noel and I waited until the den had cleared out and everyone went to their beds. I was too tired to ask who was where, but I knew Marilyn and Matt would be in the front bedroom. She always liked the mattresses there even though they were twins.

"Noel, do you want a good cup of tea?" I asked.

Tea – our family always made tea. Tea when there was a celebration and tea when there was stress. If a problem arose we instantly put on the teapot. It was a tradition that undoubtedly had roots in our Scottish background. We were all heavy coffee drinkers, however, tea was what we made when we needed to talk, to laugh or to cry. This was the time for tea.

Noel and I sat talking for some time that evening. The steady crackling of the little fire was comforting and the big over-stuffed chairs inviting. We were puzzled at everyone's behavior, however, concluded or believed it was because of the strain. We talked at length about how our mother had come to this point. Noel sipped tea and sat on the sandstone hearth in front of the fireplace. The radiating heat gave comfort to her back and she could light cigarette after cigarette and blow the smoke up the chimney, tossing the burned butts into the embers even though she was not supposed to smoke in the house.

It was around midnight when we finally decided to go to bed. The weariness of the day had taken its toll and the adrenalin rushes were wearing off. With our spirits lowered and experiencing emotional fatigue, we agreed that sleep would be a real possibility. We would sleep like logs tonight and there wouldn't be any tossing and turning. Noel went down to the room in the back and I began my mother's routine of locking up. We had performed the routine earlier but I thought I should double check. She had a variety of sliding glass windows and little cut dowels in them to ensure no one could enter. Then there were the latches and double latches. The home actually had four exterior doors to close along with turning out lights. It seemed like I had just started when there was

Noel, leaning against the door jamb in the family room laughing.

"Want to tell me the joke?" I said. I couldn't see much humor in switching off the lights.

"Kat – they've thrown our bags out into the hall," she said holding her sides and still emitting chuckles.

I was failing to see the humor here. "What?" Did I hear correctly? Our bags were in the hall? They were solidly on the bed where I left them. They were on the bed. "Nooooooo."

Continuing to laugh and motioning with her ring laden fingers she smiled, "Come here and see." She turned around and headed back down the darkened hall padding softly on the carpet runner.

I followed her in the darkness turning on the big bathroom light for a little illumination. There, in the hallway were our bags! Her little flowered satchel and my backpack had been tossed carelessly against the opposite wall. They looked like hotel laundry in the dim light and could have been laying there for hours unnoticed. Both bags had landed next to the doorway leading to our parent's bedroom. That door was open with the others being tightly shut.

My mouth must have slung right open in dismay. I was shocked! I couldn't believe anyone, let alone a family member would do this to us. We had callously and literally been tossed out of the room we always used. Everyone, and I mean everyone, knew since 1983 that I didn't sleep in my parent's room. It was where my father died and I just couldn't go in there. I hadn't been in there for any length of time since he passed. Obviously, my mother's adjoining twin bed was not acceptable at this point either. She was contaminated with something and it was only logical that the bed linens might be also.

So there we were, Noel and I, staring at each other in the darkened hall. She saw bizarre humor where I felt totally insulted and betrayed. But I couldn't stand there and dwell on the circumstances. Every bone and possibly my hair felt limp. What more could be done to us? I told Noel to get our bags back to the family room and I'd grab some blankets and pillows from the linen closet. We would just camp out on the floor in the den. It was warm, the fire still sputtering, and it was near the wall phone. A good, logical solution to an ugly situation.

To this day the question remains as to who threw our bags into the hall. From the six people in the house four were suspect. Who would have been so callous? Our mother was dying and we were in her home with nowhere to sleep. Noel's kids were in our room. I peeked in the door and both appeared to be asleep. Did they know the bags had been there? Did someone else toss them? That would have left Marilyn. Matt was off the list immediately. He wouldn't have done something like that. I think Matt would have been uncomfortable squishing a bug or setting a mousetrap. It wasn't the time nor place to start yelling about who did what where. It wasn't a game of Clue after all. I stood bewildered for a few minutes.

Dad had died in this house. He had lain in his bed in the darkened back room in pain, with no hospice and no medications. He was sipping water from a honey bear bottle because he couldn't sit up. I sat hours with him like that just to keep him company. It was one of the most difficult times because my mother kept telling me this is how he wanted to die, at home in his own bed. That part I could respect, but it was so unnecessary that he suffer like that alone in the dark. Why she didn't get hospice for him or show him more compassion, I could never understand. She was actually cooking in the kitchen and chatting with the company as they came in and out. Even when his childhood friend from the Ozark's flew in to see Dad, he took me into the hall.

"What the hell is going on here?"

I remember just standing there next to him mumbling something about my mother while tears streamed down my face. He was so kind. He took me in his arms as I began to sob and thanked him for being such a good friend to my father. Now I found myself asking the same question. What the hell was going on here?

I was in for yet another surprise and not the good kind. In both of the homes in which my parents lived there were linen closets. The one here was floor to ceiling and the entire width of the extra spacious hall. Big deep drawers that took both hands to open were on the bottom with cupboard doors and deep shelves above that. The shelves were always stuffed with sheets, blankets and pillowcases of every size imaginable. Most of them were white but there were a few prints both on the percale and flannels. Only bedding filled these cabinets. The linen table cloths and napkins were all kept in the carved credenza in the formal dining room. My mother always had linens. Some were old and mended but nevertheless the linen cupboards were always full to the brim, ready to accommodate any large group of Gypsies who should be stopping by. It has always been that way back to my earliest recollections. Some people collect shells, stamps and shoes. Mom collected linens.

You can imagine what I felt when I opened the top cupboard doors and discovered the cupboard was empty. Not a paltry few but totally empty down to the bare, painted shelves and walls. Stripped. The shelf lining paper was even missing. Mother Hubbard didn't have a day like this. This cabinet had been stacked from the bottom of one shelf to the top of another with sheets, blankets and pillow cases. Now it stood empty. For a fleeting moment I wondered if everything was in the laundry, but that couldn't be the case either. The laundry wasn't capable of holding the entire contents of these cupboards. I had been in the laundry room to get Waylon's food and there weren't any sheets there. Where were the neatly stacked piles? Where were the treasured pillowcases we had embroidered as children? Where were my aunt's crocheted cases so lovingly presented each Christmas? The only thing on those four shelves were two feather tick pillows the family had since the early 1930s. I think that they had been stored on Dad's fishing boat and the traditional ticking had orange stains on them. Yuck! The last thing any of us would have chosen.

The nightmare here seemed to be endless. I fetched an afghan from the living room sofa and took it back to the den. Noel was mumbling about the lumpy den sofa and moaning each time she moved. She could handle it for a short time but not all night. I tossed two throw pillows down on the floor on the area rug near my grandmother's pedestal table. This would be our bed for the night.

I was quietly praying this would be one of those times that a hard surface would be better for Noel than a soft one. I put the afghans and a blanket I found over Noel and myself as we lay down. We must have looked like orphaned children bundled up in colorful blankets in a nomadic tent. We weren't quite as colorful and definitely not as photogenic at the moment. I didn't bother to change my clothes but just slid my bra off, unbuttoned my pants and fell down on my stomach fully clothed.

It seemed barely a millisecond that my head had been down when the phone rang. The old princess phone was on top of the table that we were under and clearly within hearing distance. The startling jangle raised me right up and I grabbed the receiver in one swift motion. It didn't have a chance to ring a third time.

I glanced at the clock on the little shelf and it registered 2:00 a.m. We had had less than two hours sleep. Waylon went streaking across the room with a yowl. Apparently he had been sleeping on my feet and when I jumped at the sound of the ring his kitty nervous system also jumped him into flight. He was moving pretty fast for a cat with an injured leg.

By the time the doctor on the other end of the phone told me gently that my mother was failing rapidly, Marilyn and Matt were standing in the hall dressed, car keys in hand. How the hell did they get there so fast? Marilyn had her purse over her arm and was holding a three-ring binder close to her chest. They too must have been sleeping restlessly in their clothes waiting for the call. How in the world did they even hear the phone ring down the hall and in their room? They were all prepared and actually moving toward the front doors to leave.

"Hold on," I said grabbing my bra and jacket simultaneously.

I leaned down toward Noel whispering, "Do you want to go?" The pain in her eyes was apparent. Pain not just from her back but the pain that lurks deep in your heart stretching its fingers into your mind and seeping into your very soul. This pain could not be erased with Aleve. Noel simply shook her head no and without a word I knew. We didn't need a long explanation, it was one soul connecting with another wordlessly.

I sensed that these two standing poised in front of me like dogs waiting for a chase were not going to wait long. Basically a shy person I needed to get the bra back on before going much further. I quickly turned my back on Matt and slid my bra back into its proper place, spun around while zipping my pants up and the three of us scurried out to their waiting cars.

Fortunately, Marilyn and Matt's cars were the last parked in the drive making them the easiest to maneuver out. It was Sunday morning, the day Marilyn told me she had planned to leave my mother alone.

Chapter 6

DAWN

The events of the last 24 hours were more than bizarre and there was so much going on I had to "pick my fighters" as the cowboy would say. I had to decide what to focus on and what to let go. Right now I had to focus on my mother. The puzzle pieces seemed to be spread all over the floor and I didn't have time to assemble them in my mind.

When I called Marilyn the Thursday before from Montana, I had asked her, since she had said she was leaving Mom's, if she had made arrangements for health care. Her answer had been, "No." I asked if anyone else was coming to take care of Mother, like maybe one of our nieces or neighbors? Again a "No." Even then Marilyn's behavior was beyond my comprehension and still is. She had made the tiny little packages of food and stacked them in the freezer, but did she really think that our mother who could barely stand, could reach up and get them? Now I know that the pantry shelves were also empty. Marilyn was leaving minimal food and what little there was, Mom would have difficulty accessing.

After I talked to Marilyn from Montana I began planning to immediately contact other family members and line up some care. It was clear that for whatever reason Marilyn was unable to pull this off or see clearly the need.

All these thoughts were zooming in and out of my brain as we loaded into Marilyn's car to return to the hospital. It was pitch black out but the one thing I knew was she was more than familiar with the drive. She put her car in reverse, spun some gravel and we hurled into the darkness. She flipped on her headlights and they lit up the five acres of weeds where there used to be a vineyard.

Matt followed us down the same country road in their second vehicle. Marilyn and I spoke little as she explained Matt had a class at UCLA that day that he couldn't miss. He would stay with us for a while. After that, what do you say when you are going to see someone you love die? Our hearts and minds were wrapped in a comforting silence and I was more than happy to leave it that way. The city lights were dimmed and the streets barren of vehicles as we drove. The normal traffic signals had transformed to blinking caution lights in the darkness. Caution – Caution. We arrived about twenty minutes later, one car following the other with two pairs of headlights snaking their way to a grim destination.

As we got out of the cars at the hospital my feet felt as if weights had been placed in my shoes and I could barely pick them up. It was so sad, I wanted to sink into the ground and become one with the earth. I really didn't want to be here at all.

Once again the huge, oversized doors opened automatically and we stumbled into the inner sanctum of the hospital. The green elevator lights were reflecting on the polished floor and the place seemed actually quieter than when I was here before and how could that be possible? As before, no one was about nor visible. The flowers Julie had put on the front desk a few hours earlier were gone. We made it to the third floor easily and to the Isolation Unit. Marilyn robotically spoke into the sterilized grid on the talking wall and doors started buzzing and whizzing.

It was a rerun but without the shock factor this time. We garbed into the gloves and hospital smocks in silence and then slid our street shoes into the baby-blue paper booties with elastic. What a perverse feeling to don surgical gloves to touch the hand of your mother, the hand that fed you. It seemed almost criminal. After we got through the second round of doors Marilyn plopped her notebook on top of the nursing center's counter. I couldn't help noticing that she put her binder down first and the purse on top as if to weight it down and anchor it safely. I wondered what she was carrying, but figured it was legal paper work since she had the medical durable power of attorney and was calling all the shots.

It is a dual-edged sword in life respecting authority and learning to obey whomever is in charge. It can be so extreme that you don't question. But authority is not always right and hence you have mutinies and insurrections. I was "minding" Marilyn but starting to question her good sense and what extended to her so-called authority here.

Mom looked nothing like when I left her the night before. Gone was the sweet little lady lying on her pillow with her hair surrounding her like a halo. A great deal had been done to her medically and there was now a clear plastic tube inserted down her throat and taped to her cheek. She looked a little like a porcupine with tubes running in and out of her arms and at the base and sides of the bed. Each needle was sitting in a purple and blue bruise making her arms look too painful to touch. The awaiting doctor explained she was having difficulty breathing and they had to assist her. She was unconscious but thrashing about so both her wrists were softly restrained and tied to the side rails of her bed. The row of equipment on the shelf behind her seemed brighter and more active than before.

I stood trying to take it all in. My eyes fell to the tied wrists and then her hands. The hands that could render such beauty with her music and such pain with her punishments. I felt as Mom's entire personality was subdued by restraints. She didn't appear to have fought them with much difficulty. Nevertheless, it was distressing to see her tied down like that. The nurse didn't wait for the words to form in my mouth and could see I was questioning the situation.

"She was fighting her tubes last night and trying to pull them out," she went on to explain gently. "This is all we could do to stop her."

I stood looking down at the flannel ties encircling her wrists.

They weren't like the ones she used on us. I wondered why after all, did she tie us to the kitchen chairs. I never questioned that point in our history, ridiculously thinking all children were tied to their chairs. I had accepted it readily at the time and hadn't reflected much on the practice until I looked at her wrists now tied tightly to a piece of cold metal.

As an unquestioning little girl I would even wait patiently for her to finish her series of knots behind my back when I sat in the dining room chair. I did see her tie Noel differently on an occasion. Noel's arms would be crossed across her chest and her arms tied like what later I learned would be a straightjacket. Noel couldn't wiggle free at all and when that was done it wasn't at mealtime.

Surely my mother's motive for restraining us wasn't borne of fear that we were going to fall out of our chairs. Children don't fall spontaneously off their chairs during meals. It couldn't have been because we spilled or slopped or she would have put bibs on us. No – this practice of restraint went on until I was at least seven years old making Noel over nine. I honestly don't remember if Marilyn was tied to her chair, but I suppose she may have been.

My mother used her tea towels, now referred to as dish towels. They were large white ones that I think she got from my grandfather's bakery. She would fold it in a triangle, put the entire front around our abdomens and then tie us through the vertical spindles on the back, tying the knots behind. There was no escape and heaven forbid were we to move. I suppose the whole chair would have gone over with its precious contents right onto the floor. We must have known this so we sat very still. Our arms were free, of course, so we could eat or nibble at the usually unpalatable meal. The meals presented to company were entirely different but the daily fare fell far below that.

Honestly, occasionally the slats of the chairs would crack and break. Mom would blame it on her one and only "fat ass" friend for putting "her butt in first." I also found this fascinating because her friend visited so rarely. How could she possibly break so many chairs, my young mind would think? Not too long after, Dad would be busy in his shop with wood glue, dowels and clamps once again repairing a chair. What did he think? Was he also buying the story that gentle Juanita had broken the chairs again? I'm sure he didn't know his children were being tied too tight, little bodies encapsulated night after night like cocoons in dish towels that could barely move.

It was such routine I would even look down to see which day of the week was embroidered on my current restraints. Did I get Monday saying it was Wash Day or Thursday's Cleaning Day? As soon as we could reach the ironing board it was our job to iron the pillowcases and the tea towels.

Mom probably thought that restraining us would train us to not leave the table until the plates were clean and everyone had finished. So there we sat chewing on the unpalatable dribbles until everyone had finished, or whatever was snuck under the leaf of the table was put in the garbage later.

As these recollections flooded my mind I looked at her now sleeping body. She wasn't a threat to anyone anymore — not even herself. I turned to the nurse.

"Please take those off her. She doesn't need them."

I reached for her hand as I had the day before and felt her return grip so tightly as if she was gripping onto life itself. Somewhere in her haze she was reaching for me to hold her like a frightened child. And hold I did. I kept talking to her and telling her I was there with her for this journey. Marilyn stood on the opposite side of the bed stroking our mother's hair but still not speaking to either of us. Her silence was pervasive and hung heavily about the room like dark velvet drapes across sun-filled windows.

Mom had been rendered to such a fragile state and here she was gripping my hand. I had heard of a death grip, was this it? This poor woman who had given up on God and believed all spirituality was myth. She had no philosophical prospects of an afterlife and I'm sure was terrified. I couldn't help but think of the lyric again from Mary Hamilton... *The death I was to dee (die).*

A new nurse came in and introduced herself to us telling me that she was not just my mother's nurse but she was also going to be mine. I don't think at that moment I had the full impact of what she was telling me. She was a lovely woman of Mexican descent with a gentle smile. Her pure brown eyes were doe-like as she explained that my mother's blood pressure was steadily going down and what that meant. She then continued to explain each of the monitors, their jobs and how I could read them myself. I couldn't help but notice the simple cross she was wearing. I felt like God's angels were speaking to me through her and I could trust her completely.

Marilyn continued to stare into space and scarcely acknowledged this warm woman whose love just flowed forth. She had ceased even looking at me and occupied herself with Mom's hair.

For three hours we sat as our mother, step by excruciating step, descended into another realm. Descended might not be right word — transcended would be more accurate. The sun was gently lighting the sky as dawn began to break the darkness.

It was 5:00 a.m. when Matt said he needed to get going. We all left the death ward together and took the elevator to the basement coffee shop. Again, and not surprised, nothing was open. There were the vending machines though, but I didn't have enough change to even buy a cup of coffee. Matt slid the coins into the machine and one by one handed us paper cups that held some stout thick stuff but not hot coffee. Apparently it hadn't been restocked yet for the weekend. Whatever, I sipped it and felt some warmth down my throat as we sat in the unlit shop. The chairs were hard plastic and we squared off around the small table.

Marilyn looked at her coffee, her face contorted and she put her head down on the Formica table with a muffled sob. For the first time in hours she made a full sentence. "I feel like I killed our mother," she cried.

Instinctively, I reached across the small table to take hold of her hand, but she snapped up and recoiled her arms from the table.

I took in a deep breath to level out another surprise. Good grief, they were coming one after another and I had yet to adjust to it all. I wasn't expecting a statement or admission like that, however, I was reaching out to comfort her and that too was rebuffed. Matt put his arm around her shoulders. I'm thinking, well yes, you made all the wrong calls in spite of the advice you received from two different nurse friends and the research I was doing on MRSA up in Montana. You disregarded it all moving consistently against her instead of for her. Not much was done right. Nevertheless, I felt compassion for Marilyn at that moment. Yet in my head I heard the song by an old friend, Steve Gillette, like some kind of warning.

Don't trust nobody whatever you do, that is what the gamblin' man said. He never knew what he told me was true 'cause the very next mornin' the gamblin' man was dead.

I told Marilyn I thought she did the best she could do. It wasn't exactly the truth because I was wondering what actually *could* she do? Yet there I was again saying to myself, why would she say this? Did she have an active role here and/or what is she hiding? I wasn't angry but a calm suspicion took hold.

Even the hospital was suspicious when Marilyn brought my mother back in, driven in her own car by the neighbor. They clearly marked her admission papers *positive* for suspected elder abuse. I wouldn't actually know that until almost a year and a half later when I finally got the requested admission paper work, but it was there. Right now I was looking at a distraught woman, but also felt for just a brief moment, that she had just let her guard down and a confession slip.

My mother was readmitted to this hospital the day before suffering from malnutrition, dehydration and in a state of hypothermia. I was looking at her current medical records while we were in her unit. Didn't they think I could read? Yes, I felt genuine sympathy for Marilyn, however, that sympathy was conflicting with what she told me.

The fabrications and webs my sister Marilyn wove throughout her life were really quite convincing. She did appear intelligent and well informed to most. She was so convincing that I had bragged for years how my sister had graduated from UCLA with a 4.0 average. You can imagine how embarrassed I was when in doing research for my book I found out that not only did she not graduate, she never made it past the first year. Her being a teacher was also a stretch of the imagination. She did teach quilting to adults a few nights a week for a couple of years — but never held a teaching credential. So I became the liar bragging about her accomplishments and accolades. Of course, I didn't know then what I know now.

Matt cleared his throat and announced that it was time for him to leave. I'm sure he was relieved to have an excuse to flee this apocalyptic scene. We walked him out to the exit and then with heavy hearts returned to our mother's bedside upstairs in the Isolation Unit.

Once again we took our opposite places on each side of Mom's hospital bed. I couldn't stand the thought of not touching her again. I felt like I had already been denied the opportunity to tell her I loved her one last time or even to speak with her again. I pulled off my sweaty blue latex glove and held her hand to my breast like a treasured jewel. Holding her just so, I closed my eyes and began the Lord's Prayer, whispering the words just enough so that she might hear me recite the traditional words.

> *Our Father, which art in heaven, hallowed be thy name. ...*

As I got to the end — to the amen, gasping and grasping my mother's hand the finality of it all came crashing in and I began to shake like a sapling leaf in the wind. My entire body from head to toe was uncontrollably quaking and a sob emitted from the very depths of my soul. I felt light-headed and wondered how long I could possibly stand. Something inside me was dying right along with my mother. Before I could collapse entirely there were warm arms around me holding me up. I could sense and feel the pure infusion of love, *the agape,* the highest form of love from God, at its finest definition. Someone was holding me up and their spirit, their firm strength, was soaking into my total being and giving me strength. I was held securely for several minutes while the sobs raged on and on finally leaving me drained and weak.

Then gently, the person who I later called "Angel Nurse" pulled a green padded chair towards me and sat me down. She looked at me carefully and into my soul. It was the lovely Hispanic woman who had earlier told me she would be my nurse. My blood sugar level had dropped from two days of little food, less sleep and the inability to even bathe. The physical facts, coupled with the emotional ones with the impending loss of my mother had finally caught up with me. Patting my hand and ignoring my sister, Angel Nurse dashed out of the room briefly only to come back in with some orange juice and crackers. I heard her offer the same to Marilyn, who just shook her head no. For a while I sat in the chair hastily dragged up, my legs still shaking and tried to recover. I was gathering shared strength from my God, the Angel He had sent me and some sustenance in my stomach.

The situation at the death camp only became more complicated and dire as the hours dragged on. Mom was losing the battle yet each time the nurses and doctors came in to give us updates and keep us informed they were met with the obstacle that Marilyn had withdrawn into a zombie state and would stare at them apparently not registering their information. Knowing she was the legal durable power of attorney they had to address her. She was supposed to be making the medical decisions, however, her inability to focus and her departure from reality here revealed her mind also was no longer there. Possibly she had just shut down mentally in an escape act of self-preservation. These would only be guesses on my part as to what was going on in her head. Whatever the reason the doctors shifted tactics and started talking to me instead of her. They gave her polite, cursory glances as if she was included, but the questions were being asked of me. Questions which were the basis for me in the first place to refuse my mother's request that I be her medical durable and executor of her trust.

Did we want more blood tests?

I answered, "No. No more needles, no more poking. It can't help her now." I couldn't look at her black and blue arms and think more vials taken out could in any possible way help her. More tests seemed a waste for one and all and just more discomfort for my mother. No, we were way beyond that now and it seemed like a bizarre draconian act to take more blood.

They all agreed while quietly making notes on her chart.

Did we want extreme measures taken to keep her alive?

"No." I squeaked out with tears in my eyes and a lump in my throat. "She didn't want that. She was quite clear about that one. It is in her paperwork." I nodded towards Marilyn's white plastic notebook on the counter assuming that is what it held. Those coils behind the hard cover held the future of all of us.

Chapter 7

To Trust or Not to Trust?

Looking at the digital information floating across my mother's hospital monitors, my mind reeled back to the day many years ago when we sat on my redwood deck in Tuolumne County, California. She had come up for a visit and everything was perfect, it was the time of year in the Sierra Foothills when it isn't too hot and it isn't cold. The sky was postcard blue and we all felt happy to be alive.

She had lowered her head and the light through the pergola caught her white hair and made it glow. The lines in her face were a little etched and she was appearing at this point to look all of her 75 years.

"I think when I'm old I'm going to come and live with you."

I had always told her as a little girl that she could live with me, sit by the pool and eat bonbons. She used to laugh at that one but this time she was serious and I didn't really respond while waiting for her to fill me in.

"You know I can't live with Noel. Well, you know perfectly well why not there." Then her voice lowered and she almost appeared embarrassed. "And I don't want to live with Marilyn. There are some problems there." The last part of her sentence was hardly discernible and I stretched forward to hear as her volume dropped.

She just started shaking her head and a teary mist came to her eyes. I thought if I gave her a moment to compose herself she might offer a further explanation. Not wanting to be with Marilyn? The obvious favorite for all our youth?

I got up, slid through the sliding glass door and whisked myself quickly into our one little bathroom where I retrieved a box of Kleenex. When I returned she had shifted her position on the bench and regained some of her composure. She wasn't going to offer more of an explanation and in my inevitable, but now regrettable manner, I didn't press her for further details.

To this day that nags me. Why didn't I ask? The old "don't pry" was not whispering in my ear then — it was demanding loudly, "DON'T PRY!" So, by not prying I never knew what prompted my mother to not only ask me to be the trustee of her estate, but also why she wanted to come live with me, four hundred miles from her home and Marilyn. She hadn't really asked, which also was cute — she just announced.

After my mother composed herself she told me she was taking a workshop and making her own living trust. She thought she might make Daniel, her first-born grandson, executor of her estate. I think she was fetching for my reaction at that point because she couldn't possibly think Slither could do it. Had she no idea of what a bottom feeder he was? Maybe it was the traditional European thoughts of male hierarchy that were her motivation. I told her I thought it was a poor idea.

"Why?" she queried.

"Well, Mom, I hate to tell you this but Dan would put your entire estate up his nose in a matter of days and no one would ever get a penny."

"Why, what do you mean Katrina Lynne?" Calling me by my full name and looking at me through incredulous, narrowed eyes. Mom had lost the sight of one eye to shingles and sometimes when she looked at you it seemed odd, especially through her bifocals in the light. Noel had begun referring to her good eye as the "'evil eye" but they had never gotten along, and there was no forgiveness on either's part.

"Cocaine, Mom. Cocaine. You've heard of sex, drugs and rock

n' roll? That is your grandson there." I thought the direct delivery was the best.

Interesting that she didn't argue with me or even ask for proof. I think she wanted her suspicions affirmed. She prided herself on her inquiring mind but didn't question much more here. Maybe she didn't want to hear the gory details. Deep down Mom must have known I was telling her the truth and had been suspicious for some time. There had been repeated cases of missing money around her house as well as other clues.

It was me who actually saw the now notorious photo of two of her adult grandchildren snorting cocaine off the mirror in her master bathroom. They were so loaded they didn't realize, or perhaps didn't care, that they had been photographed.

Mom made a deep sigh and got quiet for a moment then surprised me by asking if I would be the executor. Maybe that had been her plan all along and she just wanted confirmation. My mother could be rather cagey at times — actually at many times.

I didn't answer her right away but continued on about Dan. "Mom, I don't think Dan has had asthma for years. All that sniffling he does is a result of long term snorting and that isn't medication in his inhaler." I paused and decided not to mention the other grandchildren who had done the same thing.

Then I asked her, "Are you going to put the 'pull the plug' clause in your will?" She knew what I meant. Permission and request that life support systems not be used on her at any time.

"Yes, I don't want to be on life support machines, you know that. If it is my time to go, I want you to do it. No machines or high drama for me."

I pulled my patio chair around so that I was facing her and looked her in the face. I explained that I couldn't guarantee at random without knowing the situation at that time, to actually terminate her life. I wasn't like that. I couldn't give her a carte blanche promise because I always kept my promises. A promise like that certainly would depend on the circumstances. I didn't have a crystal ball to see into the future and thus I would have to decline the responsibility. I was still a practicing Christian and took the Ten Commandments seriously. How do you define killing in the "thou shalt not" section? I almost could laugh at the age-old rhetorical question, but at that point I couldn't. The question will always remain as to why she asked me to be her executrix. That was a great leap and deviation from the traditional pecking order. It didn't appear to be an impulsive act and anyway, my mother was hardly anything in her old age like impulsive. She weighed her decisions, right or wrong.

I recommended an impartial person but Mom went home, finished her trust and fatefully or fatally made my sister Marilyn her durable and her executrix.

My mother could be so cold and linear at times. It is amazing how we can look at someone as if we have put on a costume mask. All the different personalities we seem to carry around and then switch to fit the demands of any situation or occasion. Behind the mask I put on I was watching the video of the family in another role, days and years apart. I was flipping back and forth and now my memory went back even further when for some reason, I became my mother's confessor. Oh, the things she told me she had done — one was literally terminating my own beloved great aunt's life.

It was the late 1960s and my Aunt Lillie was very ill. She was in a convalescent home about a two-and-a-half-hour drive from my parent's. Mom was visiting her frequently and I knew that my aunt was terminal. However, my mother said one day she just unplugged, literally disconnected the life-support equipment from the electrical sockets by Aunt Lillie's bed. Now this was the late 1960s. There were no alarms or digital monitors for the nursing staff to check. Mom proceeded to tell me that she just sat there quietly watching the life drain out of the woman who loved her like her own child. Once this premeditated and admitted act was completed my mother then confessed to sticking the plugs back into the wall and leaving. She actually got in her car and drove the two-and-a- half hours home to Yucaipa. Then, when she got the phone call pretended to be shocked and upset. Now was that a mercy killing?

No, my mother was actually bragging when she told me this. She got away with it and felt justified doing so. She was never even suspected. There was no consultation with doctors or other family members. She just expedited a death and showed no tears and had no regrets. Isobel saw nothing wrong with what she did.

Poor Noel, when she heard what happened to her favorite little aunt she wept and wept. She too knew the truth and we both understood fully the extent of our mother's capabilities.

Now the doctors were asking me if I wanted to do the same with my mother. We were at the apex of those decisions Mom made fifteen years before and circumstances were obviously very different.

The doctors wanted to disconnect the medications they were giving her to continue life. They had ceased communicating with Marilyn who was alternating between staring and glaring at the medical staff. She escaped into her mind and was somewhere else. I gave them my approval and thought Mom would truly be in God's hands now. I was calling the medical shots and feeling guilty that if I had taken on the responsibility originally, maybe she wouldn't be in this situation.

It is said hindsight is 20/20, but is it? Even the rear view mirror of a car has limited visibility. After talking for the last time with the doctors I gave and signed the orders to withdraw slowly the life support machines from our mother's body. The indicators overhead had shown no brain activity for quite a while. Her still and motionless shell was just being maintained through science and technology. Her spirit, her soul were long gone having moved to another plane.

I went out to the nursing station and also requested my mother be cleaned up. There was a thick discharge from her mouth and her eyes looked so dry. I felt she should be more presentable "meeting her maker." The nursing staff came in and gently worked around to make her appear more comfortable. Her face was washed, eye drops put in and her hair combed neatly on the pillow. There was now a sense of peace about her face. Her arms were gently placed across her abdomen and the blankets pulled up so she appeared to be comfortably sleeping.

JOURNEY

Sojourners are we
The Bedouin and Thee
Matildas worn
Discarded caftans torn
Baggage found, lost, accumulated
New, battered
Empty handed

Travelers through life
Spirits
Holding hands — holding hearts
Arms open and then arms folded
Eyes wide in wonder
Held closed by silver coin

Comforting one another in storm
Rejoicing at Celebration
Crosses held with David's Star
Saffron Beggars while Mecca gathers

Brothers, sisters, lovers, mothers
Graceful movement
Tinted hues of hands pale silk - dark leather

Sand sifting slowly through the hourglass
Fleeting Time

Lessons taught, learned, forgotten and forgiven

Mankind always moving
Lost and Roaming
Some with Compasses - Direction knowing
Nomadic souls all propelling

Chapter 8

OUR FEARFUL TRIP

It is said the soul weighs 20 grams. Apparently, there have been people who have measured and weighed others as they leave this life. I know that as our mother's spirit left her body and was winging its way to the God she did not believe in, my eldest son's silver-winged airplane was simultaneously landing at the Ontario, California airport. They were crossing in time and space, one with and one without their body. Tears rolled down my face as I watched a plane out the hospital window and glanced at my watch. I cried not for myself now but for my son. He wasn't going to be able to say goodbye to the grandmother he loved. He was arriving, as Lee Hazelwood's lyrics would say, *"just in time to be too late."* I was sad for them both, my mother who had lost the opportunity to heal her family and my son who loved her dearly. I checked my watch again and, yes, that was exactly what was happening. They were crossing paths.

I looked at my sister who was registering absolutely no discernible emotion that I could see and I was truly worried about her. She looked like a white marble statue, she was so unmoving. I wanted to reach out to her, but she pulled so tight within herself I honestly feared she would hit me if I tried to embrace her. She had never hit me in her life, but it was a knowledge I had gained by working with so many animals over the years: It was the capability of attack that I saw in her eyes. My sister was no longer, nor had been for some time, in a rational state of mind. I was at a loss how to help her.

For some reason I started to quote her the poem we had all

memorized in the 6th grade. It was Walt Whitman's *Captain* that he wrote about Lincoln's assassination.

"O Captain! My Captain! Our fearful trip is done. The ship has weathered every rack, the fight we fought is won." I misquoted it, but it mattered little. "Do you remember it, Sis?"

Marilyn continued her million-mile stare without a word. What was going on in her mind? In her heart? Did she hear me at all? Well, I thought our mother was our Captain, she piloted the ship of our lives and indeed at times it had been a fearful trip and yet at others, smooth sailing and beautiful days. There was a great sorrow in having her come to an end in such a way.

How does one explain the sense of loss, sorrow and pain? It goes deeper than tears. It is for lives unfulfilled and opportunities missed to heal and forgive. It is for the inability to exhume the deceptions long buried and clear the air with confessions. There would be no chance for resolve once a person has moved on. I've told many over the years that it isn't the grieving for what is lost, but grief for what cannot be regained. It was heartbreaking to realize the broken and torn fences in the family could never be mended now. I had tried over the years and still held hope there would be admissions and apologies. Now they would never come. There would be no reunification nor honesty.

My mother and I had become close, but there was always the distrust and history that prevented a truly honest, comfortable friendship. With my mother it was always the dance but not the dance partner. Such a deep sense of disappointment struck me and I felt so terribly — so terribly alone. Through the haze and horror of loss I managed to keep part of my brain separate from my emotions and approached the attending doctor. Again I found myself breathing deep into my belly and stretching out for the inner calmness that dwelled there. I imagined I was holding my mother's hand and that gave me courage.

"No reflection on the care here," I emphasized. "We (I used the term loosely, intentionally) need some clarification as to what happened. We need an autopsy." I continued, "Please see that she is not cremated before this happens."

He nodded and made a few notes on a form, expressed his sympathy and then made his excuses to leave. There were others to attend to, the other motionless bodies behind glass doors in the unit of death. Staff members were coming into the room, turning off equipment and straightening her bed. The remaining tubes and attached needles were gently disconnected as if she could still feel.

One of the staff asked me if I wanted to go back in and say goodbye to her for the last time. I was still leaning on the counter after the autopsy request. I declined. To me, as I have said, a body is a shell and the person inhabits that shell for a while and when it is no longer of use they leave it. I thought of the scripture in I Corinthians where it says, *"We shall not all die, but in an instant we shall be changed as quickly as the blinking of an eye..."*

Marilyn spent some time with my mother's body and then shuffled the few feet to where I was waiting. I was just reading what I could of the paperwork left on the counter. A new nurse came out from behind the counter to talk to her. You have to admire those who work this kind of unit and their compassion and understanding extending to others. She really looked sympathetic as she addressed Marilyn. "We need to know where to send your mother, dear."

Marilyn was still staring, holding the closed white binder now tightly against her chest. Finally she managed to speak but literally spit out the words, "I don't know the name of the mortuary."

"Marilyn," I said gently, "open the book. The information should be in there with Mom's paper work. It is the one in Yucaipa when you get off the freeway. Mom pointed it out all the time. I just forgot the name."

Everyone within earshot looked rather startled as Marilyn's face moved from placidity to instant red hostility. Her lower lids scooted up like a reptile's to make her eyes seem squinty. Her mouth finally opened and she practically yelled, "NO! I CAN'T DO THAT!" then stared at them with her jaw set.

Suppressing shock the nurse quickly looked at me pleading for help. The message unsaid was quite clear. She was at a loss as to how to react to Marilyn's outburst and yet needed the information. This shouting wasn't the usual grief pattern they encountered. I quickly asked the nurse if she could hold Mom a bit here and that I would call them from the house once we got there. I felt sure they dealt with a variety of reactions when it came to grief and this would just be one more response to put in their books.

As Marilyn spun and headed to the exit, I glanced back at Mom's room just as the blue privacy curtains were being drawn closed.

Chapter 9

RUNNING

Now I've seen horses bolt for the barn more than once, but keeping up with Marilyn at this point was proving a bit of a challenge. After she shouted to the nurses she grabbed her things and dashed for the exit. She tore off her Hazmat clothes and threw them into the bins at a lightning pace. I was trying to keep up and having difficulty pulling my elastic booties off; they had caught on my shoes and were reluctant to let go. I couldn't really blame her for her sudden movements as it was a classic fight-or-flight response from the scene like a deer being chased, yet for a split second I thought she might leave me.

On the way to the elevator I offered to drive the two of us back to our parent's house. Actually there was a little self-preservation in the offer because I didn't think she was safe. I had made that error when my father passed and I drove 300 straight miles crying the whole time. It was horrifying to think later that I had no recollection of being on the road and it was more than dangerous. People definitely need to assist others under such circumstances. Marilyn assured me she was all right, but I knew different as her rapid emotional shifts were becoming alarming.

As we got to the main floor she said she wanted to stop in the hospital chapel for a minute. This again was uncharacteristic of her as she frequently reaffirmed her atheism. She felt, like my mother, that to be an intellectual one must see faith as myth. I personally thought that was rather misguided but ceased those discussions years ago.

If she needed something more powerful at the moment then so be it. It was encouraging to me that she might want some spiritual help, yet when I told her I knew where the chapel was she again gave me that wide-eyed "how did you know that?" look. Was this a charade, an act? But, on the other hand, if she wanted to pray now seemed like an excellent time. I said nothing further and Marilyn walked stiffly into the chapel.

She made no attempt to sit near me nor even in close proximity. I slid into a small pew in the back and she passed me up, sat in the front facing the stained glass windows with the bouquet of flowers, turning her back on me while still clutching the white binder to her chest.

I had already said multiple prayers for my mother and continue to do so. Right now I was experiencing a sense of empty hollowness. I was just waiting for Marilyn and hoping she would regain some of her former self and become the Marilyn I knew and loved.

When she finished whatever she was doing, praying, meditating or just collecting herself, she rose and walked up the aisle without even glancing my way. I jogged behind her to the car like an obedient pup, got in and closed the door. The chasm of silence between us was growing. She wouldn't respond to my questions or even participate when I tried to converse. She did make one statement, however, she did not want to talk to anyone else that day. She was quite emphatic about that. I replied I understood and would be happy to make calls for her to let people know of Mom's passing.

For what happened next there is no explanation. I have always thought in lyrics, poetry and quotes. My mind is stuffed with them. Growing up in Los Angeles I had the opportunity to attend the Philharmonic every Saturday, so when I wasn't thinking in lyrics there would be a classical music score going on in my head. I walked around with my own sound track but what Freudian demon started playing in my head now?

Ding dong the witch is dead the wicked witch. Ding dong the wicked witch is dead…

I wanted to scream, how could I stop it? I wasn't that calloused. Please stop it God – give me another tune. Change the channel. That isn't how I felt … But it continued.

Chapter 10

HELLO-GOODBYE

When many of us make that final goodbye to friends and loved ones, we often think of when we first met them, that first "hello," and then we tend to set up a timeline, so to speak, in our minds. My immediate thought was, when did I meet this lady, Isobel? Oh, I don't mean my birthdate but rather my first recollection.

My first vivid recollection of my mother was of she and I sitting face to face. I was in my wooden, cream-colored high chair that had circus decals on the back. I was very little of course, being in a high chair, and I remember her as a pretty woman, but with a dark determined look on her face. Some have said this is impossible until I also describe to them where my crib was and what it looked like. I could tell them exactly where everything was in our house. There were no photographs of these items, they are all moving pictures in my mind.

This particular scene took place when I was about one year old I'm sure, but before I was speaking, at least not in sentences. It was evening and quite dark outside, I was always afraid of the dark, but that is another story. The rest of the family had finished their dinner and we were alone in the kitchen. I remember hearing my sisters playing in the background. Mom was angry I hadn't eaten my vegetables. In my baby-like voice and manner I tried to explain to her I didn't feel good. I was moving my head back and forth and trying to close my mouth. The food, whatever it was, was now cold and definitely not good. I didn't like the texture and I most definitely found the flavor disgusting. She had pulled her chair in front of me and forced spoonful after spoonful of green lifeless gook into my mouth.

I was crying and trying to tell her I was sick, or maybe sick of the situation I found myself in. She didn't believe me, of course, and continued resolutely with what I considered in my little mind as torture. Finally and thankfully I vomited! Beautiful green disgusting vomit right onto her. Bull's eye! I wasn't the least bit revolted, in fact I remember feeling distinctly satisfied and that successful revenge had been accomplished. The ordeal ended with her jumping up, running to the kitchen sink and making gagging noises. For me it was the big, "I told you so," and in short order I was released from captivity in the highchair and no more food was forced into me that evening.

Food in our home had a dual purpose, one was sustenance and the other control. Now, she could put on a lavish meal and some of our friends thought she was Adele Davis and Julia Child all rolled into one, but our daily fare, when Dad wasn't home, was spam, sliced tomatoes and sometimes a dollop of mayonnaise. Most of the growing-up years my father worked swing shift and it was just the four of us at our meals. Mom had not learned to cook in Scotland, married young, and really boiled most of our vegetables until they turned dark green and mushy.

Asparagus was the worst. Now that I grow my own I can't wait until early spring to enjoy the rich succulent and tender spears. Mom would place bundles standing upright in a pot of boiling water, literally killing them, and we had to eat that stringy muck or be punished.

Food when I was growing up didn't have the preservatives it does today. It was normal at our house that our bread boasted a light greenish mold. No fear of not getting enough penicillin, Mom just cut off the moldy sections and made us eat it anyway. Now maybe it was economics, but she would buy two and three loaves at a time and believe me when we got to the last one there was a ripe musty odor about it. There were daily bakery trucks coming up our city streets, milk was delivered and fresh vegetables were available. My

Aunt Lillie and her husband owned a small grocery store so I have no explanation for why we had so much rotten and stale food.

We also were rationed milk. True, we were children of World War II and I still have my ration book, however, my mother continued the rationing well after the war. I wasn't allowed a full glass of milk until I got into junior high and then I would encounter her wrath for "drinking it all up." She, on the other hand loved buttermilk and would drain it right out of the quart container. Our glasses were the 4 ounce cream cheese jars you still see in the markets during the holidays. She would set these on the table, filling them with milk before she began preparing the meal. Sometimes they would sit there for more than an hour. We learned early to take a tiny sip first to check freshness before drinking. Ohhh, the taste of sour milk, I wretch at the mere thought! It gets you somewhere between the ears with a tingling feeling long before your toes want to charge up to the stomach and force it out! Even if we ran to the bathroom sink off the back porch and spit it out, the taste would linger for several hours. It was an experience to avoid at all costs.

My sisters and I devised an elaborate ruse at mealtimes. One of us would get her attention while the other would slide whatever chewed garbage we couldn't swallow onto the extension leaf of the table that hung slightly below the top. We would then wait in our beds at night for her to go to her own room and then one of us, taking turns, would sneak back into the darkened kitchen, reach up under the table and remove the glob of whatever had been left. We either threw the rotted stuff into the kitchen trash or flushed it down our little half-bath toilet.

Marilyn really got in trouble when she was found out. We all knew if we were caught in the act we would be beaten. Each flush brought held breaths that it would all go down and not flood the bathroom. No wonder we were all skinny. Snacks were NOT allowed either, three meals a day, served on time and no eating in-between.

But, to the woman's credit and there are credit feathers given, she became interested in cooking around the time my sisters hit junior high school. We actually went to cooking classes together and I was so happy. I think it was an extension of the Girl Scout program. Also about the same time we were bringing home recipes and ideas from our home economics classes. Noel actually took over the cooking duties when my mother went to work. It was her job, the dutiful indentured servant, to have dinner on the table promptly at 5:30 p.m. Noel actually became quite a good cook with her limited ingredients and could whip lemon Jello and canned milk together to make a great dessert.

Because of our sparse and sometimes unpalatable meals, coupled with the "no snacks" rule, my sisters and I became somewhat little street urchins. We each had places to go up and down the block where we could be assured of something to eat. Marilyn would go to her friend Patty's house, I would go to Linda's and later the Piligian's. Then, there was the nice Mexican lady next door who always, and I mean always, had donuts. As I grew, I spent less and less time at home and more and more time with the neighbors and friends. I rotated around them all so I wouldn't be thought of as a pest or a burden.

Some of Mom's ideas were just rooted in ignorance. I don't think she meant to be mean, but she had some strange concepts. Her ideas on hydration and drinking undoubtedly played a major role in her last illness, but also in my early years played a critical role in two of my sunstrokes.

My first heatstroke was when I was about eight years old and Dad wanted to show us the desert in the middle of summer. No one had air conditioning then and we definitely weren't given any water. Mom didn't drink it herself and thought no one else required it. After a few hours of driving across the great Mojave Desert I passed out in the back seat. My sisters must have started yelling and Dad quickly found a service station somewhere out there. I remember him plunging his hand into a big red Coca-Cola cooler and pulling out a bottle of coke. Revived, I thought I was going to get a real treat but instead he put the bottle on the back of my neck. The cooling affect was immediate and then he went and got another. I don' t remember getting to drink that one, but I do remember they were heating up fast as he kept doing it until the color came back into my face.

My next sunstroke was when I was twelve or thirteen. It wasn't Marilyn's fault, it really wasn't. She was doing what every normal sixteen-year-old girl or boy does, visiting and talking with her friends. I felt honored being dragged along with her, spending the day with teenagers at Manhattan Beach. As soon as we arranged our towels in the sand she went off on a walk. I fell asleep in the sun without any protection, reading my book. It was several hours before she returned and started shaking me awake. By then my white, alabaster skin had turned the color of a cooked lobster and the burns were already blistered turning a deep purple red. Poor Marilyn felt so awful she got me to the car and drove me straight home. I couldn't even put my back against the seat of the car it hurt so. When we got home I went to my bed and lay, stomach down, on the cool, white percale sheets, drifting off into a slumber.

Somewhere in the night I woke up unable to breathe and with my heart racing. I was gasping and shaking and I could hear Noel in the distance calling for Mom to help. I was definitely confused as to what was happening. Mom got me to sit up and started bringing cold washcloths and applying them to my forehead, arms and gently on my back. Still I wasn't given any liquids, maybe she was worried I would vomit. Some of what happened that night isn't clear, but it is obvious that I had a sunstroke and an intense one. It was life threatening, however, no one was aware of that at the time, or if they were, they didn't act on the situation or even call a doctor. As I mentioned before, my mother did suffer from the illusion that she possessed a great deal of medical knowledge. Well, we all have experienced situations where "we could have died" right then and there, but we didn't.

It was for all these many reasons and a hundred more that I never left my children alone with my mother. For years I took them frequently for visits when I was assured my father would be there. When they were old enough to fend for themselves, they would have occasional summer visits without me.

I would pack snacks, bags of peanuts, raisins and granola bars in between all their clothes always instructing them to eat the snacks only when needed; I also safety-pinned a little money and our own phone number. My youngest was seven and the other nine before they got to go "fishing with Grandpa" and I worried about them the whole time. If Grandpa hadn't been there my children wouldn't have been either. He was their guardian angel in more ways than one.

The food thing does paint a picture of my mother's character. Around the holidays each year she would buy a bunch of fresh fruit, arrange it artistically on a huge platter or straw cornucopia with grapes draping over apples, bananas and oranges. It would be placed in the center of the dining room table and sit there, like a still-life, quietly rotting. We were not allowed to eat any of it. We would walk around it until the grapes started to shrivel from age and the under layers of bananas would darken and freckle. When there were visible signs of decay, we could have some of the fruit and only then with her pre-approved permission. I was glad years later when plastic fruit was substituted. This allowed Isobel to do her "food arrangements" without the food going bad. She hung plastic onions and peppers about her kitchen as decorations. Me? I hang *real* garlic braids and *real* dried parsley from my cabin beams, part storage, part remembering to use them, but never just for decoration to hang and rot.

Mom also arranged her baked goods. She got that from working briefly at my grandparent's bakery. She would spread the cookies out in a fan pattern on the always handy paper doilies tucked on the plates. Not only did she arrange food decoratively, but she counted how much she put down. Heaven forbid all hell would break loose if some unsuspecting child took one of the cookies left enticingly as bait at their eye level. It happened to all of us. It also happened to me as an adult and I was so flabbergasted that I nearly fell through the kitchen floor in Yucaipa.

Everyone loved Mother's chess pies. Friends and relatives often remarked about them. Two years before she died I had taken my granddaughter to visit her great grandmother. The famous chess pies were made and arranged on a platter on the kitchen table. There weren't any signs that said "'don't eat me," nor did anyone mention that they were for anyone other than company — and we were the company. In my ignorance of these matters, and stupidly forgetting the past history, I ate one or two, probably two because you can't eat just one.

As we were leaving she began putting them in a white gift box lined with wax paper and the traditional paper doilies. Marilyn was driving my granddaughter and I back to Los Angeles and we were going to catch a plane home the next day. My mother's face darkened with the ancient infuriated look as she counted the chess pies. Watching this I got a mischievous look and that sent her over the top.

"You did it didn't you? You ate Dan's chess pies," she growled angrily at me.

"Excuse me, Mom, but did you really make two dozen chess pies just for Dan? None for me?" I was trying to lighten her mood. This was no time for an argument, especially in front of the granddaughter. I was attempting to be a role model of good behavior and really thought that most of Isobel's very bad behavior had been in the past, however, my granddaughter also was never left alone with her. I am sure my mother never suspected or even wondered why the kids didn't stay with her. The best excuse ever was we were four hundred miles away. I always tried not to hurt her feelings — quite the balancing act at times and this was one of those times.

Here it came. The old familiar "drop dead" dirty look that fortunately the kid didn't see. She handed the box to her, and get this — told her not to let me have any, that they were for Dan.

Now, I have to be perfectly clear. This wasn't done in jest or as a tease as some families do. Many would have torn off the lid and had the dessert consumed before they reached the main road.

No, this was done with all the seriousness in the world. The poor child's face dropped, torn between what she saw as two old ladies. I'm sorry now I didn't just reach over and tilt the entire contents over my mother's head. Noel surely would have. Such pettiness would not and should not be tolerated, but tolerated it was. However, somewhere on the path of life I had become a little more intelligent. The way to handle this situation was ignore it and let my granddaughter sit with her precious cargo on her lap for the trip to Los Angeles, then deliver them into the hands of Dan the Creep. The Chess pies were for Slither.

Chess Pie Recipe

One cup of raisins
One cup of chopped walnuts
2 eggs
3/4 Cup of granulated sugar
6 Tbs of milk
3 Tbs of butter
1 tsp. of vanilla

Put the first six ingredients in a saucepan. Cook for one minute after it boils stirring constantly. Remove from the stove and add vanilla. Pour into baked pastry shells.

*I like to use a Swedish Sandbakkels shell for mine. Sometimes my mother just put pie dough in a cupcake form and baked those. Enjoy and share!

I have to come to my mother's defense here a bit. She did try to be nice, but it is apparent that didn't come naturally to her and she had to work on it. She did many nice things though and the story of the "horse cake" was one of them. I was about eight or nine and going through my horse crazy stage. It was my birthday and my mother wanted to bake the cake herself, fascinating because even though my grandfather was a baker, we never had store-bought cakes. We were a do-it-yourself gang. Mother wasn't the artistic one, that was my dad, so she labored for hours over a little icing horse head in the middle of the cake. She had a model and really did work all afternoon on it making the head out of melted chocolate. She was so proud of her accomplishment and I was equally delighted as both of us viewed it as a work of art. I couldn't wait for my young friends to see it.

Mom set the cake in the middle of the kitchen table and everyone came in to admire it. Within an hour there was a shriek from the kitchen! We all rushed in to discover my mother looking horrified at the cake and I burst into tears! The horse head in the middle of the cake had been eaten out! Not the edges, just the complete middle like someone had taken a giant hand and scooped it out. The whole thing was utterly ruined. Who would have done such a thing? Everyone acted horrified and the only conclusion we could come up with was it had to have been our little dog.

In retrospect, the dog, who did misbehave at times did not have priors of climbing onto the kitchen table. It was a small dog and couldn't even get up onto a chair. Dogs normally either drag something off the table if they get that far, drop it unceremoniously on the floor, or escape out a door before they consume their stolen items. Dogs also start at the edge and munch forward.

This was just the center. Just the horse head and just the chocolate, nothing more. The story was told over and over and at last over the years with some humor, the dog always remaining the culprit. I never believed it was the dog and believe it less since I've now been a dog owner for over fifty years. Not the dog!

Chapter 11

The Return

Yes, it is amazing what goes through one's mind at the time of death. Marilyn and I, once so very close, were driving wordlessly back to the Yucaipa house. We approached my parent's home with the usual crunching sounds in the gravel and noticed the sun was well up now, hitting the Spanish tile roof and cascading across the walls.

I had called Noel from the hospital to let her know it was all over and she in turn had notified the grandchildren. The driveway was littered with a collection of vehicles, from Noel's old truck to a Mercedes. As soon as Marilyn turned off her ignition she stoically marched into the house without acknowledging anyone at the door, brushing them aside as she walked in.

"I'm laying down and I want to be alone," she spit out between clenched teeth. "I don't want to talk with anybody." With that she sailed swiftly down the hall into my mother's room slamming the door. The slam reverberated down the hall as an exclamation mark. Did anyone actually jump at that sound? The rest of the family stared in silence at my bedraggled appearance. I'd had no sleep, no shower, no change of clothes and little to eat for two days. I'm sure by now I wasn't smelling very nice.

My son Brad was the first to step through the small throng of onlookers and hugged me tight. "How ya doin', Mom?" he asked. I answered that I was better now that he was here and that was the truth. Somewhere in our lives we had changed roles and this son and I had become good friends. He was the anchor of my stability in stormy times, and there had been more than just a few. We continued hugging each other and held hands as we moved through the house out to the covered veranda in the back.

Mom had neglected the outdoor space for some time simply not having the physical ability to maintain everything. The collection of potted succulents were gasping for water and I put that on my mental list of things to do. Noel was sitting on the stairs leading out to the rose garden drinking a Coke and smoking a cigarette. I reached over, grabbed her pack of cigarettes and lit one up. It had been ten years since I quit smoking but I hadn't forgotten how to light one. I inhaled. "One hell of a day I'd say. Marilyn is in the back room exhausted. I told her I'd help her make some phone calls later. She wanted to lie down and I don't blame her."

"Do you? Want to lie down?"

"No. I'm tightly wired and too glad to see all of you." The smoke from the cigarette was making me a little light headed and dizzy. Noel's family had always been an extension of my own and I cherished each time I got to see them. I hadn't any daughters and I used to tell them I would just borrow them as my girls. I had seen them frequently as they grew up, at least every few months if not more. Many times our two families had vacationed with each other and all our holidays and momentous occasions were planned as a group. In our early thirties Noel and I had both migrated to northern California, she closer to the coast and I into the Sierra Nevada foothills. We were about a two-and-a-half hour drive from each other.

Cyndie came and sat with us, her jaw still swollen and slightly disfigured from a wisdom tooth extraction. She wanted to know all the details, since nursing was her business, and Brad too wanted to know what transpired. I asked them if they really wanted to know because it wasn't a very pleasant story. Both were affirmative and sat quietly waiting to hear the gory details.

Slowly, I recounted the events and told them both. Yes, I did give permission to withhold the life support drugs and that Grandma did finally pass on peacefully never regaining consciousness. I also told them that just for clarification of what happened, I believed we needed an autopsy. It wasn't an easy tale to relate, but I didn't omit a detail.

They both seemed to fully understand that their grandmother would never have recovered and that we could have kept her in a vegetative state longer, but saw no purpose for it. I told them that, essentially, their grandmother was brain dead, her spirit having left her body before I painfully made the decision to terminate all artificial life support systems.

Various relatives began arriving and filtering in and out of the house. They rotated about the rooms in low and whispered conversations, all believing Marilyn was getting a well-deserved rest. After a few hours of this, I decided I needed to call the hospital and let them know where to take my mother. I tiptoed down the green runner in the hall to look in on Marilyn. When I opened the door and looked in there she was, sitting in the middle of the bedroom floor with the phone book propped open in her lap. Marilyn chatting away as if she were arranging a quilting show. She was talking to our cousin and when I made a face to her and held up my hand in the phone sign by my ear signifying I wanted to talk to her, Marilyn just frowned at me and bade Frances good bye with an angelic voice.

That simple act of defiance brought back the flood of memories of my mother doing the same thing. Mom would be yelling and screaming at us for some reason or smacking us around and the phone would ring. With a look of fury that could cut through metal, she would raise a pointed finger in the air for silence and we froze on the spot. Then, still holding that position, she would put a smile on her face and with lilting grace in her voice answer as if she was God's angel. "Hello," the saccharine greeting dripping off her tongue.

I was maybe six or seven when this repeated performance actually began to fascinate me. I started observing my mother's behavior and would step back from it affecting me personally. How could someone switch personalities and moods so rapidly? She spun on a dime, one moment shrill threats where we thought our deaths were imminent and the next she was pleasantly talking to our Aunt Lillie or one of the PTA ladies. Even at my young age I realized there was more involved here than just good acting. Mother had the calculated ability to change masks faster than any channel surfer could change their TV programming.

Now I looked at my sister on the floor of my mother's room mimicking the identical behavior. "Marilyn," I reiterated, "I told you I would help you do this. We all thought you were resting."

"I'm calling people to let them know."

From the look of the room, she had been at this for some time. Neither of the twin beds appeared slept in. Both were made up and the toss pillows arranged exactly where they had been the night before.

I thought it strange she had put herself immediately in the position of the grieving daughter. Was she gaining something she needed from friends and relatives that she didn't want or couldn't get from me? We had lived in different sections of the U.S. for more than thirty-six years. Maybe she didn't know that I still spoke to and corresponded with all our relatives. Perhaps she thought she was the only one with a connection. In retrospect, I don't know if we ever talked about it.

In a letter she mailed to me months later she said she was assuming the horrible task of informing people of a death in the family and if I had wanted comfort in talking to people there was nothing stopping me. Well, yes there was. There was an angry woman with the single phone line in the house and full possession of the only phone book. An angry woman with a look on her face that said she could hurl something at me any moment.

I just shrugged and told her I'd take care of the overseas group. Our family was huge, eclectic, and Scottish. I always said Scotland's best export was her people, after the whiskey. We had cousins I corresponded with in Scotland, the Shetland Islands, Australia, New Zealand and South Africa. That would keep me busy. It wasn't that I derived some sense of purpose being the bearer of bad news. I'd rather be the bearer of good news any day, but when it came to our "overseas family" I was the bearer of all news. No one else besides me had corresponded with them regularly. The immediate group had shown little interest even when kids their own age came to visit from South Africa. They didn't know their names or make any attempt to stay in touch and, personally, I felt it was their loss, but then no one asked me about it.

I left Marilyn in the back room. There was nothing more to do or to say; I went back to the family room to visit with so many I hadn't seen in a long time. All the little ones had mercifully been left at their homes in the care of others, as this was a gathering time strictly for the grown-ups.

No one really realized when Marilyn left the backroom and collected Cyndie. It appears that Marilyn had set up command central amongst the dressers, old sewing machine, and first-marriage wedding photos in the recesses of my mother's room. What she failed to realize fully at this point was that the younger generation wasn't caught up in the web of living with deception. We had spoken little about our past tragic experiences and our troubled childhoods, having only shared the good times and the laughable stories. The younger members of the family had been more open about their mistakes, obstacles and dreams. Did Marilyn really think that Cyndie wouldn't tell me later that she had been summoned to the backroom? Of course she would tell me, she wasn't a deceiver. As a nurse she just predictably and immediately came out and announced, "Hey, Marilyn doesn't want an autopsy."

"Oh," I replied, noting mentally that Marilyn had been with me when I requested it and hadn't said a word.

Cyndie continued, "I told her that in my heart I didn't want one either, but my training from a medical standpoint said a strong, yes, that we needed one. Mom," she said turning to Noel, "she told me you didn't want one either."

Noel who was listening piped up. "I don't like the idea, but I haven't talked to Marilyn about it. Why would she say that? An autopsy is a desecration of the body, but I agree we need to find out more of what happened here. I really don't want my mother cut up. It makes me sick just to think about it, but I believe we need to do it."

The rest of that day is foggy to me. The sweater I had on was way too warm for March in southern California and I was sweating. My scalp was itching and my hair was matted. I decided to take a long hot shower and try to regain my senses and some dignity with soap and shampoo. I borrowed a T-shirt from my son and slipped into the main bathroom of the house, the only one we were allowed to use at the time.

Someone had taken caution tape and crisscrossed off the door to the bathroom that my mother most frequently used. We weren't allowed in. I vaguely remember wondering who got the caution tape and where? The only time I had really seen it was on TV and once for a joke when a neighbor put it across his driveway. The explanation from Marilyn was this, "Mom's bathroom was contaminated." Pretty silly explanation but my dull brain wasn't thinking of everything. Mom did shower in this bathroom rather than the large one, but she peed in both.

The hot water cascading down my back was medicinal. My muscles began to relax and I reached for someone else's shampoo. I didn't bring any of my own and had stuffed only my camp toothbrush in my backpack. I closed my eyes and let the steam cleanse my lungs while the soap and water removed miles of the last few days. All done and refreshed I wrapped the only big towel around me and started going through the vanity for some toothpaste. It wasn't in the drawer I remembered but I did find an old squished tube. Interesting, I thought, things were all moved about. Strange because my mother never rearranged things. Tables and chairs, dishes, linens and food were always in their original places. Sitting on this vanity for the last twenty years was a small copper tray and five bottles of perfume. The bottles changed from time to time, not from use but when someone gave her a new bottle. What everyone failed to realize is that they were on display as appreciation for the gift. Mom didn't wear perfume. I perused the group of bottles in a variety of shapes and helped myself to a little White Shoulders while checking out my appearance in the huge mirror that extended the entire length of the double vanity.

Why didn't someone grab a little rag and Lysol? A simple fix for the little bathroom, however, Marilyn had given the command to "stay out," and all the kids, including myself had obeyed dutifully as if it was a government mandate. Besides, none of the younger set cared much for domestic work. Noel was trussed up like a turkey and I was stumbling about. Looking back I'm sorry I didn't crash into that bathroom and check out what the big mystery was.

What we all decided to do though, for a while, was give Marilyn a wide berth and leave her alone. Everyone had noticed what we considered erratic behavior and it was mutually agreed that it was probably due to stress, after all she had been the one most of the time taking care of Mom and the house.

Chapter 12

MARILYN

Marilyn was every parent's dream. After years of trying to conceive, she was the first babe in Mom's arms, long awaited, cherished and adored. Academically, she was way ahead of the pack and was promptly put in advanced classes in elementary school. She embraced the years of junior and high school with total enthusiasm and was on every third page of the year books. In a school with a student body close to three thousand kids this was no easy task. She was on honor rolls, won awards for academic achievement, joined clubs and participated in plays and music. She was a popular girl surrounded with friends and admirers. Though she didn't participate in any sports herself she could be found at all of these events yelling and cheering until her throat was hoarse.

Our parents allowed and encouraged us to think of Marilyn as an extremely talented young lady, which she was, and later a woman who had a sensitive nature. She designed and made many of her own clothes, and was provided a dresser with a key that locked so Noel and I could never borrow her bounty. Each day as she left for school, she closed and locked all her drawers. I'm sure she would have locked her bedroom door if that had been possible. True, Noel and I would borrow her stuff when we could. She had a great collection of scarves, and as an early teen, I became successful at picking her locks.

I think there was enormous pressure on Marilyn growing up to be the best in everything she did. She had the ballet, acrobatic, piano and art lessons. But with the lessons came the price to perform and then to get the blue ribbon. She developed tremendous headaches and nose bleeds as a kid and looking back I'm sure stress was a major factor.

Marilyn had an early magnetism about her that attracted men and boys and subsequently was never without a boyfriend from the time she was ten and in the sixth grade. She would have them carrying her books and coming by the house on bikes, scooters, and later cars. In her teen years she was always the loyal girlfriend, keeping each young man for at least two or three years and always "going steady." When one exited the stage there was another in the wings to quickly step in and hold her hand.

She was the pride of us all when accepted to UCLA as an art major. Marilyn's steady beau all through high school joined the military right after graduation and Marilyn went off to college. They planned to marry when he returned.

That dream bubble burst with her back surgery and her adoring new suitor married her happily as she was pregnant with their son at the age of twenty.

Marilyn wasn't poor in the physical appearance department and always had an adorable hourglass figure with large breasts, a tiny waist and ample hips. Her skin had remained smooth and unlike me, she got by without glasses. As she aged her hair remained dark with a few silver strands giving it a peppered, sophisticated look. Her seamstress talents and sense of color found her dressed attractively at all family events. This was of course when she was "up."

After the birth of her son she would slip for periods of time into the depths of depression, go without bathing, her hair hanging limply with a stringy greasy look and to put it bluntly, she would stink. With no makeup she would look pinched and drawn, but when the occasion arose she rose too and was the starlet of the room, voicing opinions and dropping names as if she was on center stage. Looking back I realize that she did not remain in the limelight. She severed ties with most all her high school friends and chose not to attend any of their functions. Was she embarrassed she had to get married? Sad she had lost her high school sweetheart? Combinations of all these things? Not being able to see completely nor understand another's heart and soul we will never know.

Marilyn was one of those articulate people, appearing well read, intelligent and educated. I bragged about her for years. "My eldest sister, the 4.0 graduate from UCLA." Where did I get that? Noel said the same thing. We were so proud of her achievements and never were corrected on this statement by anyone.

Even though she was attractive to all kinds of men, she wasn't satisfied with her own physical appearance. In a way this may have been compounded by our mother's statements. I asked Mom once why she labeled us and she said she had read somewhere that parents should emphasize a child's strong points, so Mom did this frequently. Marilyn was the smart one, Noel the pretty one and I was the one with a good nature.

The flip side of the coin was that we were criticized continually about the way we looked and that is a fact. Marilyn was told her hips were "too big" but good for babies and her hair was a mousy brown. My speech impediments were so blasted and laughed at that I began to fear opening my mouth not wanting to be ridiculed for my pronouncements. I wasn't sent to speech therapy, just made fun of to the point I would stammer and stutter. I was repeatedly told I had "table legs" and a "pot belly." Noel was told almost daily how "difficult" she was. I began to think I was just a giggling, pot belly pig, Marilyn, an unattractive but brilliant genius and Noel beautiful but ornery.

Marilyn thought her nose wasn't right and as an adult eventually had plastic surgery. The surgery proved disastrous because her body absorbed the transferred cartilage and it just ended up a different version of the original one. I never saw anything wrong with either the first nose or the second. I told her I loved her just the way she was, but Marilyn thought it was horrific and was depressed.

It seems to be a generational thing with parenting. I've talked to other peers and they have said the same thing. We were rarely told what was right about us, but rather our shortcomings. Our report cards were not messages of praise but condemnation. It wasn't, "Hey, good job, almost all A's." It was, "Why did you get this B?" Heaven forbid we were some kind of idiots that we rated the average C. It was junior high when I realized that nothing I could do was going to be good enough and I definitely could never be as good as Marilyn, so I decided to have some fun instead and indeed I did. It was my choir grades that got me into college. Marilyn appeared the least affected by the barrage of criticism to some extent, or was she? Where and when did she break?

As I said in junior high she slipped a disc doing acrobatics. With that and a few other events she elicited quite a bit of justifiable sympathy as chronic pain developed. The family started referring to her as *"Poor Marilyn,"* a prefix to her name that remains to this day. The family didn't even realize it in conversation how often they habitually said *Poor Marilyn* as if Poor was her first name and Marilyn her middle. Even our mother did it in her later years. Anytime she was talked about, good or bad, she was *Poor Marilyn.*

The summer before Mom's death I even questioned Noel. "Do you realize that you always refer to her as *Poor Marilyn?*" Noel was amazed at my observation then started to talk about her again, catching herself with the "poor" and started giggling. The question was, why and from whose perspective did she merit the prefix? She wasn't poor due to economics. She wasn't poverty stricken even though, like all of us had landed on financial hard times over the years.

Perhaps it was *Poor Marilyn* because of her son Slither. Dan was her only child by choice. She would often lament that she had lost a babe at five months and that was true. Everyone felt terribly sorry for her, but what they didn't know is she also terminated another pregnancy just a year later. Remember, Marilyn and I were close and I knew more about her than most.

Marilyn's attraction to men began at some point to overlap.

She sought and got sexual attention with multiple partners in and out of our society's social expectations. She told me once, referring to sex, that you don't buy a dress without trying it on first. This girl had the whole dress shop! And a high-priced one as well because her choices were always professional men: lawyers, professors, news editors and psychiatrists to name a few. She crossed color lines and age barriers and was caught literally with her pants down more than once. She even accused one brother-in-law of uninvited advances, however, I can assure you, they were clearly invited. Some might have called Marilyn promiscuous.

I don't believe Marilyn ever really wanted a career or, on the other hand, perhaps she wasn't capable of one. That is a hard call to make. She simply never managed to keep a job for one reason or another. There were always plausible reasons given. The bottom line is the girl was never consistently employed and was assisted by parents, husbands and friends pretty much her whole life. She also used her house numerous times as collateral and had the art of refinancing down to a science.

The coupe de grâce of her second marriage was when she invited the current lover and his wife to dinner along with she and her husband. Oh my, you have to admire her nerve. Of course, the wife blew the whistle and all relationships collapsed when the deceit was discovered.

Yet Marilyn helped the needy, often volunteering at a soup kitchen during the holidays. She took in a foster child for a while and later an entire family of illegal immigrants from San Salvador. She did make some profit in these situations, however, in her heart they also were for humanitarian reasons. What baffled me was the foster child for as soon as he turned 18, he moved to the east coast and was never heard from again.

Some of the things Marilyn did left me at a loss for an explanation. She could appear so brilliant but then do incredibly silly things as if she had no common sense. The front house was rented to the folks from San Salvador and Sis built a three-level house where her garage had been in the back. The kitchen, laundry and entrance were on the first floor, bathroom and living room on the second and one bedroom and a loft, accessible only by metal spiral staircases. In order to pee you had to negotiate stairs, unless of course you were in the living room, up from the kitchen or down from the bedroom.

She also had a sense of humor and her Christmas cards that year included a picture of herself covered in sheet-rock dust wishing everyone a white Christmas. Then, before construction was completed she stopped, built a floor to ceiling cupboard the length of an entire wall in the middle section of the house. For weeks she washed, pressed and folded fabric, sorting it by color and pattern and filled the cabinet with it. This was during her quilting period. Perhaps she needed a break. Yes, at times she exhibited what is referred to as obsessive compulsive disorder (OCD), but it didn't appear from the outside to be debilitating.

Now the woman was fully cognizant of her own physical limitations. Her back problems plagued her for years and here she was building herself obstacles. The stairs to the loft were tiny little pie-shaped wedges and you had to hang onto the railing and place each foot carefully. *Poor Marilyn* even fell down them a time or two. Why would she do that, build that way?

It was her strange and almost bizarre side that evolved slowly. After the San Salvadorians left her front house, her son moved back in. Slither was always moving back in for one reason or another. She would say it was until he could get on his feet, but that never happened either. Now she calls me in Montana and tells me that she thought he'd be more independent if he didn't have a kitchen. This little woman with the back problems went into her front house, pried the kitchen cabinets off the walls and removed the stove. The only thing remaining in the kitchen was the sink. This of course didn't force Dan to leave, but rather made him start using her kitchen a short distance away in the back house. First thing in the morning he would struggle from the empty three-bedroom house in front and put on a pot of coffee in her kitchen. Since he no longer had dishes to use he was forced to use hers. He'd make himself breakfast, drink her coffee, smoke his cigarettes and Marilyn, who wouldn't allow anyone to help clean up her kitchen, was left with the mess. The perfect way to encourage someone's independence is to make them more dependent, right?

When the removal of the kitchen didn't work and Dan was still hanging around, she went back to the front house a few months later, disconnected the water heater and had it physically removed leaving a big gaping hole in the wall. All the while she was doing this home destruction she claimed to have a bad back. Of course, having no hot water for showering, Slither just began taking his showers upstairs in the back house, then leaving his dirty clothes for her to wash because he no longer had a washing machine that would work. Crazy but true.

It was clear that Dan wasn't about to leave. The rent was paid, utilities were a bare minimum and most of the groceries were taken care of. When he got bored he could walk the fifty feet to a large heated home with a big screen TV. Parasites are not dumb. He could be caustic as hell, but not dumb. A bully with a purpose, but not dumb. When this lopsided arrangement didn't work for Marilyn, she would yell at him and he back at her. Their assaultive insults and yelling frequently hit a decibel level, with doors slamming and cars leaving in exhaust that carried through the air to the neighbors. Our childhood scenes continued to play out in Marilyn's home with the same script but different actors.

Perhaps she was *Poor Marilyn* because she clearly enabled Slither to a great extent. Dan had been a bright little boy and talented, but as he reached puberty she said he was "just too bright for the school system" and that he was unchallenged. As he matured he started his rap sheet of petty crimes. I don't know all the details, why he bashed in an ATM machine one night is a mystery and then there were the DUIs and the battery of a young woman. Marilyn of course, accused the young girl of false accusations and lying. When he couldn't keep a job she said he was far too intelligent and talented to be working minimal labor. Perhaps she did deserve our sympathy because she couldn't see reality. She covered up a great deal for Dan and there is so much we don't know.

What I do know is that Dan wasn't honest by any extent of the imagination. He procured $10,000 from my mother, telling her he needed a car, and then went to one of the ex-step-dads and told him the same thing. A few months later the supposed car was repossessed for non-payment. We never knew the whole story about that man's escapades. He was a delightful and adorable little guy and there was a special place in my heart for him, but his behavior as an adult was so unacceptable with me that I cut all cords.

It is difficult for me to try to explain my sister Marilyn. Like a quilt made of the many pieces of fabric she stacked, I'm not sure how it all fit together. I don't know what happened to her or when. I loved her dearly. I was her best and at times her only friend. The changes were slow and then there was the sudden, startling change a year before Mom's death.

Our phone calls took on an unexplained, caustic and negative tone. I ceased to look forward to hearing her voice and attributed the problem to possible pain pill reactions. She was scheduled for another back surgery and rejected all our efforts to help. Noel offered to come and I even told her I would take a leave of absence to assist her recovery.

What event in her life prompted these dramatic changes none of us knew, but I wasn't the only one who noticed. One niece asked what was wrong with her and even our mother commented on the change.

No, I didn't see the *"poor"* in Marilyn. She had managed most of her life not to work and I suppose in a way I resented that. I never had that luxury. She wasn't the single mother who got up each morning, got the kids off to school and then went to work herself. For very brief periods she did this, but in the long run her work record was sketchy at best.

Over the years Marilyn would tell people she was a teacher and in many definitions that was true. She was a beautiful quilter and taught quilting at an evening adult extension class once a week. When she decided to write a book on quilting in the early '80s my naive parents agreed to support her financially for another year so she could complete the project. No one did any research on the marketing at this point, which at the time was inundated with quilting books. So Marilyn took a year making several dozen, tiny 3" x 5" quilt samples and little sketch illustrations for quilts. The book was talked about for years but it was never finished. At the end she showed me the dozen meticulously crafted and illustrated instruction pages. Not enough for a book.

That was a pattern of not finishing things. She would make Noel's daughters lovely dresses for school and not finish them. Later, I would get the pile of clothes and then put in the hems or the zippers or whatever had been left out in the construction.

Who was this person? Why had she fooled so many about graduating summa cum laude when she barely got through her freshman year? We would have loved her anyway. Marilyn will remain to me an enigma and a puzzle. She has been to psychiatrists, psychologists, joined the Maharishi and participated in all kinds of self-healing and searching activities over the years. She joined Synanon in Santa Monica and said it was as an observer, but later when I researched them found it was a drug rehab. Was she into drugs?

The faiths of both Noel and myself were scoffed at as childlike or not valid for an intellectual like herself. When we tried to approach her or help her she would always remind us how "deeply she was hurt" by our talks.

Thus, Marilyn entered the circumstances of our mother's death known as *Poor Marilyn*. So many of us wanted to lovingly support her, actually wanted to help her, but she rejected all attempts. We were not permitted to mourn with her for a loss affecting us all. Not permitted even to show her love and affection that we still felt at that point.

Chapter 13

TEAMWORK

I always liked the term teamwork; my sons and I worked as a team, my horses worked as a team, I have friends who worked as a team. To me life went better with a little help from my friends. More than once I had heard the story attributed to Aesop's Fables where there was quarreling in a family. The wise father had given each of his sons a stick and asked them to break them. The sticks were easily broken. Then, the same father took a bundle of sticks, bound them with a fine string and handed them around again. The bundle could not be broken, together the sticks were strong but could be broken individually. The moral of the story being that in unity there is strength.

Cyndie, Noel's youngest, had tried to explain to me the family in southern California had separated into two distinct camps some time ago regarding their grandmother's care, but I couldn't fathom that. This family? It was incredulous to think that. No, this family practices unity, we were the bundle unbroken. Why would we polarize into distinct groups when our goal remained the same and that was for Granny to get well?

For close to sixty years, with the exception of some gaps, we had been close, in my perception and/or illusion. Like war buddies, combat fellows, brothers in arms, we had survived, laughed and cried together. My sisters and their children, when they were young had been, my very essence. They were my breath, my strength and my foundation. I saw us all as working like synchronized dancers across a stage and players at their best. Time and time again we were a team from children to adults.

I went through a period in my childhood I refer to as "the nightmare years." At that point we three girls had been moved into one room as one of our cousins was living with us while he went to college at USC in Los Angeles. That is how our family operated. The nightmares were terrorizing and I'd wake up screaming that I was being choked to death, always from behind by an unknown assailant. These went on night after night and it would have been impossible not to disturb the entire household.

It was Marilyn who came up with a workable solution to alleviate my fears. Putting her young sewing talents to work, each evening after I went to bed she would make a new little dress for my doll. Then, before she went to bed she would hang the delightful creation on a doorknob facing my bed. As soon as I opened my eyes in the morning I would see something wonderful that delighted my little girl heart. Sleep, rather than a fearful thing, slowly became an anticipated event. I'd go to bed less fearful of the dark and knowing that in the morning, stuck on the crystal doorknob would be a new doll dress. I thought it was the magical work of fairies. The nightmares dissipated for a short time — but *Help me make it through the night* was a long, continuing battle. The point is it was Marilyn, in her youthful way, who helped her terrified little sister look forward to the future. She showed me that sleep could be a friend and not the enemy. She showed me love.

She did it again when I was eighteen. I had finished my first year at Harbor Community College and my parents were moving from our childhood home. Marilyn was newly divorced and I was staying with her, working nights making hamburgers and tacos and watching young Dan during the day. It was my turn to help Marilyn out. She was also broke and would come up to the drive-through, after the rush when the boss had left, and I'd slip her hamburgers and fries. That is how we ate that summer. I really was staying with Marilyn so she wouldn't be lonely and depressed, and it was also my first planned step out of my own home.

Without communication, an easy thing since Alexander Graham Bell invented the phone, Mom just packed up her house in LA and randomly threw my things out. She didn't call or ask me over, she didn't even give any warnings or previews of the coming attractions. It wasn't that she piled my clothes into bags to send to

Mexico with my dad, but rather tossed much of my stuff carelessly into the trash. They became treasures to the landfill dumps of Los Angeles. Her actions were so bewildering because Mom and I had been building bridges for the last three years. Now if a child saves something for seventeen years it obviously must be of value to them. That is simple logic or "a given" as they would say in science. What is obvious here is that she didn't consider my feelings at all and they definitely were not part of the equation. Her decisions were mandates to be carried out, rarely thinking about others as she held the positions of Queen Dictator and Editor-in-Chief all rolled into one. She vacuumed through my room with a vengeance, carelessly tossing away my childhood.

On the top shelf of my closet, my mother found the real stuffed Koala bear that my grandfather brought me from Australia for my first birthday. The Koala had come with a live kitten and both were placed in my crib with loving hands. I have no idea why she threw it out. I was saving it for my own children and am sure I told her that more than once. I called him Coca-Koala and he was a well-worn precious treasure to me. Much like the Velveteen Rabbit, Coca-Koala had been so loved there appeared to be more leather than fur left on his body. He was definitely tufty in spots and I smile when I think of him. I had slept with him for twelve years and always kept him on my bed for the remaining years I was home. I had only recently put him in my closet. I had taken only a few clothing items to my Marilyn's, telling my mother that I would come home on my next day off and help her pack. When I got there I discovered that she had thrown much of my stuff out in the garbage, including my favorite all-time toy.

I was crushed, dismayed and speechless when she made the pronouncement. I actually went out to my faded '38 Dodge and sat quietly crying. The sense of loss wasn't totally over the toy, but the catastrophe of a destroyed treasure, the only tangible thing I had from my grandfather who had passed away just a few months before. That little hard stuffed animal I clung to nightly for many chaotic years, was gone. The comfort in a sea of chaos who I thought was safe in my room. How could she? Didn't she know or think? But then, nothing was safe there in that house, not even us.

After I ceased crying I started the engine and drove the thirty-minutes back to Marilyn's feeling as if something was missing from me, a sense of loss and grief. I told Marilyn what happened and cried some more, however, I had to go to work, distraught and distressed, to make more hamburgers ... five for a dollar.

Marilyn then did something so very thoughtful and so full of compassion that I will never forget her kindness. She went out the next day and shopped all over Los Angeles until she found a stuffed Koala made out of rabbit fur. The new guy was never the same, he was much smaller, wasn't from my grandfather, wasn't real, wasn't from Australia but it was from Marilyn with love.

Chapter 14

AUTOPSY

The much needed shower in Yucaipa was refreshing after hours of agony. I always felt the need to splash in water, maybe that was my Pisces personality, but I indeed felt better and more equipped to take on the tasks required after a loved one dies. First was to contact someone to do the autopsy. I needed to do that research and without the aid of a computer. There wasn't one in the house and no one had any helpful devices. I couldn't procrastinate. It needed to be decided, researched and someone needed to locate a place or person to do it immediately. I called the mortuary, explained what was happening and not to do anything until I contacted them back. Even though I didn't have legal authority, I did have people listening to me.

Marilyn's hostility and anger continued. She seemed to be spitting out every word she said. She asked me if I was willing to spend $6,000 for such an autopsy. As she asked that question she turned down her mouth, furrowed her brow, her hands were on her hips in a fighting stance. I was trying to maintain a level voice, the one I used with my special education students when they were about to launch into a tirade.

I told her I didn't know what an autopsy would cost until I called around and that I had never done something like this before. She hadn't either, but I thought it best not to mention that fact. Where did she get the idea they were $6,000? Had she just grabbed that figure out of the thin air or did she really know something? Maybe she was right, however, I felt she had made some pretty poor judgment calls in the last few weeks and I needed to do my own research here. Any confidence I may have had in her was evaporating quickly.

As it was, several calls had to be made. I pulled the old Yellow Pages phone book out of Mom's cabinet and started looking up Autopsy. From watching television cop and forensic programs, I thought it was just a simple call to the powers that be and the whole thing would be a done deal between the commercials. I was to quickly learn, there is a whole world out there I didn't know about.

Since Mom's autopsy request was not made by the police or a court, we had to find a private autopsy group. That was my first lesson. I didn't know there were private autopsy people who actually did it for a business. My next call was back to Community Hospital to get their recommendations. I figured that since they deal in death on a regular basis, they must have a list of qualified people. As I had their receptionists on the phone I simultaneously looked up the name and address of the mortuary where Mom had made her own arrangements some fifteen years earlier. With the mortuary information now available, I told the hospital where to take Mom, or who would pick her up, and then to double-check myself, I called the mortuary again also getting their recommendation of individuals who did private autopsies. I was cross referencing information while at the same time informing both the hospital and the mortuary of our intent.

Marilyn in the meantime was still protesting around the house that this was silly and no one wanted it but me. Thankfully, as she was drawing an entourage around her, I didn't have her hot dragon breath down my neck and I could make my calls alone and focus clearly. I started jotting down information on the scraps of paper I found in my grandmother's round table. I went down the list of recommended individuals until I finally talked to a pathologist who performed private autopsies. She sounded sympathetic on the phone and then she asked, "What kind of autopsy do you want?" I thought there was only one kind, like those I typed up so many years ago when I worked in claims for an insurance company. The kind that started with the "Y" incision. I balked and asked for an explanation.

The young pathologist explained to me that since it wasn't a forensic autopsy ordered by the police, I had the option of doing a simple clinical one to determine the cause of death. She paused and said that she could also do one that included a toxicology report. A toxicology report would cost a slight bit more and take longer because it included a lab analysis.

What is the difference I asked? The doctor explained that a forensic autopsy, like we see in the movies and on TV, is to see if there are any legal or medical problems that might warrant a coroner's exam and inquest. These are usually done when there is a homicide, suicide or accident with unexplained loose ends and those almost always included a toxicology report.

A toxicology report would also tell us what chemicals might be in our mother's body. Well, undoubtedly there would be many drugs considering the vials of antibiotics and the other things pumped into her.

I couldn't think through why I might want a toxicology report. Toxicology was, after all, the study of poisons and why in the world would I need that? Later I would regret that decision. At the time I was worried about Marilyn and her being critical of me for spending so much money. I wanted to be praised for thinking and not vilified for acting on the situation. Everywhere I had turned in the last twenty-four hours I had been harshly criticized.

There was also another factor. Marilyn over the last five years or so had repeatedly told Noel and I that our mother didn't have any money and that one major medical issue would wipe her out. I had no reason to doubt her and believed that Mom lived paycheck to Social Security paycheck. Her house was paid for, the car was paid for. I did know she had a little savings account but I thought it was little.

Considering all this, I asked how much the autopsy would cost and her quote was under $2,000 so I made the decision to go ahead with the minimum. I gave the pathologist all the necessary information and okayed the basic procedure without the toxicology tests. Then I called again both the mortuary and hospital explaining to each who would be doing the autopsy, and repeated that the cremation needed to be postponed until completion. The first phase of investigative cogs had been set in motion.

Noel said she was going next door to tell Mom's neighbor Esther the sad news. Brad and I decided to take a walk in the southern California sunshine, both coming down from the northwest, which was still in a winter weather pattern. It had been an exceptionally long season with too many successive days of gray skies and either wet or snowy weather. I needed this time alone with Brad anyway. We frequently spoke on the phone but we hadn't actually seen each other in months. Besides, there were things I knew about his grandmother's will that I had to share with him, primarily, one very upsetting fact and that his brother Vince in Australia had been totally cut out. I'm sure this would be shocking to all and excruciatingly painful for Vince. His grandmother's reason for such an action was hard to fathom and I was always holding out hope that she might change her mind. I had talked to her about it on several occasions.

Chapter 15

PANDORA'S BOX

Mom had given $10,000 to every one of her seven grandchildren at some point in their lives with the exception of Vince. For two of her favorites she had provided college educations along with free room and board in addition to the money. Both my parents had even provided vehicles for some members of the family, but not for all. There was always the conspicuous favoritism. I tried my best to keep my sons out of the mix so they wouldn't feel as though they were loved less and distance certainly helped. My sons were my dad's favorite boys, sharing the love of the outdoors and finally the love of the sea. Mom, however, had different views and since Dad was long since gone, he couldn't help or defend anyone now.

It was becoming clear to me that I was about to open Pandora's box. The ugly truths of our family and its twisted background were coming unraveled, along with some of the members. All these thoughts were going through my mind as Brad and I walked past house after house on this extraordinarily beautiful day. I recalled the fields of flowers that used to be out here, horses grazing and the big barn where we took our Christmas pictures when the kids were tiny. "Have you ever heard of Pandora's Box, Brad?"

"Yeah. Isn't it a club in L.A? Or used to be?"

"Yup – that's true," I said looking at my feet and smiling, "But there is a Greek legend about the first woman. She wasn't named Eve like in our bible, but Pandora. All the Greek gods got to participate in her design and she was given a bunch of graces, various charms and wiles." I giggled out loud, "Kind of like all the guys getting together and designing the perfect woman."

Brad also chuckled. He had just met a young lady and felt strongly that she might be the proverbial one. I continued with the story as we walked up the hill.

"Pandora was given a box. Some say it was a jar and I can't remember if she was given instructions to keep it closed or not, but of course she didn't. Normal curiosity came forth and no sooner had she been given it than she lifted the lid. Out flew the most disgusting things earth had ever seen: greed, vanity, slander ... you name it. I think regret was in there too. Anyway, Pandora was left with only one item in her box and that was hope. My point is Grandma's will isn't fair." I paused while I let this analogy set in and also braced myself for the next part.

"Son, your brother was not included in the will. He was cut out. I'll make it up to him, but it is going to sting badly. Your grandmother was never fair, and I mean never. She just couldn't forgive Vince for going to Australia. I talked to her occasionally about it and really thought she would change her mind, but she didn't get a chance to change her trust even if she did change her mind."

Brad didn't say a thing. As it was, one of Mom's other neighbors was out in her yard just at that moment and so we gave her the bad news. She said Isobel was always sweet to her and I replied that so many had said that. Brad and I headed back to the house.

Vince was cut out for a variety of reasons as explained by Marilyn in a three-page, single-spaced letter she sent him five months after Mom passed away. Marilyn accused him of lying, deception and child endangerment when he left his daughter with her mother. None of these things were true of course, they were just false accusations Marilyn made to justify why he was denied anything in our mother's estate. What was true was that he failed to send his grandmother regular photographs of his daughter and owed her one hundred dollars. Marilyn belittled Vince for transgressions he made at eighteen years old and made him out to be a total slime bag. Perhaps she was mixing up Vince with her son Slither. It seemed the cocaine users of the family got their inheritance but my son Vince, who did not have a drug problem, was denied. The truth was he was working hard at the time to get custody of his daughter, an eventuality that came to pass within a few months.

Brad sucked in his breath and I could tell he needed a little more time to process all I was telling him. We both looked down at our feet and I started to laugh because I was walking in his socks. I had forgotten socks too in my haste; his were white and had gray padded toes. The ends hung off in my shoe because his foot was so much bigger. They were comfortable and clean, but we must have been a hilarious sight for anyone not knowing our present circumstance.

So many people felt that my mother was a nice person. She had practiced and refined her social exterior graces so convincingly that her mask, her other side, was never seen except by her daughters and one other friend. Our Aunt Lillie had once told Noel sympathetically, "Your mother isn't quite right." Boy was that an understatement. My mother was a fantastic, well-rehearsed actress.

Over the years I had developed the standard answer: "Thank you. Many people feel that way," when people told me how nice she was. I still use it. What am I to say? "You've got it all wrong. She was a crazy sociopath." They would have thought I was the one who needed to be carted off to the padded green room with the soft lights. I hid the truth from relatives and friends for decades — literally decades.

After we were out of earshot of the neighbor I continued the conversation gently with Brad. "The trust gets worse, Son. Auntie Noel's share is all tied up and Marilyn has complete control over it. Complete control over every penny of when and where Noel gets anything, if anything at all. I haven't told her either yet. It's going to be so sad and I'm the best one to drop that bomb." This responsibility had weighed heavy on my heart for years.

We approached the house and passed the huge pepper tree with the spring green limbs hanging to the ground and the huge bed of ivy that I thought was a great habitat for snakes. I always had a fear of rattlesnakes, but at least they give a warning before they strike. The home was naturally cool as we entered and we could hear the muffled conversations in the den. There was talk of what to do with the house, which presumably would be empty, and the possible installation of security systems. Someone suggested lights and another a police check. The roundtable discussion continued and Brad joined his cousins whom he hadn't seen in some time. It was a bittersweet reunion and unknown to any of them, it would be the last.

I went into the kitchen and once again opened the refrigerator looking for something to drink. I really would have loved a nice cold beer, however, apparently while we were out, Noel had gone to town and bought some Coca-Cola. She was opening one, I grabbed another and she motioned for me to follow her out to the back veranda. Again we sat on the steps in the sun rather than the dusty furniture in the shade. Noel pulled out her cigarettes, lighter, and lit one up. I reached over, flipped the Marlboro pack open and also grabbed one, sticking it in my mouth. The flame reared up in front of my trifocals but I sucked it down. At first it felt and tasted great and then a slight dizziness began again and I coughed.

"It's been a long time since I've smoked," I said, only intending to have one more. I glanced across at the low chain link fence dividing my mother's place and her neighbors. Out here in the country the two of them built their houses within fifteen feet of their property lines. Those two had a strange relationship, I thought. Mom would never invite the woman over for a meal or to watch a program together in the twenty years they had both been widowed. It was only the last year or two they occasionally would go to town together, the blind leading the blind, and do some shared marketing.

It was Noel who always talked to the neighbor Esther and Noel who took her a birdcage when her old one broke. Noel and Esther got along and she was the only one of us invited into her home; Noel was the only one who thought to go to Esther's home. It was appropriate that Noel told Esther of Mom's passing, since it was she that informed us Mom had been returned to the hospital the final time.

"Esther said something really strange to me Kat," Noel started in a rather shaky voice.

Oh no — here it comes I thought. "What's that?" I asked taking a sip of coke and inhaling the smoke.

"She held onto my hand, looked me in the eye and told me to get a lawyer."

There was a pause. I took another drag off the cigarette and a sip from the cold can. "I know why," I confessed, still not wanting to tell her. My heart was racing and I was saying a silent prayer for a little strength and the right words — and God I need them quickly. Life had been unfair to Noel all along, starting in the cradle. This would be another heavy blow and I was reluctant to tell her. At the same time it would be best coming from me.

"She said she had read our mother's trust. She actually witnessed it."

"Noel," I began with a sigh, taking my time to find the appropriate words. Lord help me I prayed again silently. "I'm so sorry Noel. I never wanted to tell you this. I've known for a while and I thought our mother might change her mind, but if she had wanted to she didn't get a chance. We had talked about this again last August. The will is not fair. In fact Noel, it is pretty fucked up."

I paused, geez I wish this was something more than a Coca-Cola in my hands. "Noel, she put your entire share in the hands of Marilyn." Biting my lip I continued letting that part sink in. "Marilyn is your fiduciary."

I felt like I had dropped a sledgehammer on her heart and my own eyes were misting for her. There wasn't much more to say and

Noel looked as if I had punched her hard in the stomach. I could hear another car moving up the gravel in front of the house. We sat there together on the hard steps as the message of horror was slowly sinking in. She wasn't going to be able to be in charge of her own accounts or her own money. She was going to be treated like an invalid, or worse yet, a special needs individual. She would be at the mercy of the erratic, hostile Marilyn. The same Marilyn who had in the past stolen some money from Noel.

"Why the hell did she do that?"

"She thought you couldn't handle money."

Noel's demeanor went from sorrow to anger. She threw her cigarette down on the ground, smushed it with her foot, and her face hardened. She began to shout angrily and understandably as a wounded animal that roars. "Well, that is the biggest bullshit I've heard in years. I've raised my kids on little or nothing. I paid all my debts and worked two and three jobs at the same time to do it. Why, I showed HER where the bargains were, the second hand stores and the canned food places. I couldn't handle my money? I never had any money to handle!" Noel's voice started shaking at the end and it was obvious she was on the edge of tears.

Visions of her ever owning her own home were crashing down around her. She, too, was moving from hurt to anger, a protective move I'd seen her do so many times over the years. She lit another cigarette, sitting back down and biting hard on the filter. She inhaled with a vengeance taking another long drag, and so did I.

"Why did she hate me Kat? Why?" Her eyes looked like an injured small girl once again in trouble, eyes I still look at every day in a photo to remind me of what we all had been through.

Mom had given me the tell-tale photo a few years earlier saying I could keep it because it "wasn't a good one." What she meant was it wasn't what I refer to as Kodak lies. Everyone wasn't lined up, posed in some nice outfit and smiling. This was a candid shot Dad had taken years before in front of his beloved banana trees.

Eight-year-old Marilyn is all dressed in a neat little outfit standing, smiling. Her socks are pulled up evenly at her ankles and she has on a fresh white blouse. Her hair is swept up on each side and held with bows. Standing next to her in the photo is the younger but larger Noel with a dirty disheveled dress and uncombed hair. If you look closely at her sad face you will see a large bruise over her left eye. She is trying to hold my hand. Noel's hair is also swept up on one side, but hurriedly styled and held back partially by a lopsided bow. I'm in the photo with them, my hand-me-down underwear visibly falling down and I'm attempting to pull them up.

The tell-tale black and white photo was a story in itself. I've had it on my dresser for years. Every day I kissed those little girls goodnight before I slept and waved to them good morning. Sometimes I wish I could go back, be a time traveler and tenderly hold those little girls and tell them to stick together, that everything would be all right.

"I don't know Noel, I don't know why she hated you." We never knew. We had talked about it before. It was Noel who our mother had tried to drown. Even Marilyn, who for years had denied the abuse and still does, remembers that night.

The incident, a life changing and horrific event, happened like this. As young children we were never allowed to leave our beds once we were put in them. We used to lie under the covers and whisper to each other for hours every night, but we all feared ever putting a foot on the wooden floors once we were "tucked in." Even in the summer our bedtimes remained early and strictly enforced. We would lie there listening to our friends playing outside in our city neighborhood.

I was a baby then, making Noel about three years old or so. She was particularly thirsty that summer night and called to Mom for a drink of water. Now as I mentioned before, my mother had strange concepts about liquid not only for herself but also for her children. She apparently didn't experience thirst herself and didn't tolerate it in others. Mom controlled her body by what she would put into it and said we should always do the same. We were rationed the amount we got to drink and unless you wanted to drink from the outside hoses, it was never enough. Noel's request this particular evening crossed the invisible line of tolerance. The feeble request for water from Noel went out repeatedly and unanswered. Noel got a little louder believing her mother didn't hear her.

When Noel's pleadings weren't answered, she understandably went up in volume and intensity. She was afraid to get out of bed and pour her own drink so she just repeated her needs louder and louder. She could have tiptoed out of bed and made it the fifteen feet to the half bath adjacent to our room, but she was terrified of the repercussions if caught and she was too short to reach the sink and get water from the faucet.

Mother, fed-up with Noel's simple and repeated requests interrupting her solitude, trounced into our main blue tiled bathroom and pulled the drain of the tub closed. She turned the cold water on full blast and began filling it. Then she doubled back into our bedroom her face twisted and livid dark red. She pulled Noel from her youth bed by the arm and slung her up off the floor kicking. Remember, Noel was around three years old at this time. My mother started screaming that she'd give Noel all the water she wanted. With both of them now screaming, Noel from terror and my mother in anger, the wailing and vicious sounds blasted through the house waking up Marilyn. With the tirade of words continuing, Mother then threw Noel into the tub of rushing ice-cold water, grabbed her by the hair and held her head down under the water with her other arm across her back.

Poor Marilyn awakened thinking she was having a nightmare. Never a quick one to wake up, as soon as she realized what was happening she went running barefoot into the bathroom. Marilyn clearly remembers pulling my mother off Noel whose wiggling and splashing body she was holding under the water. Marilyn told me this herself and I would say her ability to do that would have been pure adrenalin.

"Don't kill my sister! Don't kill my sister!" Marilyn shouted above my mother's screams. The frantic pleas from the five year old must have bounced and echoed off the tiled walls of the room. Marilyn's screams were successful because they pulled Mom back to reality away from her descent into uncontrollable fury. Finally and fortunately for all, our mother came to her senses and released the death grip on the terrified and fully traumatized Noel. I believe it was Marilyn's intervention that saved Noel's life that night.

Noel came sputtering to the surface and Marilyn helped her out, dried her off and gently led her back to bed. In her normal pattern, one I witnessed many times later, I believe my mother probably left the house, as she always did after one of her "episodes." We never knew where she went, but we all agreed she would go off in the night for hours at a time leaving us alone.

Marilyn and Noel were both traumatized by this incident for life, each bearing their scars differently. They knew their mother could terminate their very existence and breath at any moment. She claimed always to love us, but every so often something dark and evil would occur in her behavior and we learned early on not to trust her.

There were other reasons for the lifetime distrust that went deeper and could be said to be more sinister. Things they never talked about to anyone except on rare occasions, which they shared with me. The code of silence is incredibly strong with us and has continued throughout our lives, and those of many others who have experienced similar things.

Because of the age differences there were a few tales I didn't know about nor remember, but that was one that both Marilyn and Noel told me on separate occasions. It was why they knew drowning was a real possibility the night she tried to drown Noel. If both ladies hadn't told me this I probably wouldn't mention it as I wasn't there. However, it further illustrates the wicked side of

Isobel and her capabilities.

Marilyn and Noel had already witnessed our mother kill an entire litter of kittens. She didn't want the cat to have kittens and was surprised by their arrival into the home. However, the kittens stayed, nursed and grew. Noel and Marilyn were allowed to play daily with the cuddly kittens and of course they bonded with them. Each day they held them and brought them up to their faces, gleefully feeling the soft fur on their cheeks. Mom had made a cat box for the litter using a few rags in a cardboard box and put it into the utility closet on our back porch with the door slightly ajar so the mama cat could get in and out and care for her babies. After the kittens' eyes were open, which had to have been almost two weeks, my mother took the box of kittens and my sisters into the same blue tiled bathroom I grew to hate.

Mom was in one of her "black moods" as we called them. The bathroom door was closed and locked forbidding any exits by children or kittens. Then, with teary horror-filled eyes my sisters were ordered to stand and watch while Mother drowned each kitten, one by one in the toilet. She actually knelt in front of the toilet, and held each kitten down in the water until it stopped struggling, then laid them on the floor. This went on until there was a tiny row of dead wet kitten carcasses lined up in front of my terrified sisters. It was seared into their memories forever. Mother kept saying over and over that the kittens had been bad and that the same thing would happen to little girls who were bad.

Oh yes, the code of silence. I never spoke of this to anyone and I'm sure my sisters didn't either. The first time I said anything was the night of June 20, 2001 when the news came on the television that Andrea Yates had drowned her five children in the bathtub. My mouth fell open and I started crying and said to my husband, "My God. Oh my God! I hope Noel isn't watching this." The old wounds were torn open and the puss came festering out. I told him the story of my mother trying to kill Noel. He sat quietly listening and then said, "Well that explains a lot." We never talked about it again.

Now I found myself years after Andrea Yates, sitting on the back steps of my parent's dream home, staring again at this injured woman child, tears welling up in both our eyes. I don't know why my mother did these horrible things, not just as a young woman, but her whole life. I knew of no one who ever treated children, let alone animals, in such a non-feeling, calloused way. How could I answer Noel? Why did Mom hate her? I had no idea.

Knowing all the past horrors and having them paraded again in front of my mind, I was at a complete loss for words. I just reached out and touched Noel's hand and looked into her eyes as if they were my own.

"I love you, Sis. I'll make it right. I promise you that." I then drew my breath in and lowered my head. I really wanted to run somewhere else. Why? Why? Why such viciousness? I didn't know. "There is one more thing," I said, almost whispering.

"What's that?" Noel said as if I could possibly dream up more injuries for her.

"She put a clause in the trust." I paused and looked again over the rose and iris garden. Oh, I thought, every rose has a thorn, perhaps we should get a lawyer. "There is a clause — a section in the trust where anyone contesting the will or trust will be cut out."

"Whaaaatttt????" Noel said her eyes widening. "Cut out! If I fight for my rights I'm fuckin' cut out? That is the worst kind of control and it comes right from the grave! Fucking unbelievable!" Noel started to shake and as she got up the movement caused her to feel light headed and dizzy. She reached back to steady her hand on the block flowerbed. Her knees weakened and she quickly flopped back down with a groan.

I could see that Noel had been pushed to the edge. Talk about too much information. I was reluctantly delivering blow after blow with what I had known for years, but internally hoped that Mom might see her way clear to make some changes. She and I had talked about it less than six months before when I last visited her. I told her in the kindest way possible, in a quiet voice, that she was being unfair and unreasonable to her family. Her trust needed to be reviewed by a lawyer. Noel reached again for the cigarettes, threw back her head and gulped the rest of the Coke. The thought occurred to me again that I'd sure as hell like to be tossing down something a little stronger, but this was my father's house and we didn't drink alcohol here. Damn! I needed a little painkiller myself. I'm sure if Brad could drive the car we could go get some beer, everyone might profit from a little liquid relaxation.

By this time we heard Marilyn's voice trilling from the den inside. She must have finished up with her endless conversations on the cell phone she produced from her purse. Everyone seemed to be gathering about her even though she hadn't called them together formally. Oh yes, the bees were gathering about the honey pot and everyone knew on which side their bread was about to be buttered. I suppose since Marilyn was in charge we all were lingering just expecting her to do something. Was she going to put this proverbial car in gear or were we to continue idling?

Marilyn stated she still couldn't find our mother's mortuary arrangements. It was an announcement not directed toward anyone in particular but the air around the family group in general. She was again gripping the white plastic notebook to her chest and her look was a cross between an innocent child's and a maniac, one eye twitching. The thought occurred to me that maybe she had taken something narcotic, perhaps a prescription. I didn't know, yet as my habit, I was searching and finding excuses for people. I had become the classic enabler and was aware of it. Yes, I said to myself, it must be the pain killers, maybe she was still on the painkillers from the last back surgery. Her pupils were dilated and she had a far off thousand-mile stare.

Without my voice sounding bossy or dogmatic I simply stated I had already called the mortuary. After years of training, first with criminals in the prison system and then with young children, I had earned how to ask questions and make statements without intimidating the other person. How to look with a non-threatening relaxed face. I went over to my mother's wall-length bookcase, reached down into the far right of the cupboard section by the window and pulled out several little metal file boxes. Mom had three, all the same size but in different colors. One was muted green, another rusted brown and a tan one. There were signs of age about the thin twisted metal handles, however, the boxes were sturdy. I plopped myself down in front of her built-in TV, which pretty much placed me front and center on the bare oak floor facing the rest of the family.

"Marilyn, this is where Mom keeps all her paper work." I looked up to see her face register surprise. Was it surprise that I knew where things were or surprise that she didn't? Oh yes, I too knew where the cookies were hidden, she had to have known where this stuff was also. Now Marilyn had been executrix for over fifteen years. She had been here frequently while I was only a guest who dropped in for a few weeks each year. I sensed that Marilyn was surprised that I knew about the paper work, what it contained and its location. My own surprises from Marilyn were soon to come in rapid order, after all, we were in the land of twisted secrets and lies. However, at this point I was still excusing her for being in a state of grief and exhaustion. I dismissed the daggers of her invading look and opened the first metal box. In front of the room, full of witnesses and for everyone to openly see, I began thumbing through the age yellowed envelopes and papers. Mom was meticulous in some respects and her organization here was admirable. Each worn but large manila envelope was labeled with its contents. Some I didn't bother opening. I came to one labeled "Life Insurance."

"Hey look at this," I said, "She has a life insurance policy." I didn't know about that so the revelation was made to all. Instead of opening the life insurance policy, I set it back to take an inventory of the general contents. At the bottom of that file, under the larger envelopes was a pile of little envelopes all measuring about 3 x 5 inches. Again, in my mother's neat block printing was the label of their individual contents. One in particular caught my eye. It said, "Silver matchbox belonging to James Alexander McFarland." I picked it up and opened it in front of all assembled. Marilyn finally sat down in Mom's chair and watched me in deadly silence. We all looked at the silver box. I didn't recall seeing it before. It was very old, from the turn of the century and was definitely silver, though badly tarnished. There was a tiny drawer in it that slid out and must have held small matches. There were front grooves for gripping and a plain oval section in the center with the engraved initials JAMcF. I held it lightly in my hand. "Goodness. This belongs to the cousins in Scotland. What on earth would our mother be doing with their father's matchbox all these years?"

No one answered that question. They really hadn't been too interested in the family history and weren't running the inquiries that I did. The question just hung in the heavy air of the room. I asked if anyone minded if I took it and returned it to the cousins since I corresponded with them frequently. There didn't appear to be any objections, just a few affirmative nods here and there. I slipped the matchbox into my pocket.

In the meantime Noel had come in the side door from the patio and had positioned herself in the far corner, leaning against the wall and just listening. I'm sure she was still recovering from the shocking facts I had revealed to her just a while earlier. After I asked everyone if they knew about the matchbox Noel crossed the family room moving toward the kitchen saying she was going to put on a pot of tea. As she got closer to me she leaned over and said quietly, "She probably stole it." Now at this point, her statement seemed a little off the wall, was it just sarcastic anger from Noel or was there more I didn't know?

I should have known better than to question myself. Over the years this family had interpreted anything Noel said as bizarre and she was discounted way too frequently. However, when checking each of her statements out, every one of these stories had been found to be true. It was her delivery the family disliked. Maybe it was that, "tactless, in-your-face honesty," they didn't like. I had at times been just as guilty as the rest, buying into the myths and legends perpetrated by my mother, that my sister Noel was erratic and unstable. Noel actually was one of the most accurate in her observations and statements to the group. Tact just wasn't one of her assets. Nevertheless, her passing comment was filed into the back part of my brain. At this point I didn't want to believe it anyway, I had just lost my mom. A mother whom I loved even though I knew of her vicious side, but a thief?

When I returned to Montana I immediately wrote James McFarland's daughter and returned the silver matchbox. She had been very young when her father passed away unexpectedly and yet her letter proved to be much more interesting.

Dear Katrina,

The matchbox is another mystery. Neither of us can understand why a McFarland memento should have landed with Isobel Graham in California, but we thank you for taking the time and trouble to send it on to us. We feel sure that having three daughters of her own our mother would not have given anything of her husband's to anyone other than her own children.

Incidentally, James McFarland did have a silver matchbox which we inherited and which we have since passed to our nephew in England.

It will remain a mystery and life is one big mystery any way isn't it?

With Love,

S. McFarland

Reading the letter I thought, much to my horror, "My God,

she did steal it." I read the letter over and over again. A souvenir? I knew someone else who "collected" from other people's homes she visited. Just a nick-nack here and there, something small to tuck into her purse.

Chapter 16

AUGUST BEFORE

The summer before my mother's untimely death I went to visit her. After Dad's passing I fully realized how precious life was and that Mom would not live forever. I visited her once a year by myself and that was fine as my husband found cities abhorrent and was miserable in California. At first I went somewhat out of duty and obligation, but by this time I also went out of love. What was unique about this trip was Marilyn's announcement when she picked me up at the Ontario Airport.

"Look," she began apologetically, "I'm going to have to leave you in Yucaipa for four days. I'll come back and get you." She took a breath.

I didn't want to comment because Marilyn had experienced a more than stressful year and I wasn't the only one who noticed how constantly edgy she was. Two nieces had also mentioned how she had been appearing erratic and angry. Her third marriage was on shaky ground, she was planning another back surgery, and Slither had been arrested again. She was mad at me because I had let that one accidentally slip out of the bag when I was talking to Julie. I could tell by Marilyn's pinched face and rather abrupt manner that it was best not to respond to her comment at this moment in time. I could still read her facial expressions like a book, or at least I thought I could.

She continued with her explanation that was nakedly honest. "Kat I can't stand her for more than two days! She is driving me nuts."

Sighing I said, "OK." It wasn't a problem for me, I thought she'd fill in the blanks when she chose to. Marilyn, after all, spent the most time with our mother as she was living within driving distance.

"I'll come back in four days and then stay a few. We can help her clean up around there. Mom can't see all the little messes and cobwebs anymore."

We switched our conversation to Mom's health issues and actually how proud we were of her staying alone up to this point. I told Marilyn again that Noel and I planned a meeting so all of us could discuss Mom's future needs and medical care. I also told her I wanted to buy Mom homeowner's insurance for her house and that I planned on talking to Mom about it. It seemed a logical idea as I was finally able to make my own bills with a little extra cash each month. I explained to Marilyn that since Mom was having people in to clean and garden she actually was in the position of an employer. She needed homeowner's insurance in case someone was injured. There was an abrupt change on her face and she darkened. "You want me to force Mother to get homeowner's insurance?" she snarled.

I felt like the prosecuting attorney had just made her opening statements and I was on the defense. Interesting choice of words, I thought, *force*? "No," I started enunciating my words slowly, "I want to buy it for her. She is foolish not to have it now and I just want to protect her."

"She doesn't want it! I've discussed it with her."

"Marilyn, it is foolish for her not to have it." I continued to explain as if I was talking to one of my third graders, "She could be sued and wiped out if any one of those people were injured. They are running power equipment, working on wet floors and the list goes on and on."

"Are you accusing me of being stupid?" She looked over and gave me the dagger look while she continued to drive. I could feel icicles stabbing into my heart and she sliced me open with her glance. "You're just worried she might lose some of the stuff you covet, like her house, and what little money she has!"

"Hey!" I started, a little bit firmer and admittedly a little louder, "Get a grip. I don't want that house and I never did. I never lived here and never wanted to. Is that clear? My objective is protecting our mother not protecting something I want. Now I have tried to do this from Montana and simply can't. I need your help with agents down here, but obviously you don't want to help. OK. I get it!"

"She is sharp as a tack and making her own decisions. She is her own woman and you are not forcing this issue."

"Well, I love her, but I'm not stupid either. She is a foolish old woman." I put the emphasis on foolish. "Her last handyman couldn't finish the job because he was going to jail and his wife was definitely casing the house when Mom invited her in for a drink of water."

"You don't know that!"

"Yes, girlfriend, I do," I retorted. "Criminals and bottom feeders were my business for years before teaching and I still can spot a felon coming from a mile away."

I was losing the conversation and it was clear this was not real communication, but once again like volleyball, a volley of words with the objective of slamming down hard on the opponent. The two of us had been at it for an hour and we weren't going to agree on this matter. Mercifully, we then pulled onto Mom's driveway and the conversation ended.

Mom of course was expecting us because I always kept her informed as to times and days, but she was still unable to come quickly to the door and had left it uncharacteristically open. We went in shouting down the long hall, our voices echoing a happy chorus of greetings. It was a nice contrast to the agitated exchange of a few minutes ago. Marilyn instantly donned a new face, pleasant, smiling and sweetly asked our mom how she was.

"Oh, God," I thought, "another Academy Award winning performance." The family dynasty of actresses continues as drama and pretense is passed down to another generation. This woman could change colors faster than a chameleon.

Yucaipa is located in the high desert of California. The summer temperatures always hover in the high nineties and in August frequently goes to three digits. It is a dry heat, but unlike Montana, it does not cool down at night and sometimes doesn't cool down at all. My parents didn't believe in air conditioning, but the thick-walled home retained the cool night air they let in before closing up for the day's sun. This worked most of the summer until the blocks and insulation heated to such a point that they radiated their heat at night. Usually I was uncomfortably hot when I visited my mom, but it was a trade-off; school was out and I could leave my ranch.

Mom's vision had reached a point that bright light was difficult for her to deal with, the result being her drapes were closed most of the time. Darkened rooms with shut doors and windows had been her decor of choice as she aged. I had the feeling I was entering a cloister instead of a desert home. It actually made my skin crawl because I lived in such an open place, looking at mountains and meadows through huge undraped windows and skylights year around. I had to move slowly down the hall while my transition lenses lightened from the bright outdoors.

Mom's appearance somewhat startled me as she had significantly aged in the last year. No one wants to see their parents fading and those changes are more apparent and defined when you don't see them on a regular basis. She was a flower withering in a vase even though she had done her best to fancy herself up knowing I was coming. Her face had the worn lines of battling pain and losing. Her right hip was deteriorating from osteoporosis and she could barely get around without excruciating steps with accompanying gasps and groans while grabbing onto various pieces of furniture for support. Isobel had always been blessed with good health up until now and for the first time she was able to relate to people with physical sufferings. Remarkably, she had even apologized to Noel saying she had no idea Noel was in such pain with her back. Mom had to experience pain herself before she could believe it in others.

In many ways it was fine with me that Marilyn didn't want to stay with our mother and me. I could spend some quality time with Mom and perhaps help her a little while I was there. Maybe I could make her laugh like I did before I left home. Marilyn made us all a cup of tea, went to the bathroom and then made her excuse to leave. I don't remember what fabricated reason she gave but she left immediately promising to return in four days.

It became crystal clear that my mother shouldn't be alone anymore. She hadn't installed any safety devices sent by her extended family. She had two wall phones each at opposite ends of the immense house. A few months earlier her blood pressure problem dropped to dazzling lows. She did have the sense to call 911, but then crawled some fifty feet to the front door, probably with purse in hand and lay there until she was picked up. I wanted to hook her up with a home aide or nursing group a few times a week, but thought I'd wait and discuss that with Marilyn and Noel when we got back down to Orange County for our planned meeting. Seeing her living conditions and fighting with my sister, I had again some regrets for not taking on the job as Mom's durable and executrix.

The days with Mom were jewels. We laughed and talked and watched movies together. We literally went through all the photo albums starting from the 1920s and I marked some of the pictures to be copied. Dad was an amateur photographer in his youth so there were great ones of him and his family before he married my mother. He kept those in his own brown leather album with a white stitched cover. He had collected the brown sepia-toned pictures of himself, his grandparents in the Ozark's, and later a photo of him as a very young working cowboy in Colorado. Then there were all the little black and white photos of Marilyn as a toddler. There were just a handful of Noel because film during WW II was rare and Dad was also working two jobs. I don't believe I ever saw my mother even pick up a camera. How fun, the family history as told by Kodak.

In the early 1930s Dad had bought a Super Ikonta 532/16 camera. It was the first quality camera that was small and affordable to the public. It only held twelve shots, and as I said, film became a rarity within the decade.

Somewhere in my life I had become my mother's confessor and I believe the only one she told as much truth to as she could. As she sat parked in her favorite chair and I on the floor near her, she told me stories of her childhood, the early marriage years and more. I started taking notes and questioned her like a reporter doing interviews and was so glad I did. I needed to get my facts straight and also wanted to put it in writing as genealogical research for future generations. It was our history, the personal history unique to our group.

What I was to learn was a little more than I bargained for. The information gained and exchanged in the next four days put together some pieces of the puzzle. We grew closer and I formed a deeper picture of this complicated woman. Mom was quite open in her old age about her emotional difficulties as a young girl, but at the same time she successfully excused her own bad behavior.

She told me stories that had any of them happened to me I would have buried them deep within the recesses of my mind never to escape. Mom, however, thought some of her stories rather funny and related them with a sense of pride. She didn't view herself as a spoiled child but rather an entitled one.

One was about a fellow school student she didn't like. There was some rivalry between the girls, and Mom told me how she took some scissors to school one day, grabbed the little girl's braid from behind and cut it off. When classmates didn't do what little Isobel wanted she would leap on them, knock them to the ground and punch them. She told me how one little victim almost died. School had let out and the two girls were on the steps going down to the street. The girl angered my mother for some reason, so Mom jumped on the other girl and choked her so hard the child passed out. As she related this particular tale she smiled and appeared satisfied that an ambulance had to be called and the little girl transported to the hospital.

Mom didn't say that she was terminated from the Aberdeen school system but logic tells me she was. The final coup de grâce for the school was when she slammed her classmate's head into an open and on-going lab experiment cupboard, then pulled the sliding protective window onto the child's neck preventing her from escaping. The student was saved from the toxic chemicals by a quick thinking teacher who pushed my mother aside and pulled the girl out. Fortunately, again they were able to resuscitate the little victim. Mom was laughing as she related that story. She wasn't sympathetic or embarrassed at her own behavior, but rather pleased she had successfully rendered a just punishment for whatever crime she perceived the girl had committed. I was horrified, but knew from our history that her story was perfectly true.

When we asked Mom what school she graduated from, she would always hold her head high, look a bit down her nose and announce that she had graduated from the Aberdeen Academy of Music, as if it was an exclusive school for young prodigies. That school was in fact a simple studio where music lessons were held without recitals or performances. She went there for her weekly piano lesson. Mom manipulated the facts with these statements but didn't actually lie, a talent she taught all her daughters. She didn't offer why she did the things she did. She just confessed to me about doing them, like biting the dentist. Then she would smile like they all "had it coming."

It is the old question of nurture vs nature. Was Mom born with these tendencies or were they shaped throughout her childhood?

Isobel was born in the fall of 1915, nine months after the Scottish celebration of Hogmanay. My grandmother would always get a giggle and say something about a toss in the hay with the handsome soldier who was my mother's father. It was WW I and the young lovers felt an urgency to grasp life, fearing that any moment it could be taken from them. Unfortunately, my kilted grandfather could not return from France to marry the pregnant nineteen-year-old Mary for six months. This was an embarrassment to both families, his much more prominent than ours. Grandma Mary stayed with her parents on the third-floor flat until the birth of Isobel.

In 1915 Scotland started to become unraveled socially and also in our immediate family. Her brave young men, at the front of most battles, were being lost at an alarming rate. In April of 1917 Grandma Mary's family got the news that her brother Alex had been killed with the Scottish Borders. Almost one month to the day the family received another letter from the Gordon Highlanders that her young husband had lost his life in France. Soon after that her brother-in-law was killed by a sniper. A year later two more of the uncles were lost in the North Sea. Before WW I was finished, Scotland had lost 150,000 of her young men and those left standing came home with deep physical and emotional scars. Armistice Day came just after my mother's third birthday, "the eleventh hour of the eleventh day of the eleventh month, 1918."

As all this death and devastation swirled about, baby Isobel still needed attention. She was cuddled, cajoled and passed around and everyone poured their love into her. She was dressed in imported clothes undoubtedly provided from her father's family, while around her the family was struggling.

My grandmother, Mary Campbell, was now a beautiful, twenty-three year old widow living with her parents. To earn a living and contribute to the family's meager budget, she apprenticed to one of her spinster aunts who was a milliner in Aberdeen.

Then, the patriarch of the family, my great grandfather, who provided emotional and financial support for one and all, fell from a ship mast where he was working and sustained major injuries. There was no welfare, no medical insurance or workman's compensation and the family fell on hard times. The Shetland uncles sheered their sheep and sent it to Aberdeen where my great grandmother spun and began to knit. She knitted sweaters, socks and scarves. She knitted day and night selling her goods until her husband recovered enough from his back injuries and was able to get employment by making picture frames on Hobart Street.

The remaining sons, attempting to help out by not being additional mouths to feed, headed off to South Africa to alluring tales of riches. The family experienced more goodbyes and young Isobel more loss.

With all this going on Isobel continued to be their "bonnie princess," the receptacle for everyone's diversion and love. Any wish or whim was fulfilled, sometimes to keep her quiet and other times to amuse and fulfill the giver. She was the doll of a grieving family and symbol of a grieving country. She admittedly took advantage of this adoring group, demanding and for a time getting continued attention. When there was something she didn't want to do she manipulated the adults with tantrums, becoming incorrigible and violent, throwing items and herself about when she didn't get her way. Positive or negative my mother remained the center of attention.

In the meantime, her young mother Mary, knowing there was no real future in Scotland either for herself or her daughter, struck out for America with the encouragement of an uncle who had already set up a successful insurance company on the east coast of the United States. The plan was that Mary would get settled there and young Isobel would be sent for within a year. Mary's sister Lilly was up in Toronto, Canada and the two had been close.

So Isobel was barely six years old and starting school when she was left in the tender care of her maternal grandparents. The household did not change with the exception that her mother no longer came home at night tired from work. Her grandparents were still there in the same cozy upstairs flat. She had her same little room, but no longer did she have her mother to share it with. Her father's family was still visiting frequently and Isobel would be taken out to their farm on the outskirts of Aberdeenshire.

My mother related to me that she was so angry that her mother got on a ship without her that she flung herself onto the pier and laid there screaming and pounding her fists up and down. It must have been quite the scene. Really, the Scots continued to have one problem after another yet managed to give Isobel piano and art lessons. It is possible those funds were provided by her father's family as she was important to them also.

She told me that when she was eight, her beloved paternal grandfather died. He sent word to Aberdeen that Isobel needed to be brought to him immediately and so she was delivered to the Boathouse in Fintry where he lay from a burst appendix and peritonitis. She said he kindly told her he was going on a long trip, one that she could not follow, but that he loved her and would wait for her. Shortly following his death she received a letter from the states saying her mother had found new love and was to be married.

Adversities continued to befall the Scottish family and my mother continued to be sheltered up to a point. My family has a long tradition of helping one another. Only one child of the grandparent's remained in Aberdeen, Aunt Fiona, my grandmother's other sister. It was she who had married James Alexander McFarland and whose daughters I wrote and visited.

James Alexander also died unexpectedly of a burst appendix and peritonitis. He was quite young, leaving Fiona with three little girls, the smallest being a toddler. It was determined that the now aging grandparents who rented the flat, would move into Fiona's large home and take care of the wee ones while Fiona took over James' business. It appeared to all as a win-win situation, all that is except to Isobel. Not only was Fiona left a home and business, she also had the rare commodity of a car!

Mom told me she was infuriated. Everything the grandparents owned was sold including the piano my mother thoroughly believed was "hers." She said it broke her heart even though she was told she could use Fiona's piano anytime, it was newer and of a better quality.

Looking back, Mom admitted now she may have been unreasonable about the move and there were things she may not have known. The flat they were living in prior to moving to Fiona's would be what we call in the United States, a tenement. It was, however, the only home Isobel had lived in and remembered. At Fiona's house my mother was able to have warm running water and a room of her own with an attached bathroom. She was within walking distance of her old home and her friends. Living with the McFarland's provided a better life for my mother and her grandparents. She had cousins near her age to play with and Aunt Fiona, a lady entrepreneur as a role model.

Chapter 17

LEAVING SCOTLAND

In the darkened cool den one of those four mornings in August my mother told me about the death of her Scottish grandmother. I was closing up the windows for the day attempting to keep the suffocating heat outside while Mom sat in her overstuffed chair sipping the only cup of coffee she would allow herself that day.

She said her grandmother had been ill and in bed for some time, long enough for one of her sons to return from South Africa and the others from the Shetlands to visit her. She was in an upstairs bedroom and Mom described in detail the blue and brown medicine bottles lined up on the dresser. She told me how she walked by them again and again running her fingers across them and how the old doctor with the black bag visited the home daily. She said that her grandmother was quite lucid and knew the end was near.

What I found chilling in the "death of Grandma" story was that my mother admitted to "not feeling a thing" when the lady died. She even said how relieved she was when, at the age of sixty-five, Grandma passed away. Isobel knew that with her grandmother's death she could come to the United States at last. Her grandmother's death was essentially her passport to freedom.

As soon as the elderly lady was pronounced dead, Mom told me that she went into their private closet, took their money stash, went out shopping and bought a new, rather sexy green satin dress.

When she returned to the mournful family Aunt Fiona was

more than infuriated with her. There was not only the disgust that my mother had taken money that wasn't hers, but double disgust when Aunt Fiona saw the dress and its inappropriate style for a young woman. Fiona, a single parent running a business, taking care of her own three small children, her sister's child and her parents, was at the end of her patience with spoiled-rotten teenage Isobel. Fiona's brother's ticket had run out and his boat back to South Africa was to depart the day after the funeral. He had found another "Shetland woman" to replace his deceased wife and wanted to marry her before they boarded ship. Isobel had bought the dress for the wedding to be held the day after her grandmother's funeral.

As my mother related her teenage misdeeds she actually smiled. I thought if I had done anything like that I would not have lived to tell the tale.

Apparently, Aunt Fiona spent the night sewing rows of ribbons and lace across the front of the sexy green dress making it more modest and as my mother related, absolutely ruining it. The following day Isobel began to plan her trip to the United States while the other family members sat grieving after burying their mother, wife and grandmother in the cemetery in central Aberdeen.

I can say, there is sometimes confusion as a teenager on how to behave at a death and I myself was confused as to what to do when my own grandfather died. I was not encouraged to attend his funeral nor even talked to about what my role should be. So, I went to the beach, as it seemed a safe place for me that day. No one asked me what I wanted to do nor gave me any inclination of what I should do, so I just grabbed my towel and left them.

Barely seventeen, Isobel gladly left all she knew and boarded the steamer *Caledonia* to cross the Atlantic. She even shared the story of her brief on-board romance with the ship's radio operator and how they would lay, arms around each other at night on the deck and look at the stars. She laughed when she said it all came to an abrupt halt when her uncle met her at the dock in New York, cleared her through customs and escorted her by train personally to her birth mother now living in California with her two little half-brothers.

Mom was chatting with me like I was an old girlfriend, confessing misdeeds one after another. She was honest about the conflicts she had with her own mother and some of her peers in what she called "the old country." It was amazing how candid and open she was during these four days. Her masks were set aside and I found myself talking to a real woman with fears and pains just like the rest of us. We laughed, we cried and we hugged as she reminisced.

During those four days I made the proposal to insure her house for her and explained my reasoning. I told her it was for her own protection and I would take on the full financial responsibility, but Mother rejected that idea completely. I suggested some in-home help, maybe just a few days a week and again she said no.

The cat food cans were starting to smell in the hot kitchen so I decided to take her garbage out to the garage. I got the automatic door opener, went outside and up to another level where the garage was separate from the house. Inside sat her old blue Dodge and next to it the garbage cans. As I lifted the lid I looked up and hanging on a nail above the cans was the strap.

I found myself staring at it. I hadn't noticed it ever before yet I recognized it instantly. Good God, a souvenir? I thought possibly she put it there for self-protection and imagined her wielding it against a phantom attacker. Why would anyone want to keep such a symbol of cruelty? I had heard of murderers keeping trinkets, but that was on TV. Mom actually did it. Well, I sighed, at least it was hanging in the garage and not the living room.

My father, at my mother's request, made the infamous strap. I don't know why he complied for that would have been totally out of character for him. It is the only thing he did in his lifetime that completely befuddled me and one with which I was in complete opposition. Maybe he thought its mere presence would be a deterrent. He made it for my mother to beat my sister Noel with. Did he know that?

The strap was black leather, shaped like a paddle, about eighteen inches long and three to four inches across. It was one-fourth of an inch thick and possibly made out of an old belt. The top part was cut out for a handle and there was a hole drilled into that. In Los Angeles it was kept on the stinky back porch in what my mother referred to as the utility closet, where she kept her irons, brooms and other items. Just to the left of the utility cupboard Dad put a nail and hung the strap there. I remember the day he made it. I was horrified then and still am, the thought turns my stomach to this day and will forever. My mother wielded the damn thing with precision. It slapped hard always hitting the back of our legs and butts where it raised furious scarlet welts and bruises.

After one particular brutal beating on Noel, I decided the strap had to go. I had to get rid of it once and for all and with its disappearance I reasoned, the beatings on Noel would stop. I waited until the household was asleep and crept in the dark, barefooted, in my flannel nightgown to the back porch cupboard. Lit only by the dim streetlights I reached up and removed it from its nail holder. As if I were a snail, slowly, slowly opening doors I crept back to my room. I think I held my breath the whole time and my heart was beating practically out of my chest. I even had to tip-toe past Noel who had cried herself to sleep. I lifted my mattress and slipped the horrid thing underneath. Then I crawled in on top, pulled the blankets under my chin and lay there shaking. I did it! It felt strange to have it there, but I did it. I may have been six at the time and I know that I didn't sleep well that night.

I was in fear of being discovered and beaten myself. I could hardly eat breakfast the next morning and was more than relieved when I could escape to school. But, the strap under my mattress wore on my mind the entire day. When I got home I even had to check that the monster was still there. It was. I hadn't been discovered yet, but the second sleepless night my fear of punishment continued growing. On the third day I could take it no longer. My stomach hurt and I was consumed with fear. My fear overpowered the dismay of watching my sister getting whipped.

The third night I re-ran my entire earlier performance, but in reverse. I waited until everyone was asleep and the house silent. Then I removed the strap, retraced my trail to the utility cupboard and rehung it on the nail. I was a coward and ashamed of myself even at that young age. Self-preservation was greater at that point than saving my sister.

Now, some fifty-plus years later I was staring at the same damn strap hanging on another nail and visible to all who entered the garage. It hung there as a painful reminder, her scepter of power collecting dust, but nevertheless it was never removed.

I decided to talk to my mother openly, with kind words about what I felt about my childhood and the beatings she rendered to all of us. She needed to know exactly how I felt and, furthermore, I needed to get it all off my chest and uncork the emotions I had carried around for so long. I needed to tell her that I loved her and forgave her, but that what she did was terribly wrong. I took a deep breath, probably several, and asked God to help me choose the right words. I turned from the sunshine and re-entered her cavernous home.

"Mom," I said, stopping in the kitchen, "do you want something to drink?" I swung open the refrigerator door and stuck my head in just a little further than necessary, fanning some of the cool air onto my perspiring brow. Then I picked up my shirt and flapped it up and under my breasts and bra. I was sweating like a pig and the baby powder I put on that morning was no longer absorbing. She would think those actions unladylike.

"No dear, I've had enough liquid for today."

"Uh, Mom, we've had this conversation before. You need to drink more water. The doctor told you that and look at the beautiful decanter Cyndie got you. She wants you to drink just one a day." I had noticed the tiny etched drinking glass that Cyndie had gotten to match the decanter. It hadn't come from the dollar store that was for sure. "You know Mom, just little sips. You don't have to guzzle it all at once."

"I don't want to. I just have to pee then."

"That is the idea." I looked at her with my most impish grin. Shaking my head I laughed, "You are the ornery one aren't you?"

I popped open a Shasta root beer and the tingle felt good sliding down my throat and tickling my nose.

"Hey, I want to talk to you about something a little more serious." I sat down near her so she could both see and hear me easily. "Were you battered as a child? Did your grandmother in Scotland ever beat you?"

Mom was surprised at the question. "Well, no. When I was real bad she would shake me by the shoulders and tell me I was a little bitch, but she never beat me. Why do you ask?"

"Well, Mom, I don't know if you have ever heard of the *Battered Child Syndrome.[1]" I paused and then cautiously continued into the marsh of our lives. "You know by today's standards the punishments you gave us when we were kids would be considered child abuse." I paused again and waited for her reaction. I wasn't

---

1 The Battered Child Syndrome is frequently misinterpreted by the general public. It is commonly thought that a battered child will abuse their children or that the abuser was a battered child. There is a great deal more to it than that. It is not necessarily a continuing chain of events. There are millions of survivors who have gone on to lead healthy lives and raise their children differently. Most victims, I would guess, do not want it public knowledge because of the stigmas and assumptions involved. Along with that is the "code of silence" and in spite of the facts, they possess a loyalty to their abuser, and they aren't willing to talk about it.

going to expand and wanted to avoid the blame game. She thought for a minute before answering.

"That is silly. I only did what I thought was right."

There was no need to crush the old lady. As I said, I loved her and I could clearly see there was no apology for our years of hell. I was at least getting an admission from her at eighty-six years old, the punishments did occur. I had made some headway in my own quest. I continued, but onto a slightly different topic of parenting or the lack of it.

"Mom, why did you send me to Bret Harte School? It was horrible. Did you know there were fights every day? Did you know that I was scared shitless for three years? Did you know that Mrs. Piligian knew it was so bad she picked Henry and me up every day after school, and then transferred her other son out?"

Mom shifted her weight in the chair and leaned closer to me. "No dear I didn't. I really didn't know it was so bad. You said Mrs. Piligian picked you up every day. Why did she do that?"

"Henry and I were terrified to walk home. We met each other outside the big fence where we were separated. You remember the big chain link fence between the boys' and girls' yards? It was twelve feet high and built to cut down on some of the fighting. The boys and girls were separated, segregated you know." I took another breath, composed myself and continued like I was telling her a story she had never heard.

"My boyfriend's hand was crushed in a penny stomp. The kids were so mean they just kept stomping his hand while he screamed in pain. My food was stolen almost every day at lunchtime. Did you know that? I went to work in the cafeteria just to eat!" I lowered my voice because I could feel myself gaining momentum in my anger.

"We walked out of PE way too often with our skirts over our heads being frisked. Frisked, Mom, actually frisked for weapons and stolen things. There were cops at the school routinely and you didn't know? You didn't know my purse was stolen and that Dad gave me a knife to protect myself? I was terrified Mom. I spent every day wrapped in that ugly brown coat, reading under the bleachers. I read every damn book in the fiction section of the junior high library and even made it across the aisle to the non-fiction. You didn't know? That is how I escaped!"

She started laughing at that point, giggling in her chair. I had to join her too for comedy relief because she was saying, "Well, at least something good came out of it. You turned into quite the little reader." True, true. I lived in Fantasyland because Adventureland was just too damn frightening.

At least I hadn't held my thoughts in any longer and that water had flowed under the bridge was many years ago. I thought parents should have had some idea of the school environment their kids were in.

My school years held few warm, nostalgic memories. I'm still a bit envious hearing others relate the fun stories from their school days and the friendships they still cherish. I just wanted the hell out of there and the hell out of Los Angeles completely. I wanted to cut those ties and run baby run. Eventually, I made it all the way to rural Montana.

Mom said she was amazed at my story and sat quietly while I related my tales of woe. "I truly didn't know honey and I'm so sorry."

I'm glad she said that. At least she saw there were some errors. The school was one, but our beatings were not to be apologized for. At least she knew how I felt, so I got up, hugged her and told her how much I loved her and appreciated all she had done for me. I sincerely meant that all was forgiven. I hoped that my sisters could forgive her too.

"Oh, dear," she continued, "I appreciate you. I've loaned a lot of money out to this family and you are the only one who paid me back every month, faithfully on time." Mom's voice was a little shaky now and she hesitated for a moment. I thought maybe all the information I had just given her may have been a bit too much. My curiosity went way ahead of me but fortunately my mouth stopped, no sense creating more grief for her. Who else had borrowed money and who had not paid back their accounts? She had been more than generous in the last ten years, generosity which I was led to believe resulted in her diminishing bank accounts.

Just about then I could hear Waylon the cat yowling at her door. I unfolded my cramped legs, got up and let him in. He headed straight for her in the easy chair and she leaned over, stroked his head and I could hear him purring contentedly.

"I'll feed him Mom." I smiled and reached down to pet him too. Marilyn hated this cat and she frequently told me so. I went into the kitchen to find his bowl and was looking around on the floor when Mom instructed me through the louvered window.

"His bowl is in the cupboard next to mine."

"Next to yours?" I started to laugh. "It's bad enough I feed my old cat in a special place, but I don't share my bowls with her."

"I'm not sharing. I just keep them there."

"OK. OK. So I can feed him the rest of the Friskies in the fridge?"

"Yes, dear, that will do nicely. And pour him a little canned milk. He likes that."

One could easily talk between the kitchen and family room in this house because my father had built in a window-sized opening between the two. "Anything else while I'm in here. Are you sure you don't want any water or soda or tea?"

"No! I'm perfectly all right."

"Well, I'm not. I need copious amounts of liquid, then I locate all the bathrooms. Think of me as the bathroom inspector."

Mom laughed again and it felt good. We were having a fun time in spite of the conversation and we both were relaxed. But, when I returned to the den I could see by her set facial expression that she was thinking something serious, as if the subjects I had brought up weren't serious enough.

"I'm worried about your sister Marilyn," she began. "I have been for some time."

I decided not to jump with both feet into this conversation, but to wait and let my mother express herself. I had had my turn. "Hmmm." I was waiting for the other shoe to drop. Hmmm is the good old, ambivalent, non-threatening sound saying, "I heard you."

"I just don't think *Poor Marilyn* can handle all the responsibility of being executor of this estate."

"Well, for starters Mom, your trust isn't fair and there are going to be problems." I was gentle as if I was telling someone they had a fatal disease. In a way it was fatal. Mother, without legal advice, wrote the trust herself and had included some pretty dastardly things. She had taken an afternoon workshop at her local library and thought, as she often did, that she had all the information to do it herself. It was like seeing an accident about to happen and being powerless to stop it. But I continued with each word thought out carefully. "Mom, there is a solution to this dilemma and I agree with you, it may be too much for Marilyn. You could get an impartial person like a bank or a lawyer to be the executor."

"I don't want to give them all the money," she said firmly.

"Mom," I tried to explain, "I don't think they cost that much and it just might save your family some grief and definitely save Marilyn." I couldn't help thinking that perhaps her trust had been crafted intentionally to create dissent. She loved to stir up more than one pot. Mom certainly hadn't thought the trust totally through, then again, maybe she had. I had seen this old lady in her prime pit people against each other and she was quite good at it.

She would pretend to be on one side and then feed each venomous gossip about the other. She vicariously enjoyed watching the children of her brother fight over his estate. She would sprinkle salt on their wounds and then later, after the screaming stopped, she would say, "Oh my, what a shame." Yet she had taken an active and vicious role manipulating and fueling their emotions. Her own trust was crafted as such a weapon. Marilyn would be in charge of sister Noel and those two didn't always get along. Cutting Vince out was another definite problem, but one for which I had already had a solution. I would just give Vince his share right off the top of anything I got. Vince would get his share, however, it would never heal the deep stab to his heart.

Was my mother thinking that she could actually break the bonds I had with my sons, pitting one against the other? She was mistaken there. Her daughters' relationships may have been tenuous and slightly unraveled, but the relationships I had with my sons were set in cement. I believed we weren't about to break them over anything as petty as money. "You know Mom," I began, with these thoughts flying through my brain like bats, "you are putting Marilyn in a bad spot. She isn't very stable, you and I both know it. She has been up and down emotionally like a yo-yo for years and lately that has gotten worse. She is actually afraid and has told me, that no one will like her. It just isn't fair to Marilyn to put her in charge of an unfair will and she doesn't have the ability to do it. You need to contact an attorney and get some advice."

God, I thought, my mother isn't intentionally putting Marilyn in a position as the final coupe de grâce on her brain is she? Mom knew Marilyn was fragile, she didn't want to push her over the edge after she died did she? I knew she demanded and expected to be in control, but the rest was pretty confusing.

"I'll think about it," was my mother's response.

I hope so, I thought to myself, but I knew how oppositional Mom had become in the last few years, or maybe she had always been that way and I hadn't noticed. My recommendation for motion lights was vetoed, homeowner's insurance was vetoed, and more household help was flushed down the drain. Knowing this I should have done reverse psychology like I have occasionally used on kids, but then that is hindsight. I should have told her that it was a great trust and the best ever written. Everyone would just love the way it worked and Marilyn would do a wonderful job as the executrix. I'm sure she would be open and honest is what I should have said, Marilyn who for years refused to talk about this. But then I was holding out for the meeting we had planned with Noel. Surely three seemingly intelligent women could make a plan. You know the joke: The Three Wise Women.

Chapter 18

WHILE SHE WAS DOWN

Did Mom know she was close to the end of her life? Was she aware she was cleaning her own slate? I will never know. In many respects I'm flattered my mother trusted me with her stories even though at times it was more information than I wanted to know. Those four days together remain precious in my memories.

There also was my genealogy research that extended beyond birth dates. Even as a child I was always asking what this or that person was like, what they did for a living, etc. To verify things I collected certified birth, death and marriage certificates. Some documents clarified questions and others opened up more mysteries.

So while I had my immobile mother to myself, I asked her about one other puzzling death in the family and that was of my dad's mother who died in her early forties. Growing up we were told she died of leukemia.

"Mom, why did you tell us kids that Grandma Graham died of leukemia? Her death certificate says cause of death was peritonitis. The leukemia wasn't discovered until later, if at all, and at that time those tests weren't all that accurate. What happened there?"

Mom began her tale. She said that Grandma Graham had a polyp removed from her colon. She had come home from the hospital and was feeling fine, however, after a week at home became very bloated and constipated. She wasn't too sick because she was planning on going fishing the next day with her eldest son, but the bloat was uncomfortable and causing cramps. Then my mother related to me that it was she who called the doctor and he told her to, "Stick something up her rectum to relieve the bloating."

Now I'm thinking, "Oh God, she didn't stick the douche nozzle up her butt as a little hydrotherapy for her hated mother-in-law." My mother continued her story by telling me that is exactly what she did. However, afterward, her mother-in-law suddenly took a turn for the worse and had to be returned to the hospital.

My mother would have been twenty years old at this time. In the three tumultuous years she had been in the United States she had enrolled and been kicked out of nursing school, worked as a clerk at my grandparent's bakery and continually fought with her own mother. She had a relationship with a young man who had no intention of marrying her and then Mom admittedly married my dad on the rebound. Those two had been married only one year.

Mom knew little of housekeeping or cooking and her mother-in-law had tried to help her. I'm told by others that Grandma Graham was a kind, spiritual woman, but didn't put up with any nonsense; she and her new daughter-in-law conflicted right away. My mother admitted she just didn't like her.

When Grandma Graham was returned to the hospital, it was apparent she wasn't going to live as the infection was untreatable. Remember, this was 1936 and the medical world has advanced greatly since then. Her teenage daughters gathered around her bed along with her sons. All four of her children told me she recited the 23rd Psalm, closed her eyes and died. She was forty-five years old.

Hearing this from my mother's lips I immediately knew, intentional or unintentional, my mother had perforated my grandmother's intestine causing the peritonitis, the same cause of death of both her grandfather and uncle in Scotland. She knew what peritonitis was and what caused it. A cold feeling went through me. Such a history all happening so long ago. I couldn't prove a thing, nor did I want to. This was a literal case of letting sleeping dogs lie and it didn't matter anymore. She told me about pulling the plug on my great aunt long ago and now this. I consulted with several nurses and they all concurred with my supposition. The bowel had been perforated.

"And Mom, the death certificate also said she was widowed. She wasn't widowed, she was divorced." I teased her by saying that they had really messed with information regarding Grandma Graham. She didn't have any answer to that. She just sat in her chair, hands folded in her lap with the "holier than thou" look and I knew not to probe any further. Mom had always made negative remarks about my father's mother. None of us ever knew her, but for some reason her spirit filled me with goodness and love throughout my life, like a guardian angel. I always felt compelled to defend her and did. Noel tells me that she asked our mother more than once to take her to the cemetery where the mystery grandmother was buried. Finally our mother did, but then Noel claims my mother pushed her onto the grave saying, "Well there she is." I did find her grave marker as a teenager. I cleared it of debris and placed a few flowers there in her memory.

My father was despondent with his mother's death. They were very close and he was just beginning to see through young Isobel's charms to the woman she really was. With Grandmother Graham's death came her orphaned daughters and it was Dad who brought them home to live. With their company, Isobel was no longer lonely and she no longer had to be tutored by her husband's mother. Again, she was in a sense free. They were all kids, basically, and none of Grandmother Graham's children could pay for her funeral and burial. Dad borrowed the money and with now three young ladies to support, he got a job with the Los Angeles Police Department.

Chapter 19

SHRUNKEN HEADS

There are times in everyone's life when you find your mouth swinging open. Whatever has occurred, you have no alternative as the muscles holding your lower jaw in place just slacken and your face falls into the position of disbelief. It is best, I have learned during these times, not to utter a sound.

That is how I felt those four days in August when my mother told me she had an abortion between my sister Noel and me. She explained it was because "Noel was so difficult" and she couldn't deal with another baby. This came as strange news because she had always told us how hard it was for her to conceive and each one of us was a miracle, a story I actually repeated several times before the truth arrived.

I was slack-jawed for several reasons, one being that the doctor who performed the abortion was the same one who delivered both Noel and me, well not exactly Noel, she was born in the car. When Mom told me this I asked her if she told my dad what she was going to do. Oh, wicked, wicked webs of deceit, I knew well when she paused and her voice changed. She said "of course" but the translation meant, most definitely "of course not." Yes, I knew this woman so well that she could no longer deceive me regardless of how hard she tried.

It matters not your or my opinion about abortion here. That isn't the issue. She lied to us about not being able to have more children. The other issue was that the doctor was our family physician for years. In addition, we also suspected with good reason, that he was our mother's lover.

You see, both of my parents had long-term relationships outside their marriage. That may not seem unusual by today's standards, but in the 1940s and 1950s it was highly unusual, or at least it was not made public. I almost think their relationships were in some way agreed upon because both terminated at approximately the same time.

I liked my father's "lady" but the family doctor always frightened me. I didn't like him. He smelled like the pungent, fruity smell of ether and his dark hair was slicked back with some kind of cream. He had penetrating blue eyes and always seemed to wear a less-than-clean gray suit that was seriously rumpled. This guy was totally different from any other male I had met in my life before and after.

He frightened me for a variety of reasons, but most of all he had a shrunken head collection that he kept in his office. No, it is true! He had been a missionary in the South American jungle and had collected them there. The heads were not out for the public to see, but he showed them to me on numerous occasions. Was I fascinated by the little mouths and eyes sewn shut with raffia strings dangling down? Did I actually ask to see them? I don't know, but I do remember being totally frightened by the collection of little dark-skinned people and big hair. The encore of the share-and-tell group would be when he reached into his box and pulled out the final head, that of a white man! Good Lord, what kid would want to go to a doctor that showed them shrunken heads? I was already a wreck between beatings, the post war hysteria of the 1950s, and the nightmares. Now I had to deal with shrunken heads in the doctor's office. No wonder I screamed at night.

The doc also had framed around his office on the high mahogany walls a collection of huge, colorful but dead butterflies. I thought that even if I was a butterfly I was going to end up dead and plastered in a frame on his wall.

Now we would never have known this man, our family doctor, was my mother's long-time lover if he hadn't been arrested and prosecuted for performing abortions. Remember, this was the 1950s in Los Angeles where laws and attitudes were quite different. Abortions were highly illegal and his arrest made the headlines. We were all shocked, or at least pretended to be shocked, when our beloved family doctor was "framed" on an abortion charge. Looking back on this incident I actually can laugh. My mother, Ms. Liar of the Year, clearly couldn't have been shocked. This was the doctor who performed her abortion. My father may have been surprised because he didn't know about either incident.

Mother actually dressed up in her finest, went to court and testified as a character witness on her lover's behalf. She proclaimed his innocence from the witness stand, telling us at home he had been framed, knowing all along that none of it was true. She was in the spotlight in court, and I'm sure the prosecuting attorney, along with the defense, would have fallen over had they known the real relationship between the good doctor and the witness.

She perjured herself royally and no one would have suspected the PTA President and the Girl Scout Leader was capable of such a deed. But indeed, she was a great actress, and a sociopath can fool just about anybody. I knew she was capable of some things but to actually go into a court of law and lie from the stand. Wow! She must have thought this was quite the coup feather. The man was convicted anyway and served time in the California prison system. His license to practice medicine was revoked.

So how did Isobel react to his guilty sentence? Her lover in jail? Well, she dutifully wrote him love letters every day. And, every day as regular as clock work, my sister Noel carried them to the mailbox on her way to school. We didn't realize at the time they were love letters. We thought she was being supportive of a person who had been innocently framed and wrongfully convicted, so every morning Noel dutifully carried the letters until one early, foggy morning.

Mom, in her haste that morning had failed to fully, "seal with a kiss" the envelope and the moist air loosened the seal further. What eighth grader wouldn't be curious to read their mother's mail? So predictably Noel opened Mother's loosely sealed letter to the good doctor and it didn't surprise her as she read the contents. Noel felt exonerated of any supposed crimes and the tables turned. At last Noel had the goods on her mother. She read the letter carefully, recognized it for what it was with all the Xs and Os signed at the bottom. Carefully, the letter was resealed, dropped in the blue mailbox on the corner and Noel went on her way to school. Later, Noel would occasionally "forget" to mail a letter on the proper day and she and I would read them together giggling over the rows of Xs and Os and Love, Love signed at the end.

For the year or so the doc was in prison my mom would sit at her piano for hours and play endlessly, day after day, ad nauseam, "Unchained Melody."

> *Oh my love, my darling I've hungered for your touch a long lonely time....*

I can't stand the song to this day. It isn't a mild dislike – I really hate that song. I have never heard it without thinking of them, so when she told me the abortion story that summer in Yucaipa I realized again what a complicated person she was. She not only lied to the court, she lied to us, and obviously lied to my father. And now, she is confessing so much.

> *Forgive me daughter for I have sinned.*

Chapter 20

LITTLE RED RIDING HOOD

Marilyn arrived as she promised, four days later in the August heat. She came in with a basket of snacks, dressed in a fresh beige shirt over her brown pants and a new fashionable pendant. She appeared happy as she showed us the teas and biscuits from Trader Joes, little cheeses and a collection of tiny sample foods we really could have lived without. They were delightful little morsels, that was true, and I appreciated her efforts, but in Montana, none of the food would be considered substantial, maybe for little girls playing with Barbies, but none of this was real.

Marilyn said she was going to spend the night with us and planned on taking Mom and I to the movies. It would be a treat for me as the only shows I had seen in a real theater the last twenty years were *Braveheart* and *Dances with Wolves*. It was so remote where I lived that I only went to the theaters if I was in a city. Mom had loved reading *The Bourne Identity* by Robert Ludlum on the air. She thought Matt Damon might be a little young for the role, but she was totally excited to be getting out of the house and into town.

For the last few years Mom had volunteered as a reader for the blind on a special radio broadcast. She had a great reading voice and manner and was sympathetic to the totally blind as she stood in that doorway herself.

Marilyn's motives were clear. She wanted to get out of the hot house and into an air conditioned theater. We agreed an afternoon show was the best choice for all of us, when the heat of the day became unbearable. Marilyn and I also decided that before we left we would do some cleaning for Mom. I told Marilyn that we had been looking at the old photo albums and if we left just a little earlier we could get a few of the old ones copied for both of us. It was all agreed upon and everyone was quite pleasant.

Feeling that we had a great plan and things were going well, I headed for Mom's vacuum cleaner. It was an old and heavy upright Hoover but it worked fine. As Marilyn puttered about I started the machine in the living room. It wasn't really dirty, but there was a fine layer of dust everywhere just from the lack of cleaning and summer accumulations. Having lived on dirt roads most of my life the dust didn't bother me. I had seen clouds of it when the summers came to a close and my dirt roads were dry, rutted and dusty.

I was buzzing away with the rhythm of the machine moving back and forth, thinking I could dance with anything and this time it was the vacuum. Around we go swirling and twirling. As I left the living room and started pushing the vac down the hall runner, I got the feeling of something behind me. It seemed unsettling like the eyes hidden in the forest watching as you walk through. Was my hearing going I wondered? It sounded like two machines and I wondered if this one was on the fritz. I turned around to find my sister Marilyn literally crawling on the floor behind me. CRAWLING! She was on all fours like a two year old, down on the ground, pulling behind her another small canister vacuum cleaner I had never seen before. She was crawling down along the hall wall using a hand tool and her hair was falling in her face. What a scene! Switching off the upright I turned and faced her.

"Marilyn! What the hell are you doing?" I'm sure I was frowning and not waiting for an answer. "Get up from there right now!"

She muttered something with her head down and at first her words were lost behind the curtain of salt-and-pepper hair. Something about the place not being filthy. I wasn't sure, then I heard her over and over again. "It's not filthy — it's not filthy."

"Hey! I can do this. I've done it a thousand times before. It's

OK." I was softening when I saw her momentary look of confusion. Was this a scene from a looney bin? In my shock I know that I was smiling because I didn't know how else to react. "We don't crawl here — get up! This is just too weird, girl. Let's go see the movie." I pulled the plug from the upright and started winding it around the machine turning my back for a minute on my crazy sister. Was this really happening, I thought? Jesus, Mary and Joseph, I've never seen anyone come crawling down a hallway pulling a vacuum. If it hadn't been so ridiculous I might have laughed out loud, however, there was such a seriousness in her face. Slowly, Marilyn rose to her feet, pushed the hair back from her face and unplugged the smaller vacuum. No wonder the southern California family was voicing concern for her.

We both made our way to the utility closet and put the vacuums away. I didn't say anything, but I thought, that was the strangest fucking thing I've seen in years. I didn't think that would fly well and besides my mother detested that kind of language and seemed to hear profanity no matter how far away.

Instead, I suggested we get ready to go and I went into the big bathroom, bent over and fluffed up my hair. I don't comb my hair. It is naturally curly like both my parent's, but softer than Mom's. I just lean over and run my fingers through it, sweep it up and slip in a clip. I didn't need to refresh much other than my lipstick and that came only after I remembered to brush my teeth. I was ready in less than five minutes.

Our mother was already dressed with makeup on in anticipation of going to town. She didn't get out much anymore and it was thrilling for her to be with her two daughters. I got the photos together that we were to copy, grabbed her by the right arm and led her out to Marilyn's waiting car. I thought that with some physical support the pain in her hip would lessen and besides there were her vision challenges; we were going from a dimly lit house to the bright outdoors.

Mom needed constant help at this point and was not getting it. I was concerned that she might just topple over like fragile glass and break.

With characteristic tenacity, Mom vehemently denied she was frail at all with an attitude that made me both proud and angry with her.

Marilyn had finally struggled out to the driveway and managed to start her reluctant vehicle. I was silently praying that she had air conditioning because to me the heat was suffocating. Mother also gasped at the hot temperature outside as she had been inside for days and wasn't fully aware of how hot it really was.

The conversation was light on the way and thankfully Staples was air conditioned, as I believe all of California is now. We fortunately found a parking spot right up by the door and I felt that in itself was a good omen. Mom had never been in a Staples store before so was unaware of the advancement of modern technology and the rows and rows of electronic supplies available. I got out the small ziplock bag that held the pictures from her album that I wanted to copy and took them up to the counter. With Mother standing fascinated next to me, I requested three copies made of each. Within a few minutes, much to her amazement, we had lovely, flawless copies in our hands, enough for everyone. I quickly paid the girl even though Mom was grabbing for her wallet.

"No Mom. It was my idea so I get to pay."

"I always thought you girls would have to fight over them." She giggled as I showed her the finished products.

"No fighting necessary. Everyone can have a copy of everything because it is so easy nowadays." I tucked the copies gently into my bag so they wouldn't bend then grabbed her arm again as we exited excitedly through the glass doors and back into the car.

The theater was in the same shopping complex so we didn't have far to travel, just a few doors down. Marilyn dropped me and Mom at the entrance and she went to find a parking spot.

The theaters in southern California had changed drastically since I had left the area in the early '70s. They no longer were individual but rather mega-complexes showing multiple movies at one time. I made a mental note that I needed to get out of town more often. Marilyn had come into the lobby and went to get tickets while Mom and I surveyed the scene. We were like a little island standing in the middle of a colorful swirl of activity. The glass enclosure was crowded with a diverse collection of people of all races and I could have stood in the lobby just viewing the people, I was so enchanted. Montana is somewhat monochromatic; it was delightful to see the different skin tones and cultures interact pleasantly with each other. What hadn't changed about the theater was the smell of popcorn and butter wafting across the carpeted lobby.

The smell tickled our noses and I couldn't help it. "Ohhh. That is too good! Mom, shall we get some popcorn?"

Her eyes twinkled and she smiled, "Oh yes! Let's do."

Marilyn returned more quickly than we expected. "We are in Theater 4 up the ramp." Then she hurriedly pointed to a wide, ascending ramp.

Mom met my eyes. We both were disappointed at the fact we might have to rush and do without the popcorn. "Marilyn, Mom and I would like to get some popcorn." I turned to Mom. "I'll get it. Do you want a Coke, a Pepsi or a candy bar with that?" and I started to laugh. I felt like we were two little kids escaping to the theater.

Mom smiled too, "No dear, just the popcorn."

"OK, but that stuff makes you mighty thirsty. Don't think for a minute that I'm going to share with you." And I gave her my big, teasing grin. I turned to my sis, "Hey Marilyn, my treat. What do you want?"

"Nothing. I don't eat that junk food."

"OK. I'll tell you what. You girls get going and I'll catch up with you. This won't take but a second."

Marilyn and Mom, arm and arm, started up the long spiraling ramp to the second floor. I dashed over to the concession stand that was empty of customers for a moment. In no time my order of two popcorns and one large Pepsi was delivered. I threw in a box of pink and black Good & Plentys just for fun. Then, looking up the swirling array of people I saw my mother's white hair sticking up and that was my beacon. I put on my best cowgirl, long-legged stride and met them at the top. It felt good to move my muscles after sitting in what I considered solitary confinement for several days. I grabbed Mom's other arm just as we swung the double doors open into the theater.

Both of us gasped simultaneously. The walls inside were painted black. My transition lenses hadn't shifted from the brightness of the outdoors and suddenly I was quite blinded. I reached for the wall to steady myself, and Mom too, as we both were experiencing the same sudden disorientation. I quickly explained to Marilyn what the problem was, "I can't see," I whispered. Both Mom and I were literally blinded and I needed a minute or two to recover. I groped along the wall trying frantically not to block any of the other theater goers who just a minute ago seemed so friendly. Now the two of us were the recipients of some unflattering comments. Finally, my glasses adjusted and we were able to find our seats.

The wide aisles of yore had been cut and the seats stacked as close as rungs on a ladder. We felt like perched birds on a wire and our legs almost dangled into the next row. I can assure you this was not what I would have called progress and was uncomfortable on several levels. The film started and we were assaulted by a soundtrack at a decibel level that felt as though it was pushing our bodies back with force. If the shock waves didn't kill us, the action on the screen would. Novices to theaters, we sat much closer than any of us calculated and the action figures nearly jumped into our laps. Mom gripped my hand harder and harder and both of us felt it was a full-on assault to our senses.

The only forgiving part of the entire two-hour ordeal was that it finally came to a climactic conclusion and the blessed theater lights came on. I thanked God for the experience finally coming to an end.

We rode back to my mother's home discussing our shared

opinions of the experience. Marilyn and Mom really didn't like the movie but I did. It was the theater environment, though air conditioned, that was too much for me. Since it was still hot we thought we'd have sandwiches at the house instead of a heavy dinner. Mom said she had some bread frozen in her freezer.

Back at the house we all shuffled into the kitchen dropping our purses and bag of photos on the chair by the front door.

Marilyn said we'd have to wait for a while for the bread to thaw when she pulled the loaf out of the freezer. She pulled the bread out from the plastic cover and then tore off the thin second wrap surrounding it. I looked over at her, raised my eyebrows and mistakenly said, "You and my Harry are just alike. You thaw the bread and make it stale at the same time."

Within a split second her face twisted, turning crimson. It was amazing how fast she reacted and I thought, "Oh my! Instant demonic." The muscles of her neck bulged, making it appear that her blood pressure was soaring and then, between her teeth she seethed in an entirely different, alto voice, "Just what do you mean by that?"

Having worked around a lot of angry people and animals, I knew not to provoke her so I backed down, stretched my arms out openly on each side and actually took a few steps back. "I was just saying you and Harry thaw out the bread the same way." This woman was breaking from reality. My mother, hanging onto one of the kitchen chairs for support, saved the moment by asking Marilyn to help her to the family room.

I realized I had been standing holding my breath for some time. I knew Marilyn was depressed, I knew she had some legitimate problems, however, she appeared about ready to kill me over what? A comment about the way she thawed out the bread? It was unbelievable, yet convinced me that my mother knew more of my sister's problems than she was saying. She had told me she thought Marilyn wasn't up to handling the estate. What more was going on, I wondered?

What I did know was that Marilyn had sought a series of therapists and counselors off and on for the better part of her life. The first time I was aware of her problems was when I was just out of high school and she was getting her first divorce. I thought it was just the circumstances at the time, but her counseling went on for years. I have no idea how it was paid for.

In her conversations she would frequently bait people into arguments and then trounce on them verbally like a striking serpent. When she got in these moods I just avoided her. Sometimes she would call me on the phone acting silly, buoyant and almost euphoric. It was fun talking to her at those times and I wondered if she had been drinking. Other times she would be in what I called the "Eeyore mood" where everything was doom and gloom and the sky might fall at any moment.

I found myself cracking off a piece of frozen bread and absentmindedly smearing mayonnaise across it. My thoughts were on Marilyn and the last year when her frequent phone calls changed dramatically. She would be hostile and I couldn't figure out why she would want to place a long distance call just to rag on someone. The calls came out of the blue and I thought perhaps it was her son Dan's troubles or maybe she was experiencing some anxiety over her impending back surgery. Whatever the reason, I sought excuses for her. It was becoming alarmingly apparent that something much deeper was wrong. When I spoke to her last from Montana before coming down I asked if she was still seeing a counselor and she told me no, that she had to get ready for her surgery. Granted it was a totally illogical explanation on her part, but it was hers nevertheless.

As I put the sandwiches together the bread mercifully thawed out in the heat of the kitchen. By the time I got back to the den everything had settled down and Mom was totally engrossed watching Bill Moyer's Journal on TV. I handed everyone their little plates with a napkin and we just sat in silence eating while watching the news. I wasn't about to rock anyone's boat the rest of the evening. Keep everything on an even keel, I told myself, no sense upsetting Mom. After a while we all felt sleepy and I turned in early with a good book in the back guest room. I put John Coltrane on the tiny CD player in the corner. The speakers weren't very good but it helped slip my soul into another place.

I've always found prayer difficult in the cities and I'm not sure why. I have managed it, but the connection between God and myself seemed more distant, maybe more distracted than distant. For whatever reason it was not working this evening so my alternative was music. I needed something to center me and tonight it was a tenor saxophone and the light jazz of John Coltrane. Finally, I drifted off into the saner world of sleep.

Morning came at last signaling it was time to leave Yucaipa. I said my goodbyes and gave sincere assurances to my mother that she was a treasure, that I loved her and forgave her years ago. To me she had become a beautiful crazy quilt pillow much like the one she made me years before. Some of the fabric was beautiful and silky, but some parts were garish and I didn't care for them at all. The tiny pieces she put together were held by a fine display of embroidery stitches all in different colors and textures. Every time I pick up that pillow I think of my mother, each part is different yet together they form the colorful mosaic of a prized kaleidoscope.

I held her gently and longer than I normally did. We weren't a family to display a great deal of affection and maybe that is why I am so needy now. I'm glad I held onto her those extra seconds. I embraced her and infused her with all the love I could give.

As we drove out the driveway Mom stood on the steps of her home, looking like a princess in the early morning light, her white hair glowing about her head. Then she blew me a kiss goodbye.

Chapter 21

FENCES

Marilyn drove out of the driveway and slowly down the road. We had just reached the five-acre property line when I asked her to stop. "Marilyn, I want to show you what I'm talking about, the neighbor is encroaching on Mom's land. Why don't you make a left here so I can show you where he graded the road."

"I can't. It is too dusty."

"Well, it isn't that dusty. It is just unpaved. If you drive slowly you won't kick up the dust."

"I can't."

"Well, then just stop the damn car and look. The man has made a graded road here that goes the entire length of Mom's property. All you need to do is put in a $3 fence post and a little sign that says, No Trespassing."

"I can't put in a fence post Kat. You know I have back problems." She gave me the final "don't you dare argue with me" stare and simultaneously took her foot off the clutch, the car lurched forward down the road.

"Marilyn, I know *you* can't put up a fence post, but there is nothing wrong with either Matt or Dan. We do it all the time in the country. There is nothing to it. You just buy a post and put it in the ground."

"The ground is too hard."

"True. We take a little water and pour it where we want the hole. Every time it gets a little hard we pour more water in it." I could see that we weren't going anywhere here, so I just got quiet.

We rode the next hour to Cyndie and Noel's new home in Orange County almost in virtual silence. There was a tension between us that I couldn't quite put my finger on. What was Marilyn really afraid of? I couldn't get my mind around her opposition and was so grateful when we finally arrived at Noel's.

Noel was delighted to see us. The house was sparkling and there was a fresh plate of cookies sitting in the middle of her dining table. She had put fresh cut flowers in two different vases in the living room and sweetened it all up by lighting a few pink, fragrant candles. It smelled like jasmine and cinnamon in the spring. After she enthusiastically greeted us she put on a pot of water for tea.

"Marilyn, I'm so glad to see you. At last the three of us can sit down and have a talk about Mom's health and some future plans for her." Noel was beaming from ear to ear.

With those words Marilyn sprung up and out of her chair like a bungee unexpectedly releasing. She grabbed her purse and moved simultaneously toward the door.

"I don't have time for this now. I have to go."

I backed off and decided to let Noel handle this one. I had already had it with Marilyn's attitude and word fights. "Don't be silly Marilyn. We've talked for months about getting together today. This is the only time Kat is here. She has to go back tomorrow. Can't you stay for just a little while?"

"No!" Then a hastily offered an excuse, "I have to get back. My granddaughter is coming today." That was the first I had heard of that.

With her hand on the front door knob she was out in her car before the tea kettle had a chance to whistle. Marilyn, again in classic fight or flight, had fled practically running.

Noel, casually reached over, raised her heavily mascaraed eyes and smiled while lighting a cigarette. She held it expertly between her brightly painted red nails and exhaled. "Well, I guess ol' Marilyn didn't want to talk to us today, or any other day as a matter of fact. You are lucky she brought you this far, you could have been walking."

We looked at each other and burst out laughing. Sometimes things are so bizarre that you have to appreciate the ridiculousness and the illogic of a situation and just laugh. Noel and I were definitely on the same wavelength.

Chapter 22

THE SURGERY

Mom's surgery was the classic joke: *The surgery was a success, but the patient died.* It had been, in some technical way an elective surgery, elective meaning she chose to have it. I don't know what her alternatives would have been. She lived alone, in excruciating pain that kept her chair-bound for days on end. Her eyes scrunched tight and she sucked in her breath to keep from gasping too much. She had to hang onto one chair and shuffle to the next to get around and really needed a walker. Her quality of life had greatly diminished. There were things she needed help with and no one to help her.

In addition, partially due to her immobility, her personal hygiene had taken a dip. It was never the best anyway, never a daily bath with her frequently saying she hadn't gotten dirty and there was no need to bathe or change clothes. Needless to say, she developed a musty lingering odor about her that so many older people seem to get and be unaware of. She hadn't figured out why so many of us gave her bath supplies and perfumes. All three of us had gently tried to tell her this. Well, maybe two of us, because Marilyn also lacked these daily hygiene skills when she got depressed and perhaps she didn't notice. With her eyesight compromised, Mom didn't see the food dribbles on her blouses and pants and she couldn't see the ants in the kitchen and the messes here and there. Even if she could have seen them she would have been hard-pressed to clean them. She was in dire need of domestic help of some kind and apparently Marilyn, who saw her most often, didn't see this need clearly. When Noel moved closer and offered to help Mom, she was rejected. Clearly the family dynamics were working against any workable solution.

Mom elected to have her hip replacement surgery. I don't know if either she or Marilyn were informed what a high risk surgery this was for a woman of her age and health. I told her, Brad told her and I can't imagine the doctors not telling her, but I'm not sure she fully heard any of us. Then again, she felt she had no alternative, and to complicate matters, we were dealing with a woman who was used to having everything her way.

The appointed day came for the surgery. Marilyn drove from LA to Yucaipa and accompanied our mother to the hospital. Then she dutifully parked herself in the waiting room for the outcome. Unbeknownst to us, Marilyn was living in her own bubble at the time. She didn't tell Noel about the surgery so was quite surprised when Noel also showed up in the waiting room. I don't know — did she not think Mom and Noel spoke at all?

"Hey, Marilyn," Noel greeted her and sat down. "How's it going?"

Marilyn just glared at her for a moment, her nostrils stained slightly brown from her cigarillos. "Fine. Why did you come?"

"Uh, well in case you forgot, I'm her daughter too. I care about how she is doing. You have got to realize how risky this surgery is for her." Noel plopped her purse on her lap and looked at Marilyn.

"You never cared about a damn thing," Marilyn said, and with that turned her back on Noel. She picked up one of the well-worn reception office magazines that interested her little and began flipping the pages nervously.

Noel just sat quietly and didn't respond. Marilyn was getting increasingly difficult to communicate with at any time. The silence between them was indicative of the growing chasm, the result being they sat, not speaking or acknowledging each other, as the hours ticked by, waiting to see if their mother was going to be alright.

I was in Montana teaching, trying to focus on needy children and planned on calling as soon as I got home. Noel would step out for cigarettes, then Marilyn would wait until she returned and go out herself, lighting the slender cigarillos one after the other on the porch outside.

Finally, there was a jolting scream down the surgery corridor where they had parked themselves. Recognizing the shrill yells of directions to the staff, Noel looked over at Marilyn and calmly said, "Well it looks like Mommy Dearest survived."

"I wish you wouldn't call her that," Marilyn spat, at last acknowledging her sister. "It isn't nice."

"Nice? For God's sake Marilyn *she* isn't nice! Did you read the book?"

"What? *Mommy Dearest*? Why the hell would I read that?"

"Because you might have a little better understanding of what we went through, that is why. Crawford's child abuse was a walk in the park compared with what we endured. She was Joan Crawford's adopted daughter and Joan beat her with wire coat hangers."

"Bullshit! You are always bringing up stuff that never happened. Our mother has done nothing but kind things for you over the years. You are an ungrateful bitch and you have made her life miserable by your accusations and hateful attitude. Give it a break!"

The two women's voices were rising in the normally quiet hospital lobby and they were drawing attention and frowns from some of the other folks.

Noel lowered her voice but moved closer to Marilyn's face. "Our mother beat us with wooden coat hangers and anything else she could get her hands on. Don't you remember your butt bleeding from being pulverized by the shoe stretcher? I could never figure out if the baby blue paint was chipped from wear or from tear."

"You are out of your mind! That never happened!"

Noel just stared at her. She had heard about the Stockholm syndrome and knew that Marilyn had mental blocks, but this was like staring at someone who was denying they had a nose on their face.

Some things in life are so clear and then again they flip. Marilyn's personal clarity had become more and more disconnected and defused from the realities she experienced. Her few childhood memories became those she created rather than recalled.

The two women changed their focus and Marilyn said she was going to go talk to the doctors alone. She strode off in a huff carrying her purse and notebooks with her. Her cell phone went off just as she rounded the corner and Noel heard her switch to a sweet, melodic voice, "Hello…"

Noel packed up her things, reshifted her back brace and began her journey home.

I phoned Marilyn just a few hours later when I got home from work. "Marilyn. How is Mom doing?"

"She's fine. She came through the surgery with flying colors and will be home in a week."

"How far did they have to put the stem in?" I asked.

"What stem?"

"You know the shank part of the prosthesis. The phony metal part they stick down the femur. How far down did they have to go?"

"What are you talking about?"

"Mom's hip surgery, Marilyn. Mom had a complete replacement of her hip. It comes with a little ball at one end and a shank on the other. They have to insert it down the femur. She had osteoporosis so bad they had to make a longer stem."

"I don't know." There was a pause and I could almost hear the gears whirling in her head, "She has osteoporosis?"

"Didn't you talk to the doctors?"

"They just said she was fine. I'm going home and she'll be home in a week. We are moving her to a convalescent facility until she can walk."

"I thought you were going to take care of her."

"I can't. My granddaughter is coming over."

Frustrated, I politely said goodbye and hung up the phone. Then I fumed about the house for several hours walking in circles. I didn't want to call Mom at the hospital figuring it was too soon and she needed all the rest she could get. I will call her tomorrow when I get home, I told myself. I'd feel better when I could talk to her in person. None of us thought this was her best course of action, but she had been determined ever since her neighbor Esther had broken her hip and had a replacement.

"If Esther can do it I can do it," was a quote from one of our discussions. I had finally talked Mom into a little physical therapy class to help strengthen and stretch her muscles, but she had let things go too long and had to sit in a chair in the class. Getting to and from the class was so taxing for her that after three sessions she didn't go. That was my mother, doing everything "her way" in spite of professional advice. But what was so troubling was she would even go the wrong way on a one way street!

You can imagine my dismay and frustration when I called the hospital the next night to discover she had been moved to a convalescent hospital. No one had informed me.

"Where?" I cried into the phone.

"We can't give out that information," the receptionist explained. "You will have to contact a family member or her medical provider. Does she have someone in charge?"

My fingers shook as I dialed up Cyndie's number. I figured

being a nurse she would definitely know more than me. She answered right away.

"Cyndie! Thank God I got you on the line. Your grandmother isn't at the hospital. They have moved her I don't know where."

"I know Aunt Kat," she said, her usually modulated voice raising a pitch. "I couldn't stop it."

"What do you mean you couldn't stop it?"

"Look Auntie Kat. I got there just as they were loading Grandma into a transportation van to go to the convalescent hospital and that was pretty unusual so close after a surgery like that. She was running a slight fever and it is raining down here. You usually don't move patients until 48 hours post-op. I went to find Aunt Marilyn, but she had signed all the papers and left. The hospital staff said they couldn't do anything about it, that Marilyn is the medical durable, and I'm only second in line. Grandma was all flushed yet feeling cold and she was a bit confused. I'm a little upset myself so I'm going to get off the phone and drive over to the convalescent hospital right now and see if she is alright. I'll call you back later."

It was an agonizing four hours waiting for the return phone call from Cyndie. A major storm front had moved into our valley and the resulting blizzard made it difficult to even see the woodshed from my living room window. Fortunately, my husband had gotten in a night's supply of wood and was busy throwing logs into the blazing fire. The television was on with voices I wasn't listening to and my mind circled in swirls like the snow outside the windows. I think I jumped when the phone rang.

"Auntie Kat, she is OK, but uncomfortable and she is running a low-grade fever."

"Who orchestrated the move Cyndie? Who would move an old lady just out of surgery?"

"I'm not sure, but Auntie Marilyn signed the paper work. This place looks OK, but it isn't the one she picked out. I don't know why she was brought here. There isn't even a phone in her room."

"No phone?"

"No, I don't know why and she has a roommate. It is late here and everything is real quiet."

It was very late, that I could agree on. The weariness of working with little children all day and the worry about my elderly mother was taking a toll. It had been several days since I had a good night's sleep. I said goodbye to Cyndie and hung my old phone back into the cradle. I vowed the next day to drive into town and buy a message phone.

The next day I called the convalescent hospital with the information Cyndie had given me and asked to speak to my mother, Isobel Graham. The individual handling their phones sounded perturbed and that I had a lot of nerve asking to speak to a patient.

"Hey," I responded just as firmly, "we are in the twenty-first century right now and I want to talk to my mother. Get her!"

There was a clunk as the landline was put down and I could hear the nurses talking that they had to go get a patient. I waited for a few minutes before my mother's weak voice came on the line.

"You shouldn't call here Kat," she said.

"Mom, you need to get a cell phone."

"I don't need a phone, dear."

"You might want to call out."

"For what?"

"For help!" I started re-thinking my demands, not wanting to upset her. When all else fails ask about the food, I thought. "What did you have for dinner Mom?"

"Oh, pizza," she sounded foggy.

"Pizza?" I tried not to gasp. "Was that all?" Then I chuckled, "Was it good pizza?"

"No," she was drifting off. "It was the kind you get at the market. It was frozen, but it was hot."

"Mom, you don't like pizza. You don't eat pizza."

"Well, I do when the grandkids come." She was fading and I could hear mumbling and shuffling in the background. "I've got to go now. They only have one phone here and they had to wheel me out to it. It's too distracting."

All I could do was envision her being wheeled back down the hall with a fifteen-foot phone cord dragging behind her like a lifeline rope to a ship. What kind of hellhole was my mother in? A hospital with no phone? I put in an immediate call to Marilyn.

"Marilyn, I just talked to Mom..."

The words were barely out of my mouth when the voice at the other end snarled in a low witchy tone, "You shouldn't call her there."

"Look, can you get someone to go buy her a simple cell phone? Just a cheap one to keep by her bed. I'll pay for it." I would have to charge it, of course.

"She doesn't need a phone."

"I think she needs a phone and so strongly that I'm willing to pay for it, but I need someone to go get it. Have the store call me and I'll give them my charge card number. Just get her a phone!"

"Well, I'll do no such thing, she doesn't want one and she doesn't need one. One of us will be there all the time."

"Are you there now?"

"No. I had to come home. Listen, you are overreacting and I'm not doing it. I have to go. My granddaughter is here and I have to cook her something. I'll talk to you later." The option of further discussion was cut off. The phone connection ended with a defined click in my ear and then nothing.

My ear was beginning to feel hot from the phone pressure. There was now a strange tingling setting in and I gave it a quick rub and then set off dialing nurse Cyndie.

She answered on the second ring. "I'm so glad you called. I just left the convalescent hospital. We've got some problems here and no one seems to be taking me seriously. Grandma has an infection and there is a big oozing blister on the site of her incision. I had to change her compression stockings because someone put them on upside down. Auntie Kat, she is a mess. She hasn't been bathed in some time and her toenails look like they belong on a dragon. I couldn't believe it when I saw her. I tried to get someone to help me, but the only people on the staff in the evenings are nurses' aides. I did check her chart and she still has a fever. I think I'll call her doctor personally in the morning."

"Oh my God, Cyndie, I don't know what I would do without you. Where is your mother?"

"She'll be at the hospital first thing in the morning. We'll take care of everything."

We said our goodbyes and I struggled off to grade some papers. My mind wasn't at all on the kid's work and I was glad I had the teacher's edition so I could simply go down the roster, check off the right and wrong answers and figure percentages.

Chapter 23

SMOKE, MIRRORS AND MRSA

My mother was not recovering from the surgery and in my daily phone calls I was told she was growing weaker and weaker. Marilyn went to the convalescent hospital and stayed with her all day every day spending her nights up at Mom's house. We were all comforted somewhat by this, but more distressed that Mom was not responding.

Her doctor finally came and saw her, ran some blood tests and determined she had contracted MRSA. When the family informed me of this I immediately looked it up on Google.

MRSA is a Methicillin-resistant Staphylococcus aureus bacterial infection, rather new and highly resistant to antibiotics. The antibiotics being given to my mother were not the ones recommended on the Internet. The phones were ringing back and forth and at every opportunity I was calling Marilyn who would block me with quick excuses and vague answers. I called Cyndie and explained what I was learning from the Internet and that Mom needed to be moved to a private room. Yes, she confirmed that, but my sister Marilyn didn't believe either of us and had to call her girlfriend, a nurse in San Francisco. Later, Marilyn admitted her friend also had told her Mother needed to be in a private room, that her infection was difficult to treat, and recently was discovered to be running rampant through hospitals across the nation.

Marilyn had already become Mom's ever present bodyguard and wasn't allowing anyone else to visit without her being nearby. This increasingly agitated Noel and she decided to get up very early one morning and beat Marilyn to the hospital. She wanted to talk to Mom alone, and see what was going on. Somehow Marilyn got wind of this and when Noel pulled into the parking lot at 5:30 a.m., she was already there.

Cyndie decided to take both her mother Noel and her Aunt Marilyn to lunch. She thought that if they got away for a while from the hospital she could explain to both of them the severity of MRSA. Her reasoning was that once she relaxed, Marilyn would understand she needed to request different treatments and see that they were carried out. Her report to me that evening in Montana was that the lunch didn't go well at all. Cyndie said she had to repeat over and over again just what MRSA was to Marilyn. She tried explaining it in one way, then another and Marilyn just kept saying she didn't get it. Finally, she took Marilyn's legal tablet and wrote it down for her. Cyndie relayed to me that Marilyn seemed disjointed and unresponsive to her explanations. She said she felt like she was talking to someone with Alzheimer's and that she repeated herself so much she started to giggle and explained she was making rolled eyes over Marilyn's head to Noel.

Cyndie went on further to say that Marilyn starting mumbling that her son had MRSA as a baby but recovered. We all knew this was impossible. It didn't really start rearing its ugly head until the 1970s when it was identified in Australia. Slither never had MRSA.

Again, Cyndie said she told Marilyn she needed to move our mother to a private room, she had tried herself at the facility but couldn't as Marilyn still held the primary permission forms. Cyndie shared with me how she was feeling pretty frustrated. With their lunch finished, she paid the bill and they all walked out to the parking lot to return to The Manor, the name of the convalescent hospital. Then she remembered she had a newly bought PDR (Physician's Desk Reference) for Marilyn in her car. She reached in the backseat and handed it to her aunt.

"Maybe this will help you," she told her. "It has definitions of some of the medical terms and medications." She told me she tried to be gentle in her approach as if she was explaining something to an eight year old, not someone who claimed to be a UCLA college graduate. "Maybe you could look up some of the things the doctors are telling you."

Marilyn took the book and gave Cyndie a smile. Then she turned, tossed it into the backseat of her car, and drove off without as much as a goodbye or thank you.

The lady in the bed next to my mom died that night. Mom was delirious at that point and didn't know exactly what was happening as they wheeled the deceased out, and in the cloak of darkness a new victim was brought into the room of doom.

Mom was never informed at any time she had an infection, I wondered if her doctor was even aware as he didn't come daily. It was up to the staff to keep him abreast and log her symptoms in on her chart. Mom was given an intravenous for bronchitis and a bladder infection and I'm not sure she had either diagnosis as I never got to see the medical records until a year later. When I did eventually read her records, I had trouble with the terms, the handwriting and the abbreviations. I would need a doctor's help to decipher much of it.

The weekend arrived and Mother was weaker when Marilyn requested she be discharged. Horrified now, Cyndie attempted to override her again and at least clarify to the doctor what was going on. She called the doctor's weekend exchange number and was told he wouldn't be available until Monday and they didn't consider a patient in a convalescent hospital an emergency unless the hospital personnel called. Who was Cyndie after all? She had no influence, no legal right, just a concerned granddaughter who had enough background to know her grandmother was sliding downhill and no one appeared to be helping her. The girl's heart was being torn out along with the rest of ours. We were all painfully aware how powerless we were to do anything. Mom's care was like an avalanche crashing down a forest wall taking everything in its path. We were just helpless onlookers, observers of a wreck with our hands legally tied behind our backs.

Mom was released from the care facility without blood work, with an infection, without the doctor's knowledge and into Marilyn's hands. She wasn't cleaned up and she wasn't checked for pneumonia. Marilyn told me her bowels were so impacted from the Vicodin painkiller that they had to be "dug out," but no stool sample tests were made.

Was the convalescent hospital to blame? Did the right hand not know what the left was doing? Did Marilyn know what she was doing? There were no sanctions ever made against the doctors, even though Marilyn later insisted there were. The hospital itself remained blameless and there were no actions taken against them, no suits I knew of. Everyone involved appeared blameless, yet the fact remained that my mother was brought home with her seemingly attentive and dutiful daughter Marilyn at her side. Looking back all I think of is *Hush Hush Sweet Charlotte*.

Personally, at the time I was relieved Mom was back in the comfort of her own home. I didn't know the circumstances yet, how she got there and my reasoning then was at least I could talk with both she and Marilyn. I thought perhaps things were improving until Wednesday when I called and Marilyn informed me that she was going home to her house in LA.

"Did you get an in-home nurse or health care worker?"

"No."

"What do you mean, no? You can't leave her there all alone."

"I've fixed her some nice little meals and put them up in the freezer."

"She can't walk let alone stand and reach into the freezer!" I was close to yelling.

"I'm going home tomorrow. I have to take care of my granddaughter," was the robotic reply.

I wanted to crawl through the phone and smack her. "Your granddaughter has a mother and father to take care of her. Who is going to take care of your mother?"

"If you care so much about that why don't you come down and take care of her?" The words shot out like rapid fire.

"Damn it, Marilyn! You know I'm the only one holding down a job here. I'll be there as soon as I can. I'll tell the school tomorrow to prepare for a sub. You can't just leave her. I'll be down Saturday morning."

"Well, I am." She hung up the phone.

I was stunned. Marilyn actually planned to leave our mother alone and head back to Los Angeles. Unbelievable. Well, it was time to act, undoubtedly way past time as far as I was concerned. I didn't wait but a minute and dialed Noel's number. I explained the compounding problems and that I'd make flight reservations in the morning.

The next morning I received Noel and Matt's dreaded calls. "Our mother is dying."

Chapter 24

CARNAGE AT THE RANCH

Usually, before a great car wreck, there is some attempt to prevent it from happening. A driver will clutch the steering wheel frantically maneuvering this way or that while putting their entire body weight onto the brakes, hoping to stop before contact with something or somebody. If the brakes don't hold or the wheels are not turned correctly, there is the resulting carnage. In the case of my family, at the moment of Mom's death, it seemed like multiple cars were hurling through space, simultaneously aiming at each other. I didn't notice if some were braking in the massive cluster of chaos or if others were actually pushing down their accelerators. What resulted was an extensive, damaging wreck to my family. Later, I would say that it was heart wrenching, as if I had multiple loved ones who were killed in the same accident the same day.

Those who lived close by left for their own homes as late evening approached the day of Isobel Graham's death. I thought it would be nice, like so many homestead families I had known, to pass my mother's house down to another family member. In Scotland we even had third and fourth generations living in the same house. I mentioned to everyone, that with Marilyn's back problems, the house would be perfect for her. It was all on one level and she wouldn't have to worry about stairs. Her home in Los Angeles at that point had a higher market value and I reasoned she could sell that one, buy out Noel's and my share and move up there. The family could still meet and use all the silver, china and spacious bedrooms they had been accustomed to as children and adults. The house could remain the nucleus of the family gatherings. I saw it as a win-win situation, good for Marilyn, good for the family and good for Noel and I. Marilyn vetoed the idea on the spot.

I walked into the emptying house. Brad was standing in the entryway bidding his cousins goodbye and looking puzzled that everyone was leaving. "Isn't there a reading of the will? Why is everyone leaving?" There was a hollow sound to his questioning voice.

"I think that is in the movies, Son. Marilyn isn't letting go of that white binder and she is barely talking to me today. All the paperwork is apparently in there. I think we should just leave that one alone right now, we've got a mess here. I sure wish your grandmother did what we talked about last summer."

"What?"

"When I came last summer your Auntie Marilyn didn't want to stay at your granny's, not even overnight." I motioned for Brad to sit down in the living room where we could talk without being heard. "Marilyn honestly said she couldn't stand your grandmother anymore and kept apologizing that she would have to leave me up here alone with her for four days. She repeated this several times. It wasn't my imagination and I'm not making this up. Marilyn couldn't stand being with her own mother. I came down here because I knew about some of Granny's health problems, the high blood pressure thing and the hip problem. I'm amazed with your granny's blood pressure skyrocketing into orbit that the doctors would even consider a hip replacement. Maybe they had gotten it under control with medication. Your granny was sly as an old fox about not telling us all that went on with her health. I thought Noel, Marilyn and I could get together and discuss some of the issues we were facing. You know, like make a plan of some kind for the future before anything bad happened. I was trying to be proactive but it was a little like screaming stop before a wreck."

"Too late there, Mom." Brad actually smiled and his brown eyes softened when he looked at me.

The two of us went into the kitchen where Noel was busy at the counter making sandwiches. "I found some bread in the back of the freezer and Julie left some lunch meat for us."

We hungrily munched taking huge bites and anticipating the next one. Then we added more Cokes and sugar to our newly adopted junk-food diet. No one had gone for milk and all we had were sodas or coffee and those were being consumed at an alarming rate, keeping the weary spirits going. Finally, we came up for air and the chewing slowed down slightly as our bellies became full.

"I told Mom to get a lawyer last summer," I explained between munches. "She said she was concerned about Marilyn's behavior and personality changes. She said she didn't trust her. That is true and I wondered if there some writing on the wall I didn't know of? I didn't ask the details but as we all know ol' Marilyn slipped a major cog or two a little over a year ago. Hey guys, I tried!"

Noel looked at me, rolling her eyes and grinning, "Well, aren't you Miss Smarty? I'm glad you talked to her." Then with added emphasis, "Not that it would do any good."

"It didn't. Or, she didn't get the chance to make the changes she wanted. I was always honest with our mother, Noel. Last summer we had nothing to do but talk for four days and it was a great time."

After saying this the loss of my mother hit me again full force. I put my head down on the kitchen table and allowed the sobs to come. I cried for the loss of my mother and the loss of what could have been. I cried for the pain of everyone and the impending disaster I could see coming.

I didn't often talk about my psychic feelings and always tried to discount them and intellectualize them away, belittling myself. It was only after I reached fifty that I started trusting my instincts, my feelings and my heart. The dreams I had of my father speaking to me about this were coming to fruition. Noel moved over and started rubbing my back gently with little circular motions. She had been comforting me this way with little back rubs since I was a youngster. In a few minutes I relaxed and began to feel better.

As if on cue we all got up, put our dishes in the sink and stepped out to the patio. Each of us smoked another Marlboro and Brad scowled gently at me. He also understood the extremely stressful situation that we were under and I'm glad he didn't succumb to the habit again as I did.

He cleared his voice and talked softly as we sat outdoors. "I tried to talk Grandma out of the surgery, I told her it was suicide at her age. She wouldn't listen to me. You know I talked to her all the time. I called her almost every week and we did have some nice conversations. I'm going to miss her, what a way to go."

We sat out on the porch for some time talking about Grandma and smoking one cigarette after another. Waylon the cat was rubbing against my leg, his little food dish was empty again. He knew who in the crowd to seek attention from. I said it was time to feed him and Noel said she wanted to make some tea so the three of us, Brad, Noel and I, with Waylon trailing not far behind, returned to the den through the side door. Marilyn was sitting in Mom's chair talking on the phone, but as soon as we entered there was a quick "bye-bye" and the call was terminated.

I went into the kitchen and started looking for some cat food. Noel put on the tea water and was scrounging around for something sweet. One of her kids had been more than nice and brought up all kinds of goodies when they arrived that morning.

Brad sat opposite Marilyn in the den and was attempting conversation. He was trying to be polite and engaging, but she was only giving him some cursory, short answers. He was looking up at the flagstone fireplace where my mother still kept some of my father's mementos when Noel and I returned with mugs of steaming hot tea. It had been a long time since Brad had been able to visit this house as an adult.

On the mantle was a green antique brass ball that was used as a floater for the fishing nets years ago. Next to that sat Dad's little inkwell shaped like a devil and his father's powder horn from the Ozark's. Brad didn't remember seeing it before.

"What's this?" He reached up and took the old powder horn down, turning it in his hand. "It has initials carved in it."

"Yes," I answered. "It was your great grandfather's. He made the powder horn when he was a boy and those are his initials carved in the side, JBG. It's not fancy," I said with a smile, "but definitely his."

Marilyn's voice suddenly rose like a Banshee from the chair, loud and shrill. It was as if an electric prod had been pushed in her behind. "Yes! And it goes to the first-born male and that is Daniel!"

We all stared at her, eyes widening and our mouths practically falling open. What a reaction! Exhausted by all the events and also feeling assaulted, I decided this time I wasn't going to fold into a limp scarf and pretend this wasn't happening. I was going to stand my ground. I had decided a few years earlier that I wasn't going to be bullied anymore by anyone else in my life. It didn't mean I wasn't filled with trepidation. It meant that no one any longer was going to lie or manipulate me while I took it all silently. Well, they might lie, but I'm going to tell them that is a lie. I had been a marshmallow long enough!

Noel had returned to the room with another cup of tea and was suddenly very quiet and taking it all in. She couldn't have missed any of this conversation as she was just on the other side of the louvered pass through. She crossed the room, curled up in the sofa, moved a few pillows to get comfortable and just observed us. She knew the history of the powder horn and the conditions of succession. We all knew the story. It had been relayed multiple times over the years since we were kids.

Breathing in, I modulated my voice and began. "Marilyn, there is another story. Our cousin Jett was given that powder horn for safekeeping by J.B. The family had pretty much disinherited the man because he left them in rather dire straits, but his cousin Jett kept his stuff for years. Over and over he told us the first one that brought him a little baby boy would get the powder horn."

"You mean the first baby with a penis brought to his house would get it. You made a bee line." Marilyn interrupted me with a snarl.

"You don't need to get crude Marilyn. My son is sitting here and it wasn't exactly a bee line. Our sons were born eight years apart. You had eight years to take your son the hundred and fifty miles to Santa Maria to collect that powder horn. I took Brad to show him off to Jett and to visit him out on the oil lease. I took both my boys many times and have pictures to prove it. Brad was the first little boy brought to Jett. He was J.B.'s first great grandson to visit Santa Maria and the oil lease."

Marilyn's face twisted accusingly and her mouth tightened as she sneered. "Where were you when we buried Jett? You only went because you wanted something."

I must have sighed deeply, weary of feeling I had to defend myself over and over again. I felt like a falsely accused defendant at a murder trial. "Marilyn, I visited Jett all the time even after he was in the old folks' home. I used to take him cigars and sit and talk with him for hours. I really liked that old guy in spite of all his idiosyncrasies. He told great stories about our dad, granddad and life in the Ozark's. I wouldn't know any of it if it weren't for him. I bounced around the Santa Maria oil leases sitting between Jett and Dad holding a NeHi soda between my legs for hours on many an occasion." I started to laugh with the recollection. I was the little girl in the bibby overalls and a head of curly hair. I was Dad and Jett's little sidekick as they checked the oil rigs. I continued speaking, "You know and I know that powder horn ..."

I was interrupted by Noel's voice coming from the corner, finishing my sentence, "...is Brad's!"

Marilyn didn't skip a beat, but you could tell she knew we were telling her the truth. She knew it too, yet she got up, walked deliberately to Brad grabbing the horn from his hands. "It is Dan's and that is that!" Brad sat in stunned silence. The only sound was Noel loudly sipping her tea.

Quiet descended on the room like a fog in a mausoleum. I got up and turned on the TV. "Maybe tomorrow we can talk when we've all rested." For now I would watch some mind numbing program that I wouldn't remember later. Right now I just wanted the insanity carousel to come to a stop, dismount the painted horses going up and down and wake up from this nightmare!

Chapter 25

SUNDAY

It would be nice to say that we all woke up Sunday morning and started fresh with a clean slate, however, that was not quite the case nor did it even come close. Because most of the family had departed late Saturday night, Noel and I had beds available. It was like seeing the vacancy sign at the last motel available after a long night's drive. We both struggled into the guest room where just twenty-four hours earlier our bags had been tossed into the hall. Neither of us even suggested changing the sheets. We didn't care who had been in the beds before us and besides there were no clean linens in the house. We just piled into the covers, me sleeping in my borrowed T-shirt and panties and Noel bringing along an actual nightgown. As we lay down to sleep Noel whispered to me, "Well the stick has certainly been passed."

I knew immediately what she meant. The unyielding control my mother had over everyone had been usurped by Marilyn. Seeing clearly this ascension of royalty, I replied, "Not a stick dear, but a scepter."

We both giggled at the concept and then I immediately slipped into a welcomed deep sleep. The next morning when I relayed this exchange to Brad, he beat us all with his quick humor when he said, "Not the scepter, more like the Claymore!"

For the readers who do not know what a Claymore is, it is a two handled massive, double edge sword used by the early Scots. The swords averaged about four-and-a-half feet in length and they were swung around in a circle striking the enemy from any direction they might approach. Scotland's hero, William Wallace's sword was 5'4" including the hilt.

A full night's sleep was not to be had that night at my mother's house. I tossed and turned and kept hearing talking in the back of my mind, not being sure if it was real or imagined. It was Marilyn talking on and on and I was too exhausted to care if she was on her cell phone or not, but I kept coming out of my sleep wondering who she would be talking to so late.

Noel told me later that Marilyn indeed had been on the phone most of the night and she couldn't sleep at all. At one point Marilyn even quietly had opened our bedroom door, apparently to check to see if the two of us were sleeping. Noel said she pretended to be and was totally relieved for the first time that I was snoring. She also said that she was frightened by Marilyn's behavior and lay still pretending to be asleep, but listening to all the conversations. She was scared when Marilyn opened our door and wondered how Marilyn could stay awake for so long when the rest of us could barely keep our eyes open?

I awoke about 4:00 a.m. Rocky Mountain Time and gave up on my attempts of solid consecutive sleep. That time was 3:00 a.m. in California. Noel was sleeping then so I quietly pulled on my Levis and padded in my bare feet down the hall and toward the kitchen. I noticed the light shining under Marilyn's door. Maybe she fell asleep with the lights on, I thought. I went into the kitchen as quietly as possible turning on the stove light and started to make coffee.

Thank God Mom still had some coffee in the house considering every other cupboard was uncharacteristically bare. It was a cheap off-brand but I didn't care, anything hot and wet would be good about now. Trying not to wake anyone I stood quietly in the kitchen, put my arms on the facing sink and tried to do a few stretches while I waited. I pulled out the pot and poured a strong cup of java while the rest of it continued to brew, then I took my cup into the darkened living room.

There was so much information and drama to digest that I just needed to sit, think and focus. I found solace sinking into one of the living room's big chairs. I didn't open the drapes as I sat sipping and silently greeting the day in the dim light. The aroma of the brewed coffee wafted through the house and I heard Marilyn's door open. As she started toward the kitchen I quietly chirped, "I have some fresh coffee for you."

Marilyn came into the living room and stared, astonished to see me, then turned without a word and went back to her room. She was there briefly then reappeared with a yellow legal pad in one hand, pen fastened at the top and a coffee mug in the other. She took the chair opposite mine without speaking. Was she a marathon woman requiring no sleep? Her attitude and demeanor continued to be more than unusual from the Marilyn I thought I knew or used to know and loved.

"Whoa!" I chuckled looking at the tablet, "You carry those things around?" I was trying to start on a light side, throwing in a little humor.

"I want to know what you want," she snapped.

Pretty early for business, I thought. The sun hadn't cleared the horizon yet and I had barely started my first cup of coffee and someone wants to launch into legalities. What I want? I want my mother alive and these bizarre shitty scenes to stop. I got up, motioned that I would be right back and then went and refilled my cup. Returning to the same chair, I looked at her as gently as I could across the shadowed room. This woman was having some major and undoubtedly serious issues. Her whole personality and demeanor had noticeably changed over a year ago. "Well, not much in the material sense," I began. "What I want from you is fairness." I paused giving a moment for my words to sink in. "Our mother was never fair, Marilyn. Our whole lives have been unfair. You know it and I know it. Our mother's trust gives you two-thirds of the property and me one-third." I continued uninterrupted but pausing every so often while I watched her write. "It was cruel cutting out Vince. Downright cruel and vicious and you know it. That action put me between my boys, and they with each other. Why? The trust is unfair to Noel. She has always worked. You are in a position now to make a difference in this family and the pain and aching does not have to continue. You can change that right now."

I decided to stop there hoping I had made my point. She could come out as a heroine. A benevolent queen, if that is how she viewed herself, wielding a scepter of kindness rather than a cruel whipping stick. Marilyn was busy scratching all this down on her legal pad.

At last she spoke. "That isn't fact Kat. That is your twisted opinion. The question is were those two fair to our mother?"

Oh my, I thought, we are in for it now. She is defending the woman she told me about a few months before that she couldn't stand to be around. Once again it was the en garde of a verbal sword fight and should I engage? I was going to lose no matter what I said or did. My mind reeled, this wasn't the kind of situation where my strengths were. I wasn't good with any of the verbal duels my family so frequently participated in. I was the one who had to digest and then process information. I was one of those who never had the snappy answer. My answers always came too late the next day when I rehashed the scene. I'd think of answers when the blood stopped rushing into my head and the inner voices no longer screamed. The quick comebacks and rapid put downs were Marilyn's forte.

I shouldn't have to defend Noel or my son. I certainly wasn't prepared for her assessments of them toward our mother. Neither had offended or cheated anyone in the family and neither had reached outright into someone's purse or wallet and stolen money in this house, but someone else had. What were their crimes? The two of them actually shared the same holiday birthday. Noel used to say laughingly that our mother didn't like Capricorns.

The absurdity of the situation was making me lose my focus. I tried to get back on track thinking of the tasks at hand. The situation was twisted, that was for sure, but the twisting was coming from Marilyn.

"I'm just saying, Marilyn, that you are now in the position to right so many wrongs, decades of wrongs." I put the ball in her court and took another drink cupping my hands around the warm mug for comfort.

"You sound like you don't trust my honesty."

That statement was designed as a hook for a fight. Marilyn was armed and dangerous and I knew it. Oh yes, raised by the queen sociopath, this one was a good student. All the bells and whistles in my brain were going off. There were no little proverbial red flags here, not at all. What I saw were huge, fluorescent, neon-red lights flashing across the wall: CAUTION CAUTION CAUTION.

Good God, I thought, I'm falling into deep shit here. I actually heard Shakespearian voices saying, *"Oh the lady doth protest too much."* I recalled the criminals who I used to work with exhibiting the same behavior of innocence when they were guilty as could be. They never took responsibility — it was always someone else's fault.

"It isn't your honesty I'm questioning, it is your fairness," I continued.

"You seem to know a great deal about Mother's trust." Marilyn had pulled herself up like a rattler ready to strike. I could feel her glaring viciously across the still dimly lit room, attempting to penetrate my resolve.

"Well," I drawled, taking some intentionally long sips of coffee while I thought through each word. Then I started to relax and thought that maybe two could play this game. Sadly, that is how I viewed it at this point, a chess game. "What you have failed to realize is Mom and I were friends and, yes, I have read the trust. We shared a great deal of information with each other." I actually started to chuckle at the absurdity of our situation as Marilyn continued writing on the legal tab.

"Hey, Marilyn," I chided with a devious humor prodding me on. "Do you want me to sign that paper like some kind of affidavit when we are done?"

The air in the room was heavy with suppressed rage. Apparently, I hadn't backed down on cue as she had expected. I had grown stronger and more educated in the many years since I left southern California. Without comment she snapped the top of her pen withdrawing the tip in an audible click. "I will honor Mother's wishes," she said, before getting up and literally marching back to her room slamming the door so violently that the bang echoed down the hall.

So much for thinking about the others still trying to sleep.

The sun by now was sliding up in the east and the rooms of my mother's mansion were slowly coming awake. I looked at the old upright piano, walked over and lifted the cover. I placed my fingers on the keys and silently remembered so much. Had there been the least amount of encouragement, I could have played it well; it was Marilyn who got the lessons. I was self-taught from hours of what my mother referred to as "pounding." I would sit and make chords and play all the songs I knew by ear. I felt a pang of guilt when I looked down at one yellowed and glued ivory key. I had done that as a young child, lifting the edge with my thumb until it snapped and broke. I wanted to mark where middle C was so I would know where to place my hand. I don't know why no one thought to put a little sticker or dot on it, so I guess I did it my way. I'm sure I paid for that maneuver dearly but I don't remember. There were so many spankings that they seemed routine.

And just why was my mother so unfair? You would think I would resent what my sisters got and I didn't, but somehow it didn't occur to me to feel that way. They were trapped in the world of expectations and subjected to a great deal more pressure than I. I had a great deal more freedom.

Marilyn's first wedding had been hurriedly planned with friends and family gathered at our church then a reception at our home. She was pregnant in good old family tradition, but nevertheless, relatives came from far and wide for the celebration. She was sent off with gifts and well wishes before the age of twenty.

Noel's wedding was almost a year to the day of Marilyn's, but a more lavish affair. Marilyn made her a beautiful wedding dress and painstakingly sewed seed pearls across the front. Noel chose Marilyn to be her matron of honor with cousins and me as bridesmaids in matching lavender dresses and heels. There was a huge reception for several hundred at the local country club. Noel also was pregnant, however, as I said, it was a family tradition although the wedding had been planned for months ahead including the professional photographers.

I do have a few snaps of my first wedding. I'm laughing as I write this. Fortunately, a friend of mine remembered to bring his camera. Because everything I did was criticized, I did not take the young man to meet my parents until we were engaged. My philosophy for some time had been, why bother? I was working my way through college, waiting tables at a local folk music club. My employer offered to host the reception and my mother said they wouldn't come if that was the case. They didn't like where I worked, a coffee house, which didn't even serve liquor. Finally, they bribed me and my fiancé by telling us that if we did not have a wedding they would give us the cost of one as a gift. I was always broke, and the offer sounded wonderful, so I acquiesced.

The wedding was simple, no guests, just my sisters, their husbands and one friend. Three weeks later my mother mailed me a congratulations card and inside was the pink slip to the car I had wrecked. It is true I used the car for school, but they owned and failed to insure it. In addition, I was injured in the accident and my parents collected the insurance settlement, which was the cost of the wedding. I don't believe my father ever knew she did this. I knew from early experiences my mother's sense of fair play was non-existent by anyone else's standards.

There was a great deal of pressure in my family, somewhat reinforced by society at the time. The girls, cousins and all, were supposed to be married or engaged by eighteen. I had total fears of being an old maid because I didn't have a serious relationship going and I was twenty. This pressure had all the potential makings of poor decisions and I was no exception.

After talking to Marilyn about fairness, I decided what we all needed in this house now was a good meal. We'd had junk food for days and our bodies, at least mine, weren't used to that kind of diet. I could hear Brad moving around the den where he had parked himself for the night on the sofa. He also didn't want to sleep in the back bedroom that once had been my parents. We've never talked about it, but I couldn't help wondering if it was for the same reason: the damn room felt haunted.

I started scrounging around the refrigerator. Between the food Julie had brought and a few other items, I was able to put together a decent meal for the four of us, the first solidly nutritious food we had had in the last few days. Maybe today, I thought, once Marilyn and Noel had eaten, we could have some *nice* discussions or at least civil talk about the estate and which direction we should take. I seemed to have an eternal spring of hope in my heart, yet at the same time that spring seemed to be more realistically drying up. There wasn't the audience now for distractions and the performances might be minimized; it was an excellent time to focus on the business at hand. Brad was an unimposing figure so that left my two sisters and me. My hope was that possibly we could begin to untangle this growing mess before it unraveled completely. It was actually Brad who started the conversation at breakfast. He was looking at his eggs and almost whispering. "Aunt Marilyn," he began, "Grandma promised me her car years ago. Did she put that in writing?"

"No!" Marilyn exclaimed as she reached across his plate for a second helping of eggs. "That is a high-ticket item." She slurped the coffee to wash down her food, dabbed her mouth daintily and looked squarely at Brad. "I'm having our cousin Joy, who runs an antique store, appraise this house. Julie's boyfriend is going to appraise the car. Kat, I want you to make a list of things you want. Noel already wrote a letter years ago saying she didn't want anything material so that is that. I'm just doing what Mom wished." Marilyn reached over and started stuffing her face with the canned peaches I had put on the table.

I wondered if there was going to be no end to her cold, mandates and her authoritative statements void of compassion. "Marilyn," I said calmly, "everyone in the family knows the car was to go to Brad. We have all known it for years. Grandma talked about it quite frequently.

Without a pause, her voice came forcefully. "No! You can purchase it!" Again she looked right through me and I noticed her eye twitching again. "I'm having a professional appraisal of the car and will send that to Brad. Actually, the neighbor down the road also wants to buy it."

I gasped, "You already talked to someone about it?" It hit home that she clearly thought all this out before our mother's death and offers had been made.

"Well, yes, some time ago." Marilyn's grief at our mother's death less than twenty-four hours ago seemed short lived. She was definitely in control now and the dispersal of Mom's belongings premeditated. The question again remains, for how long? Was it days, weeks or months before, when she said she "couldn't stand her?" Who else was behind this? I could only guess the phantom partner on the phone perhaps? What was also painfully clear was that the answer to any question to Marilyn was always a resounding "No!" What was the purpose of proceeding?

Everyone in the family knew that Mother had promised Brad the old Dodge. It was what is referred to as common knowledge. It wasn't a new car. She had talked about who got what of her possessions quite openly in the last few years. Noel's son was to get sets of some of her books. Vince was to get the tapestry chair by the front door which we all referred to as the "throne" and I was to have a small cloisonné ceramic cat that I had loved since I was a tot. It was all understood, if not in writing, or at least I suffered from the illusion it was all understood. I knew "my" cat had been in writing but couldn't recall the others.

The car in question was manufactured the year Brad was born and that is what made it special to him and his granny. Mom had taken excellent care of the vehicle. Dad had loved cars also and worked on them keeping them in tip-top condition. He taught Brad simple mechanics and later more complicated ones. The car itself had increased in value rather than decreased because as it aged it went from an old car into the world as a classic muscle car. As it aged, I kept telling Mom she could put a classic license plate on it instead of the old one and I thought it might save her a little money.

Dodge had made a four-door series of Coronets in 1967 for various police departments to purchase in fleets. Dad, not being comfortable with any four-door vehicle, found a rare two-door and he bought it immediately. My mother loved it and after Dad passed away she cared for it as he did. When her vision started going, she had a few little fender benders but each one was repaired so the car appeared as if it just had been driven off the showroom floor. She also had these repairs made immediately so none of us would know. Eventually, she'd confess to me about more than a few and that repairs were being made.

The older the car got the more male attention it drew. Mom was amazingly naive about some things and I still marvel how nothing really bad ever happened to her. She would cruise around, handbag on the seat full of cash, letting men of every ilk look at her vehicle. Some offered her money, some trades and she always drew a small crowd of onlookers when she pulled the long-bodied, blue, gas-guzzler into a parking lot or service station.

Two summers before her death I had been down for my annual summer visit. We had both been out shopping and she stopped for cheap gas in a seedy section of town when a bare-chested, dirty young man began talking to her through the open passenger window. I was inside paying for the gas when I looked out into the bay of the station to see the man now had his entire torso shoved through the passenger window and was reaching toward her. Several Hispanic men in line with me gasped simultaneously when we saw this. Their concerns were audible as I ran out the service station glass door yelling at the top of my lungs, "Get away from my mother!" I was fully launched into attack mode. The man jerked his body out as I screamed, just as my startled mother's reflexes pushed down on the accelerator. The Dodge lurched forward and then, she began in her panic to turn the steering wheel frantically. So there I was, dashing down the sidewalk while Mom was driving in circles around the service station. Had she forgotten I was there? By the time she rolled to a stop I was laughing and crying at the same time. It was like the old Keystone Cops, slapstick comedy at its best and quite a sight for the onlookers.

"You don't have the sense God gave a sparrow! That is what you used to tell me growing up!" I was a little angry and scared for her at the same time.

Mom had calmed down and started giggling. "Yes, I did didn't I?"

"Mom, you have got to be more careful. That man had all the earmarks of a felon. He did not have good intentions."

Squaring her shoulders and holding her head high, she began telling me that she was quite in control of things and then proceeded to get lost on her way home, a community where she had lived for forty years. Her excuse was, I had upset her. Oh, what an exceptionally exhausted team of guardian angels looked over her and some I believe were even working overtime.

I lost my appetite during breakfast looking at Marilyn that Sunday morning. Brad also was rearranging his food around the edges of the plate with his fork. Noel and I got up and instinctively started cleaning up the kitchen and doing a bit of tidying. We had been trained well by our mother. Marilyn filled her coffee cup again and moved to the den. While the sink was filling with warm water, I checked Waylon's plates and leaned down toward the trash with the other empty cat food cans. Whew – the stench came up and nearly knocked me over.

"Marilyn," I called out, "you have the keys to the garage and I need to take the trash up."

"Forget it!"

"What? Marilyn, maybe you didn't hear me clearly. I need to take the trash up to the garage. It stinks. These cat food cans are going to stench up the whole house not to mention attracting flies and maggots. We got a growin' Petri dish here. Nasty!"

"Leave it at the back door! The garage is closed," she answered.

I put down the tea towel and left Noel to finish up. Anger was creeping up from my feet like the old red surge. It had taken me years to train myself not to explode and send things hurling through the air. I knew I would just be striking a match into a gas can if I said anything to her now. I thought I'd walk out to the veranda to calm myself down. I walked out into the hall, across from the kitchen and looked at the yellow caution tape still strung across the bathroom door. Wasn't that a bit dramatic? Who the hell went and got the caution tape? Not only was the bathroom off-limits, we weren't allowed into the garage. The fishy smell wasn't just coming from the empty cat food cans piled in the trash; the whole scene was bizarre. I needed some time to be alone and think. Brad, always faithful, brought us both more coffee. I sat outside on the steps looking at the gray morning skies of the San Bernardino Valley. "I miss home," I said. "I miss my clean blue sky and I miss my mom."

We were silent for some time. Again Brad explained how he had tried to talk his grandma out of this operation. He somehow felt responsible that she wouldn't heed his advice. I told Brad that he wasn't alone, she rarely took anyone's advice. To say she was a headstrong woman and always her own counsel was an understatement. Brad stepped off into the flower garden, whipped out his cell phone and called his girlfriend up in Washington. This whole scene was so surreal, no one would ever believe it. I was hoping his girlfriend realized he wasn't nuts and gave him a little sympathy. He was walking around a formal rose garden while inside the house a family of crazies were acting out their parts; lies and mysteries were piling up one right after another.

I sat for a while thinking this might be the last time I would be in my parent's home. A feeling of gloom and doom settled around my heart. Brad finished his call to his sweetie and the two of us walked around the perimeter of the five-acre property. I explained to him about the neighbor using the back property as an easement and how I had intervened last summer. I told him I informed Marilyn about easements and told her of friends who had similar encroachment problems where we lived in northern California.

I reiterated how I told her that a simple fence post and sign would solve the whole deal and that she could take care of it for under $10. I had even gone down and talked with the other property owner. He wasn't the fire-spewing dragon portrayed by Marilyn or my mother, but quite the reasonable individual. I explained the situation and told him he really shouldn't have graded her property to the back of his house, but that Dad would have let him drive that way anytime. We even exchanged phone numbers and he told me he would take care of it. However, with her new personality, Marilyn seemed to want war. A major battle of right and wrong. Yes, a sign, a post and ten dollars would have solved the whole problem there.

Brad talked to me about the car and how terribly disappointed he was. It wasn't that he was receiving something the other grandchildren had not. How do you compare the cost of a car with the cost of a college education? Mom had done none of these things for him, and much like me, he wasn't really keeping score. Neither he nor his brother had been on the receiving end of my mother's generosity as much as her other grandchildren. It was just for the last five or six years she had repeated over and over that he could have her car when she no longer needed it. Brad had been the only one in the family who had an interest in cars, had a shop and actually raced both cars and motorcycles. There were plenty of cars in the family and if I counted correctly, two Mercedes parked in the driveway yesterday. No one needed this car, it was just sentimental to Brad and he was crestfallen. Financially, neither he nor I could purchase it at this time. He had a pretty level head about the accumulation of debts and ironically, both of us were paying on college loans, me being the proverbial late bloomer.

When I called my mom to tell her I graduated from college at last at the age of fifty her comment was, "You could have done it sooner if I you hadn't been so lazy."

The California sunshine was welcome to both Brad and I. Neither of us had basked in it for close to a year and we both were equally reluctant to go back inside the house. We walked together around the side of the house just to move a bit. Both of us were normally active people and all the sitting had been a strain. Just about the time we reached the front door it flew open as if on cue. Marilyn was streaming out like a wet hornet aimed at an unsuspecting victim. Her hair was flying back as she charged toward us.

"I want to talk to you outside!" she demanded pointing her finger stiffly at me. I was already outside so that wasn't a problem, but it was a "no brainer" that we were going to be subjected to another unpleasant exchange from the Bully Queen. I thought how nice it would be to punch her.

"No!" Those words came flying out of me for a change. "Marilyn, there will no more family secrets. No more! I'm sick to death of them. You can talk to me in front of anyone. No more little silver stiletto knives in people's backs. I already told you that — that deal is over." I stood facing her refusing to budge. Brad stood by my side baffled by his aunt as he had never seen this side of her.

By now Marilyn was yelling again, her face contorted and her eyes wild. "Our sister just accused me of killing our mother!" Then, through clenched teeth she continued yelling and demanding, "Get her out of here!"

Now it was my turn. I didn't even have to think. "No! I will do no such thing. She was Noel's mother too and this home is all of ours."

Marilyn's mouth tightened down, she looked at me then spun around like a top and stormed back into the house. She had no reinforcements this time; we followed knowing there was going to be another scene. Marilyn whipped into her room and came out again with a new yellow legal tablet. She plopped into one of the carved oak chairs in the dining room and gripping her pen like a weapon started scribbling furiously across the paper. I wanted to laugh at the absurdity of it all, but that little guiding voice in my mind said, "I wouldn't if I were you."

Noel entered from the other end of the room with the dishtowel in her hand and appeared very calm. "Marilyn, why won't you talk to us? We should discuss what is going on here. You aren't giving out any information and we don't know what is going on. Why aren't you reading the will? We need to talk about a funeral. We need to talk about a memorial service."

"She didn't want one," I stated blandly.

Noel looked at me knowing what I said was true. "We should do it for the grandkids."

"Damn it, she didn't believe in God and she did not want a service. She was quite clear about that," I said. "She didn't have one for our father you know." It was a real sore spot for me and one from which I hadn't completely healed. I stood in this same house twenty years before with my dying father. It was another crazy event with my mother refusing to say a prayer with my dad who was a Christian and losing his brave battle with cancer.

Dad's sisters were both there. We went into the den, formed a circle holding hands and along with my uncle and Noel, said prayers and sang some hymns. Mom, not only refused to join us but made jeering remarks. We all went against "Mother's wishes" that day and held a service for our dying father in this very house.

Marilyn repeated, like a broken record, "I'm following our mother's wishes." As she walked to the back bedroom down the hall, I couldn't help shouting out, "Our mother's fuckin' wish was not to have a service!" I know it wasn't right. I know it wasn't Christian or forgiving. It wasn't a lot of things and my only excuse, I was becoming unraveled too. My courtesy took a hiatus, but what I said was true, my mother had been adamant about no service. Adamant!

The door slammed to my parent's room again and within a minute we could hear her talking to the phantom again on the other end of the cell phone.

It wasn't clear to me why Noel had accused Marilyn of murder. I hadn't told her about Marilyn's dramatic confession at the hospital. This was something that hadn't been mentioned or alluded to until this very moment by Noel. Now the two of us, without talking, were thinking along the same lines.

I really wanted a cigarette now, and a drink, or anything else that could dull my senses. Oh, for a cold can of beer or three or four. It was barely 10 a.m. and I wanted this day over. When I was little and things got ugly at home, I would run out the door and go to the neighbor's house two doors down. Sometimes I would just hop on my bicycle and peddle furiously away, flying down the streets of LA until I could peddle no more.

I pulled another cigarette out of Noel's pack and paced through the doorway back into the sunshine, lit up and inhaled deeply. This time I was out front and sat on the edge of my mother's circular planter. In the middle was a little cherub that once was a fountain. I couldn't help but smile to see that the bright red paint Dad had brushed on the toenails years ago was still there. That was my father's subtle sense of humor, to my mother's loathing. Amazing that the red hadn't faded even though Dad had been dead twenty years. I should find such good nail polish.

I hadn't quite finished the cigarette when Noel came out of the house with her satchel, her brace belted over her blouse and her massive collection of keys clutched in her hand.

"I'm going now. I'll see you later," she snapped striding up the path towards her little truck.

"Wait. Wait. We have no car. I am out of clothes and I need a clean shirt and some sandals or something. I'm wearing Brad's socks for Christ's sake. Noel you've got to help us, we've got to go to town and the little bitch Marilyn isn't taking us there." I don't believe I had ever called Marilyn a name up to that point in my life other than "poor."

"OK, Kat. I'll take you to town and then drop you off back here. We need to get a camera and start photographing this place. Marilyn is bound and determined to take it all and I want documentation."

I grabbed my wallet, left my backpack by the door and shouted to Brad I was going to town. Noel and I literally jumped out the door and practically ran out to her truck. She declined my offer to drive and mounted gingerly up into her seat grabbing the steering wheel then pulling herself in one leg at a time. We drove down the familiar road to the smallish town where we found a Thrifty Drug Store on the main thoroughfare. After we pulled into the parking lot and stopped in the handicapped zone, Noel slid out of the driver's seat with the same caution she had gotten in with. The big box store's fluorescent lights made me squint when we walked in and then I was hit with the smell of freshly waxed floors and the overwhelming odor of new plastic.

Fortunately for me they had a big stack of rubber beach shoes in a box by the door and another stack of T-shirts for $5. There was still plenty of snow on the ground when I left Montana and all I had were heavy shoes and a warm shirt. Thrifty fit into my limited budget, with less than $10 for a new outfit.

This family really had no idea how broke I was or that I was still living on painted plywood floors in my Montana cabin. I didn't want them to know about my financial situation, which to me was so personally embarrassing. I had just put myself through college at the age of fifty and was earning a low salary at a little school nearby as the family's sole wage earner. I didn't figure my circumstances were any of their business.

I did ask Marilyn what I should do about my house payment. I had borrowed money from my mother so the house wouldn't be foreclosed. Just that statement makes me want to gag. It was the single most humiliating experience that had yet happened in my life. A house potentially foreclosed, not because I couldn't make a payment, but because of a scam I had stupidly fallen into.

My mother, realizing this and as a confidante and friend, respectfully didn't share the information of the loan with everyone, only Marilyn knew of it. I made every payment on time and continued to pay her a higher interest rate than the banks. I knew she lived on Social Security and once I was on my feet, it was my way of helping her out each month. Little did I know she had quite the savings and I honestly thought she was more broke than frugal; I wasn't privy to her income.

As I walked toward the checkout at Thrifty I picked up a disposable camera and a pack of Marlboros. To pay for everything I pulled out my trusty Master Card. I couldn't ask Noel for money, she too was on a limited budget and a fixed income. Noel was on SSI because of her injured back, deteriorating bone and the chronic compound fractures that attacked her at will. When we finished shopping, she drove me back up to the house with the intention of just dropping me off, but she had to use the bathroom before she made the trip home. The front door was unlocked and we headed down the hall together so I could change clothes while she instructed me what to photograph in the house. We stopped and looked into the room where Marilyn was staying and peeped in.

Chapter 26

THE VANITY SET

The house was quiet as we stood in the doorway to the "Ballerina Room." We weren't sure Brad and Marilyn heard us return but we could hear their muffled voices from the den. Neither Noel nor I talked as we looked around the room, thinking it would be the last time. We were, in our own hearts and minds, reminiscing about the house, its loving construction and mentally photographing what we saw.

This room was named the Ballerina Room by the grandchildren because of the cheap faded Degas ballerina print Mom had probably bought when they were little. Countless children had been rocked in this room in a chair which predated me. There were three generations of toys stored here, from battered favorites to some new additions. The basket of checkers represented hours spent playing with Dad whiling away whole evenings. I could almost hear our children's laughter as they ran up and down the halls and outside in the yards.

As we turned, the sunlight slanted through the window landing on the built-in desk and illuminating the vanity set arranged on the top. "Do you want that?" Noel asked me.

My heart went cold and my stomach tightened in a knot as I saw the set gleaming in the light. My mind propelled back decades to my childhood in Los Angeles. Noel knew why when I said, "No! I don't ever want that!"

It was Christmas 1953 when I got the vanity set. I had gazed for months at different little sets of mirrors with matching brushes and combs, imagining owning one. Sometimes they were in jeweler's windows or at Sears. Dad and I were always going to Sears together to look for saddles for our imaginary horses and then I'd go look at the vanity sets. Perhaps it signified my transition from girlhood to womanhood, a "coming of age" symbol for me. I wanted nothing more than my own fancy brush and comb set. My mother had one made from tortoise shell that she brought from Scotland and so did Great Aunt Lillie. I loved watching my aunt brush her long white hair at night after she untied her braid. She told me if I brushed my hair 100 strokes every night it would shine.

That Christmas I felt like Cinderella going to the ball when I opened the May Company box and the gift within. There packed in tissue paper with little gold stars lay my coveted treasure and I was thrilled beyond description. It couldn't have been more perfect. The gold plate shimmered around the beveled mirror and it seemed to sparkle in front of my eyes. Etched flowers with tendrils scrolled down the handle of the mirror matching those cascading along the handle of the comb and brush. I ran my fingers lightly over the etchings artistically engraved on the back. It was breathtakingly beautiful for a nine-year-old girl. I felt like every wish had been granted. It was so precious and such a treasure I was fearful to display it on the dresser, so I tucked it in the right hand corner of my bottom drawer. It would be safe there in the dark between my socks. Sometimes our heart's desires are too great to look at, yet several times during Christmas break I would go into my room, squat on the floor and open the drawer just to look.

I found another box identical to the one holding my vanity set. Both boxes were the same size with a gold criss-cross print of a fleur-de-lis on the top. I put my paper doll collection in the other box and set it on top of the vanity set in the drawer. I liked to put things in order and size, and unlike our frequently messy house, I was beginning to organize things with color and shape.

One afternoon my girlfriend down the block called to see if I wanted to play with our paper dolls. Of course I did! There also was the sheer satisfaction of being invited to play. The young girls in the neighborhood had evolved from pudgy Betsy McCall paper dolls to making our own pre-Barbie dolls, complete with designer clothes. Our paper figures were slimmed down and older. We spent most of the time coloring and cutting out new clothes from wallpaper scraps. "I'll be down in five minutes," I replied and then dashed to my room, grabbed my box and ran down the block to play.

The city sidewalks of Los Angeles were not flat at the time. They had originally been laid in concrete sections and scored to accommodate the expansion and contraction of the seismically active area. However, the work of the multiple earthquakes and root growth from trees had rendered the walks uneven, cracked and jagged. One particularly lethal section near my friend's house had a section of sidewalk which lifted at a jagged angle several inches high. It was a real tripper and we all had problems traversing it, especially on our roller skates.

So there I was, running down the street, thrilled for an excuse to leave home and feeling buoyant. I will never forget it. The fall happened so quickly that the impact of my body sprawling across the pavement was numbing, the wind was knocked out of me from the sheer force and my right knee was badly torn open. In no time there was blood running freely, covering my leg. My right elbow and forearm were equally as torn up. The physical injuries didn't faze me immediately as I was shocked and stunned while still laying on the sidewalk. Much to my horror, I saw broken glass and the metal of my beloved vanity scattered in front of my face and bleeding arms. Suddenly I couldn't breathe.

Crushed! I can say truly crushed! That was my heart at the moment. In less than a second my childish dream of treasure was shattered and the shards were in disarray all over the sidewalk. I couldn't speak. Slowly I gathered myself up feeling the weight of loss that only a child could feel. I gathered up the remnants of the broken mirror, cutting my hand further in the process, and placed it all back into the box then closed the lid.

The sobbing came from the depths of my little body. Feeling wretched and full of anguish I walked painfully and slowly back home, blood trickling down my arms and legs.

Mom must have heard me coming or perhaps a caring neighbor had called to give her a heads up on the accident. She was standing at the door looking like an angel in her blue flowered cotton dress and her hair neatly done. Her face, however, was set in stone as she was waiting for me. I struggled up the porch toward her, expecting some comfort, hoping for a hug and some consoling. She was unmoving, standing at stair level up. As I reached out for her, my mother pulled back her right shoulder to gain momentum, stepped forward and slapped my face so hard that the blow forcefully knocked me down again. Now I heard only my own sobbing through my ringing ears, the cement hard and cold underneath me.

If she was yelling I didn't hear her. As I went down I held tightly to the damaged treasure box and didn't release my grip, a literal tuck and roll. Finally, I started hearing her tirade. Frequently, even at that time, I would shut down and hear only the yelling but not the words, a defense mechanism I have to this day. Once the volume and barrage of accusations start flying, I have trained myself to tune the words out with ease.

As I lay there Noel came to the door, undoubtedly to see what all the fuss was about. Pushing past our out-of-control mother, Noel grabbed me, helped me up by my free arm and took me into our living room. She whispered in my ear to sit tight in the big stuffed chair, which I did in fear, still clutching the box with the broken vanity set.

Noel whipped around facing my mother who was close behind with her hands on her hips. She was a ferocious twelve year old and was not going to be bullied from an early age.

"Pick on someone your own size," she shouted at my mother, coming to my defense. "She didn't mean to!"

In response to that act of defiance, Mother pulled back again and slammed her fist into Noel's face. I don't know how she restrained herself but Noel remained stoic. She had planted both feet firmly on the carpet, bracing for the impact. Staring at our mother she quoted the Bible. We were, after all, Sunday school kids.

"And unto him that strikes you on one cheek, offer also the other."

There was a moment of silence. Noel shifted her feet apart, set her jaw and steadied herself. I was certain the whole ugly scene was going to end then and there. Our mother's eyes narrowed, her teeth clenched, she reared back and then swung forward again hitting my sister with full force on the other side of her face.

I sucked in my breath gasping for air as Noel tried to regain her senses. It was then my mother sprang forward like an animal on its prey, grabbed Noel's hair and threw her onto the rug. Then she jumped onto my sister's small body and pounded her about the upper arms and chest. It was brutal and frightening and I thought she was going to kill my sister, but I couldn't move from my chair, paralyzed by fear. I know I was crying and cry now for all of us.

Then a piercing banshee scream come from my feet and right up through my throat. I'm sure all the neighbors heard me, and even I was shocked. "Don't kill my sister! Stop it! Stop it now!"

How that particular fight ended, I don't remember. Probably Mom grabbed her car keys and disappeared for hours as she did so frequently. Later she would return calmer, though we'd be alone for hours, frightened and not knowing where she was.

Noel took me into the main bathroom where the first aid bandages were, washed my bloody leg and knee and then gently took care of my arm. She bandaged me as best she could and we went to our room, me with bandages all over, swollen red eyes and Noel with bright red handprints on each side of her face. We crawled into our matching beds and Noel started telling me one of her great fantasy stories. *"In a land far away..."*

The vanity set wasn't as damaged as I thought. Eventually my mother had it repaired and returned it to me. With the exception of a small, barely discernible dent on the gold rim, it appeared almost new, however, in my heart it was forever tarnished. Again I put it in my bottom drawer but never looked at it without recalling that frightening and painful day. The vanity set now represented ugliness and shameful behavior in my mind. When I left home in 1962, I left it in the box in which it came, untouched in the same dresser.

After my parents built their new home, my mother placed my vanity set in the Ballerina Room. Each time I visited her I was reminded of that day. Was that a symbol of control for her or did she not think about it at all?

"No." I closed my eyes then looked at Noel. "No, there is too much heartbreak there. I don't want it. I will *never* forget that day." Nor in my thoughts would I forget any of the other days and nights of horror and long buried events we never spoke of. I left those monsters buried way down deep hoping they would decay away. I never even told my collection of counselors and psychiatrist all the stories. They may have suspected, but it wasn't discussed. I sought help to lance the current problems but never probed the causes.

Chapter 27

NOEL

I don't know a soul who's not been battered. I don't have a friend who feels at ease.

– Paul Simon, "American Tune"

Who was this spunky woman-child who often went to bat for me, who took the blows my mother dealt? Noel was the middle child and, of course, there is a huge collection of so-called studies about middle children. What went deeper and was more complex for Noel was that almost from the moment of her birth, and possibly even before that, my mother hated her and would admit it. Worse still, she would state publicly to anyone who would listen "how difficult" Noel was from the moment of her arrival on Christmas Day. Noel grew up being told almost daily that she was mean, stupid, awkward and a bad little girl.

There is no defense for this treatment but perhaps some understanding. Mom frequently told us how challenging it was for her to become pregnant and how we all were miracle babies. Amazing that she didn't think those little miracles should be treated with kindness and respect. At twenty years old our mother had a surgery for ovarian cysts that left her with one-fourth of one ovary. She was told she would be lucky to ever conceive and undoubtedly this must have been devastating news for the young, lonely woman. She had few girlfriends in her new country and was no longer working now that she was a housewife. She told me how she practically attacked my father when he came home, trying to conceive. Finally, after more than five years of marriage and presumably no birth control, she did become pregnant. It was a flawless pregnancy and easy birth in the fall of 1939 when Princess Marilyn was born. The miracle child was doted upon and welcomed by a family who had waited a long time for her arrival. It was undoubtedly a grand event and I'm sure the happy couple spent many hours just gazing at the life the two of them created.

Two years and three months later Noel arrived on Christmas Day. She came so fast that she actually was born in the car on the way to the hospital, Dad assisting and Marilyn looking on. Did Mom resent the baby for having the audacity of interrupting the Christmas festivities? Sadly, from her birth, my mother had nothing nice to say about her.

Noel was born two weeks after the Japanese attack on Pearl Harbor. Was my mother fearful of the war and projecting that on poor Noel? The young parents had also just moved into their newly built, custom home in Los Angeles.

One of Mom's frequent complaints and stories, even into Noel's teen years was that "she bit me when she was nursing." I often wondered about that especially after having children of my own. For goodness sake, most babies don't get teeth until they are six months old and even then it is only the bottom ones. How could an infant bite the nipples of their mother?

Perhaps Isobel was suffering postpartum blues with two babies and being home alone most of the time. Dad was working multiple jobs, one to support his family and another to serve his country. He was working the shipyards of San Pedro and another shift at LAPD as a policeman. They were over their heads financially with the new house and furniture they had bought on time. Then of course there was the fears of California being attacked. WW II had burst open, shaking the confident ground of the US and propelling us onto two fronts. Perhaps my mother was frightened knowing how WW I had torn her Scottish family apart and WW II was on the doorstep again of her grandfather and cousins in Scotland.

Noel became the scapegoat of all the family problems. She was the perennial victim of my mother's raging anger, her frustration and hate. She was whipped for everything under the sun and undoubtedly never deserved any of it, if there is such a thing as *deserving* a whipping. It was Noel's indomitable spirit and her own ability to lash back that saved her from breaking under the weight of mistreatment and never becoming an abuser herself. Each time Noel was beaten the scar tissue on both her skin and spirit healed stronger, enough to withstand the next storm and the one following that. Besides the physical brutality there were the degradations of another kind: Noel was told repeatedly that she was stupid.

When we grew up, Noel would tease me and say that if I had been the first lady president our mother would have just said, "wrong political party." We would laugh but it was the dark side of humor. Neither of us ever came up to Mom's ever-moving measurement of success. A large-boned and fast growing child, Noel was sent to kindergarten at the age of 3 years and nine months. Yes, I checked the records and that is true. I believe my mother lied about her age just to get her out of the house. I would have been about six months old at the time and to hear Mom tell it, I was a lovely baby, always happy and a joy to be around. I think I was just a quiet baby not demanding much.

Thus, Noel was packed off to public school. Because she was so young, developmentally she wasn't ready to learn to read and write and quickly fell behind the other children. There were no preschools or educational television programs then, so she had no background or foundation exposure. When the school suggested she stay back a year, where she would have been with kids her own age, Mother wouldn't allow it. Later, when I talked to Mom about her reason for sending Noel to school so young, she said it was "safer" for her to be at school because of the war. I believe it was "safer" for her at school because those were the hours she was away from my mother's physical and mental abuse.

Noel's feisty spirit was a good thing. She would tell my mother "no" and defy her unreasonable requests. When she did fight back she often would bite and that was when she was dragged into our kitchen and hot peppers were forced into her mouth. Bless my sister, because with a searing mouth, tears running down her face, her nose and throat burning, she would glare at Mom, stick out her tongue and ask for more. Mom would even repeat that story to people but from a different angle; she thought it was funny.

Noel was strong, but that too evolved into a hardness and a bitterness she has never been able to shake. Any misdeed from childhood to adulthood brought confirmation of her "difficult nature." It gave my mother more ammunition to tell neighbors, educators and family of Noel's "bad attitude" and aggression. Marilyn and I, under the conspiracy of silence, told no one including our father of the beatings. Through fear and retribution for our own safety, we kept silent. That is the code, an unbreakable code of silence shared by so many battered children.

It was a vicious circle which gained momentum and grew like a malignancy. People began to expect Noel to act out in some way and she would accommodate them. This pattern went on for some sixty years and each angry and hostile event was added to the litany of prior crimes against her that could be reviewed and thrown in her lap at any time. Even Noel's kindnesses were dismissed. Her gifts were openly criticized as cheap and useless, making her feel the same way. When it wasn't physical abuse, which stopped when she was around seventeen years old, it was verbal abuse, yet her spirit didn't break.

Even in our adult years, when there were family gatherings with our parents, she would end up away from everyone, isolated on the porch smoking and drinking sodas or in the kitchen doing dishes. Sometimes she would be so upset at her treatment that she would leave the table and it would be openly stated that she was being rude once again. It is amazing how everyone believed that, including her children, without every wondering why. They accepted everything my mother told them because Queen Isobel was always right! I too was guilty at times of falling into the quagmire and not seeing the pattern clearly.

How Noel stayed reasonably sane is beyond me. If you take a puppy, kick it every day, and never pet it you are going to have a mean dog. The same is true of human beings. My sister's strong spirit and pure will kept her out of prison and somewhere she found ports in her personal storm. She still has a deep religious faith and an innate intelligence of human nature. Her introspection into people's behavior has actually made her more forgiving than most of us. Not forgetting, mind you, but she attempts to forgive. She cannot, however, forgive our mother and I can understand that.

Noel grew to be the prettiest among the three of us. The "ugly duckling" grew tall, with beautiful eyes, perfect features and she walked with dignity and poise. She modeled herself after the actresses Grace Kelly and Kim Novak, even sweeping her hair into a sophisticated French roll. We painted our bedroom lavender because it was Kim Novak's favorite color.

Men just fell all over Noel and still do. I figure she must emit some pretty strong pheromones. Even as an elderly woman the men still flock to her as if she lights up the room. In later years Mom would actually giggle and tell me, "Well, there we were at the library and as usual your sister was surrounded by admirers." Was she jealous of her? I've heard that of some mothers.

Tragically, Noel as a teenager was brainwashed that she wasn't very intelligent. Her grades were good but Marilyn and I were in advanced classes and Noel in the regular mainstream. She was discouraged from going to college. Her intellectual self-image was again shattered when an ill-placed entry counsellor at the local community college told her "some girls should just get married."

That was 1958! Things have changed and the "babies" have come a long way. Seeing no further education or career choice, Noel married the following year when she was barely eighteen years old.

Chapter 28

WHAM!

What provokes an abuser to do what they do? With my mother, once she began she lost all control and couldn't stop even if she wanted. Looking back, perhaps she was well aware of her own curse and that is why she chose, in many ways, to self-exile herself. After Mother's death, Marilyn, for all intents and purposes, did the same.

Mom's friends were always kept at arm's length and she literally had a fence between them and herself. Her whole life she would talk to the neighbor gals over the fence and those who came to the house were the wives of Dad's friends. There never was a group of women laughing in the living room nor did she meet friends for lunch or shopping. She was active in the PTA and a Girl Scout leader, but those women also did not come to the house and no one suspected what went on behind our doors, with the exception of a few close neighbors who couldn't help but hear the fighting.

A particularly vicious beating involved one of her favorite weapons, the wooden coat hanger. I have no recollection of what my crime had been, but I was convinced that my mother was going to kill me and had we been alone she may well have succeeded. For the most part, young children believe they have deserved their punishments because somehow they've been "bad." We were no exception, yet we worked as a team protecting one another to the best of our childlike abilities.

As I said, this particular beating involved a wooden coat hanger. Actually, it involved more than one. Mom grabbed me in my bedroom, coat hanger in hand, bent me over her knees and while sitting on my bed started beating me with all her might again and again across my butt. When the first hanger cracked and broke in two, she pulled me screaming across the room, into my closet where she grabbed a second. She then proceeded to drag me like a ragdoll and again threw me across her knees. The second coat hanger cracked, split and broke as she furiously hit me. For a third time she dragged me back to the closet, grabbed another wooden coat hanger and continued her tirade. I was exhausted, screaming in pain and screaming for help.

I don't know where Noel and Marilyn were that day, maybe outside riding their bikes, but they weren't in the house when my mother began this attack. What I distinctly remember is them both running into the room yelling at my mother to stop. They literally grabbed me by my arms and legs and pulled me away from her and out of the room.

What brave little girls they were, working as a duo to save me. They knew far too well that they also could be her victims at any moment. When they got me to the big bathroom they slammed the door and locked it. This was a ploy we used frequently; the same "torture chamber" bathroom could also double as a safe haven.

This particular day the three of us stayed in there for what seemed like hours. Noel and Marilyn got cold washcloths to put across my bottom trying to stop the searing pain. The welts and blisters were growing so rapidly that it would be impossible to comfortably sit down. I wrapped up in towels and lay down on the step up to the tub while my sisters sat on the floor beside me whispering words of comfort.

When the house got quiet we listened at the door, turned the lock quietly hoping it wouldn't click and made double sure she was gone. Relieved, knowing she had driven off, we could then creep out. It was toward evening and the three of us were feeling the pangs of hunger. We went to the kitchen together, got out the dried peanut butter from the pantry and made sandwiches that we each choked down before going to our beds.

It is more than a little understandable that all of us developed major trust issues. If you can't trust the first person you meet in this life, then how can you trust others? The first adult the three of us met on this planet placed us all in a state of perpetual fear. The hand that was rocking our cradle was thinking of turning it upside down with us in it. It was a long journey for all of us to turn our horrific childhoods around. Personally, I have worked years on the project and still consider it a work in progress. I thank God for the counterbalance of a great father and other positive female role models that I came across.

But now, here after our mother's death, the three of us had come together at another crossroads. Isobel had died and things were collapsing back into chaos and disorder. The trust built over many years with Marilyn was breaking apart for reasons far beyond my comprehension.

Chapter 29

AFTERNOON POLLUTIONS

I stood at the front door where my mother had so many times before. Noel was in her car looking at me sadly as I reached my hand up to my mouth and blew her a kiss goodbye, just like Mom always did when we left. As Noel drove off I had a sense of loss again, standing alone there on my parent's front porch.

A few minutes after waving Noel off I returned to the house with my heart in my shoes; I was really down. Marilyn met me in the hall and announced that Julie's ex-husband had just called and made some strange comments about the house and its contents. Later we would discover there never was such a call. That story, like so many others, was concocted. Marilyn appeared distressed as she related this information and said we should do something to secure the house. She said she was going to town to buy some window locks. Under the circumstances and yet not seeing the bigger picture, that didn't sound unreasonable to Brad and me even though Grandma's windows were all secured with custom-made dowels snuggly set in each one.

As Brad and I headed to the kitchen, Marilyn went into Mother's back bedroom and emerged with a huge roll of bills about the size of a toilet paper roll two-thirds used. She was thumbing through them and my eyes must have popped out of my head; they were all $100 bills with Ben Franklin's coy smile. I knew Mom had cash in the house but it was more than a surprise to see this much. Marilyn confessed later that she actually had $4,220 in that roll. I would guess possibly more, but it wasn't me who counted it.

Mom generally kept me abreast of where she was moving her stash as she rotated it to various hiding places, but I never suspected it was more than a couple hundred dollars. A few years earlier she had some of the money taken from the piano and once from her purse. Fortunately, when that happened both Noel and I, along with all our kids, weren't in southern California, leaving only two or three suspects.

I just looked at Marilyn, the wad of money in her hand and grinned saying, "Gee, I knew we had an inflation problem, but those window locks sure must be expensive." Obviously, she didn't trust Brad and I with money in the house, nor the garage, because just as I said that, she reached for the garage door opener sitting on the shelf and stuffed it in her purse giving me the "I gotcha!" look.

The devil got a hold of me, as happens now and then, and I just couldn't help myself. My black humor had been unleashed. I was sticking it to her at that point. "Golly, when you are searching for money don't forget to look under Mom's bedroom carpet. I know she used to hide some there too." Now part of this statement was true because Mom did hide money there, but I also knew she had moved it again; she was getting nervous with the pilfering of her cash. Secretly, as I said these remarks, I hoped Marilyn would hurt her damn back when she greedily pulled back the rug to look for more.

The tension in the air thickened and could be cut with a knife. It was actually a relief to see this high-strung woman get in her car and leave. Brad and I both could relax and breathe the minute she pulled out of the driveway. At last we were alone in the house. We could take off our heavy armor and let down our guard.

Brad made more coffee for us, mumbling that he'd like some beans to grind then the two of us went into the den for a while and listened to the steady drip of the coffee maker. Brad looked over Mom's wall-to-wall collection of books and commented on the "self-help" books and volumes covering longevity. "Why," he wondered, "did she make such poor medical decisions?" I explained my view, which was you could own and memorize book after book on how to swim, you could quote famous swimmers and Olympic winners, but you can't swim unless you get in the water.

So there we were, Brad and I alone in Grandma's house, to fend for ourselves. He wanted to be helpful and we started cleaning all the neglected light fixtures on the outside of the house. Some of the fixtures weren't functioning as they should and Brad wanted to take them apart. We needed tools and it was clear we were not getting into the shop or garage when I remembered that Mom had an inside tool drawer in her kitchen. After rummaging around the collection of twine, mousetraps and picture hangers, I found some screwdrivers that fit the screws on the light fixtures. It was a nice diversion to be outside working on something. Brad talked a lot about the girl he had met and said he might ask her to marry him. I thought it would be a prayer answered for him as I knew he was lonely and wanted to start a family of his own.

As the afternoon wore on into evening, both of us became keenly aware of how long Marilyn had been away. We began to wonder where she was since it had been way over five hours. The town was less than fifteen minutes away and both of us were sure she would be back in a little over an hour. What in the world was she doing? We had decided it was time to go in and try to make supper when she pulled into the driveway.

It didn't appear when she got out of the car that Marilyn's mood had softened. Her face and jaw were still set, along with the thousand-mile stare. She marched in the door and her body language clearly said, "Back off!" Without a greeting of any kind, nor noticing that all the outside lights were on, she dropped a bag of window locks on the tapestry chair and went directly to the phone in the family room. I trotted after her like a well-trained puppy expecting some exchange of information. Without comment she grabbed the heavy Yellow Pages from under the book case and thumbed through it for a locksmith. She made an appointment for Monday while I was signaling to her that Brad could do it. Why should we spend money when there were people right here with all the abilities? I had even installed doors and locks myself.

The truth of the matter then hit me and I asked myself, how could I be so dumb? Not only was Marilyn locking all the windows, she was changing all the locks because so many of us had keys to the front door, myself included. It wasn't the threat of an unknown intruder, we were the ones being locked out! Marilyn would have sole access to all the money, the house and its contents and literally the keys to the kingdom. Rock this boat and you will land overboard without a life preserver. The guillotine clause Mom had put in her trust gave Marilyn a power that said, anyone opposing her is out of the trust.

Marilyn hung up the phone without acknowledging that Brad could do the installations. She then went into her room explaining that she had to call her doctor and physical therapist to change appointments. She used the plug-in phones for conversations she wanted us to hear and her cell phone in her room for those she did not. It was Sunday afternoon. You can change appointments on Sunday?

Marilyn's appearances and long disappearances were more than mysterious. She was on the phone day and night. Was someone else instructing her?

"Marilyn, why don't you let me take you out to dinner? We all could use a nice break from here." She didn't respond. Without commenting, she actually got up, walked into the kitchen, and made herself a sandwich. Then she came back in, sat in front of us, bit into it and chewed while she looked at us. Who was this woman? This wasn't the Marilyn I knew. Someone else had crawled into her body.

I excused myself, went into the kitchen and likewise made sandwiches for Brad and me. Forcing my voice to sound pleasant, I asked her if she would like me to make her a cup of tea. But Marilyn exited to the back room without a word, leaving her dirty dish on the table. Once again we could hear her talking away on her cell phone. Brad and I, at a total loss of words, ate in silence.

There seemingly was no end to Marilyn's anger and hostility toward us. The happy family illusion was imploding in front of our eyes. Brad was more than baffled and almost despondent as to how he had been treated. He had no knowledge of the back stories and even if he did, all this bizarre behavior he had witnessed in the last day was difficult to comprehend. "Son," I said as gently as possible, "don't take this personally. You haven't done anything. It isn't your fault."

This was the same message I would give the battered children I worked with as a teacher. The same message I gave Noel, "It isn't your fault. You did nothing to deserve this." Battered people somehow just don't get — sometimes for a very long time — that it isn't their fault. They don't feel that way — they feel that they could have done something different or said something different that would have changed things.

Brad's deep brown eyes just registered confusion and pain. He too suffered from the illusion of a close family and didn't know that molten lava was boiling beneath the surface, or that decades old turbulence was still churning. This wasn't the time to share the sordid family history.

I did feel the need to explain a little more about Marilyn. "Honey, your auntie has a long history of emotional problems. We just never told you about it. It wasn't a dinnertime topic and I always hoped she would get better. We can't climb into her mind and see what is going on, but this has been too much for her. Right now we are just going to try and get out of here alive. I can't see her motives. I can tell you, though, she has been going to counseling of one kind or another most of her life."

My son stared at me for a brief second. "Do you want to translate all that? What the hell does that mean?"

I was tired and worse yet I didn't want Marilyn to hear me talking about her. "Look, Son, I'll explain later. For now let's just try to relax and remember nothing going on here is your fault. You have done nothing but nice deeds. It isn't your fault your aunt

Marilyn just isn't quite right. Actually, Brad, your grandmother knew this too, but then she also had her issues. The family covered for both of them."

Marilyn came out from the back at that moment, coming up for air from her endless phone conversations. We heard the door open and click closed so that was the immediate termination of our conversation. Walking past me as if I wasn't there, Marilyn walked over to my son sitting in the opposite chair. "Brad, I'd like you to write something for your grandmother's memorial."

He said he would and appeared relieved to be asked to do something. Of course he would, he was such a compassionate person and was honored she would ask him. It was interesting that she didn't address me at all. I had been the family writer for years and was published, yet I wasn't asked, nor was it even acknowledged that I might be sharing the same oxygen in the room.

It was then, on the heels of the request to participate in his grandmother's memorial, and without pause, that Marilyn made the announcement to Brad she couldn't possibly take him to the airport the next day. He would have to make some other type of transportation arrangements. Brad, who was living on a raveled shoestring similar to my own, was taken aback. No offer of explanation was forthcoming. Apparently, she couldn't create a plausible justification from her arsenal of excuses, just the terse, clipped statement stated with unblinking eyes. It was another illustration of how in control Marilyn was of all our destinies and definitely our destinations. We had no money, no car and we were at her total mercy.

We were high and dry in Yucaipa and would have to get home the best way we could. Brad's reservation home to Seattle was for Monday afternoon so we did have a little time to find rides. Maybe there was a shuttle service or taxi in this small town. We definitely would have to get on this first thing in the morning. It was Sunday night now and everything was closed.

As Marilyn finished with Brad she turned to me and spoke for the first time. She spit her words out with ice in her veins. "And you can go with him!" As she delivered that verbal blow, essentially kicking me out of a house I now partially owned, the front doorbell rang. It was the neighbors Brian Carper and his wife who sold real estate. They were there to offer their condolences for my mother's passing.

Marilyn immediately jumped into her role of the bereaved daughter, dabbing her sad eyes and telling them in a shaky voice how much she was going to miss her mother. This changing of personalities and mood on a dime was not unfamiliar to me, déjà vu of Mom.

It really was a stellar performance. Was this the same woman who just a few months before had told me she couldn't stand our mother? Was this the woman who had planned on leaving Mom last week to her own devices after a major surgery, that woman?

The neighbors went on to say what a wonderful person my mother was. Mrs. Carper also mentioned, without prompting, that the real estate was worth a lot more than the appraisal they had gotten a few weeks earlier. Brad and I, standing there in silence, heard the whole thing. Her husband also chimed in that the car was also of greater value than appraised.

Both comments left Brad and I stunned. We had trouble believing what we were hearing and yet came to the mutual conclusions we only had suspected before. While my mother was in the hospital, her home, its contents and her car had been appraised at Marilyn's request. If Mom was expected to recover, why then all the appraisals? What else was going to rear its ugly head? What else didn't I know was going on behind closed doors and behind our backs? Clearly a great deal and none of it was good.

As they began to leave the house, Mrs. Carper commented on one of my paintings, a young Amish boy eating an apple. She said how much she had always liked the painting and how it gave her such a nice feeling. I walked over to the painting, took it off the hook and handed it to her on an impulse.

"Thank you for the compliment. I want you to have it as a token of appreciation and thank you for your friendship with my mother." It was Marilyn's turn to look surprised. I walked the couple to the door, flipped on the now working outside lights and let them out. As I did Brian reached in his pocket and pulled out my mother's car keys.

"Here, I almost forgot to give these to you," and handed them to Marilyn.

These are the people who drove Mom to the hospital in her own car. I wonder what they were thinking now that I found that out. Marilyn hadn't called an ambulance or a medical transport. They had actually loaded the sick old woman with a painful new hip replacement into her own car and drove her to the emergency hospital. No wonder the suspected elder abuse box was checked on her admittance form. There was more than one reason for that, but I wouldn't know those facts for almost a year when I finally got the paper work. I could feel my stomach tighten and begin to churn with the latest revelations.

The Carpers had no sooner left and were out of earshot when Marilyn turned to me snarling, "You had no right to do that."

"I had every right. It was my painting. I gave it to my mother and now I'm giving it to her friend." I really wanted to add, fuck you on the end. I really wanted to, but that wasn't an expression that came easily to me and I'd already slipped more than once. So I just thought it and glared back at her. My niceties and rationalities for her horrible behavior were ebbing like a tide along with compassion and excuses.

We could see Marilyn was working herself up for another volley of abusive words, but instead she turned on her heels, went to her room and grabbed another blank legal tablet. Good grief, they must have been on sale for a pack of ten. I went back to the den, slumped comfortably into a chair and threw my leg over the side. There had to be a comfortable place, a peaceful place somewhere in this house. I barely sunk into the seat when the mighty Marilyn followed tossing the tablet at me. It landed fortunately in my lap and not my face. The sought after peace was nowhere to be found at the moment.

"Write down what you want," she demanded tossing a pen on top.

I put the tablet on the arm of the chair. "Well, Marilyn, I told you earlier, I don't want much. I'd like to have Grandmother's round table. OK, I'll write that down. And, I'd like the little coffee table Dad's girlfriend gave him."

"That is a trashy comment Kat, totally inappropriate now." Again I heard her swords rattling.

"I meant no disrespect to Mom, Marilyn," I sighed, "but you and I both know that Dad's girlfriend gave him the table eons ago." Mom knew it too and she kept it. I swallowed and continued, "For Christ's sake, he went with the lady for over fifteen years. It wasn't a fly-by-night, sordid affair, and I want the table."

"What else do you want?" came her shrill demand. Marilyn was prodding me back into an unpleasant reality. It was hard for me to think. I had lived as a minimalist for so long and this house was huge with valuable collections of this and that all over it.

"I guess I'd like Dad's Indian baskets and the cloisonné elephant." Later, when I remembered, I wrote her and asked for the cloisonné cat as I knew Mom had written in her trust that the cat was for me. I was just muddled at the moment and unprepared for making a list of material things I wanted. I was still in shock that Mom was dead and I could not understand all the non-stop, vehement hostility being spewed like projectile vomit toward me. With Marilyn's announcement that I was to leave, I knew I would never set foot in this house again.

The cat, yes I loved the little cat statue. As a little girl I had not been allowed to touch the figurine as it sat, curled up on the tier table of our Los Angeles home. It was Asian, made of black bisque with its little ears and tip of tail white enamel. It was decorated cloisonné, orange anemone wild flowers down its sides, and on the bottom was written with an old marker, 35 cents. It was my mother's treasure, too, and I'm sure Mom told me it was an early gift from my father. Noel disagreed and said it was given to her by a girlfriend from night school. I liked my idea better, that Dad gave it to Mom, but it didn't matter. It was perfect with not a chip on it, something I truly wanted.

"That is all?" my mother had said when she asked me at the time, and it was put in the trust.

Marilyn waited about six weeks after Mom died to give the cat figurines to Julie's daughter.

"Well, what else?" Marilyn was insistent.

"Look, two of the silver trays in the dining room are mine. I got them when I married the boys' father. I gave them to Mom years ago. It would be nice to give them to the boys now."

I looked up on the mantle. There sat Dad's little black devil inkwell. The pointed forelock was really a handle that lifted up to reveal the inkwell inside. For years Dad had old ink pens that sat in its pointed ears. It was a fascinating and entertaining piece both of us loved and enjoyed, so I just got up, as she watched, took it down and dropped it in my backpack. Then I wrote it down on her tablet. The last item I requested was Dad's police revolver. I signed my name at the bottom and handed it to her.

There is a weariness that can settle into your very bones and it had settled into mine. Really, this huge house filled with antiques and artifacts was not going to bring my mother back. There are no U-Hauls being pulled behind the hearse. My sister had become so vile that the very air seemed polluted and hung heavily in the room. With the constant chorus of "No. No. No." I didn't think

I'd get anything I asked for anyway. I decided it was way past time to try and lie down. As I got up my eyes fell on the collection of pre-Columbian heads and figurines displayed on one of the shelves, there were about a dozen of them. Dad had collected them on a trip to Mexico in the early 1950s and they were definitely a source of pride. We had taken them to the Southwest Museum in Los Angeles for verification, and, yes, they were Pre-Columbian. Since they were found before the laws changed in the early '70s, they were quite legal to have.

"You know, Marilyn, these little clay figures are pretty special. There are enough here you could give one to each family member. Besides that, they are quite valuable."

"I'm giving them to a museum!"

"Well, my dear, lovely thought," I sighed, "but perhaps you might think of the family."

Fourteen months after this conversation, I received a letter from Marilyn's attorney (he must have been mine also, because she billed me for his services). The letter stated the artifacts were to be placed on permanent loan with the Los Angeles County Museum of Natural History. I contacted the museum regarding the collection to verify their placement. I received an email from their Anthropology Division that they were never received. The value of each figure was between $2,500 and $3,000. If I counted correctly, she had in her possession antiquity artifacts worth between $30,000 and $36,000.

Dragging down the hall towards the bedroom I again passed

the yellow caution tape on the bathroom door. I should have torn down the tape and checked out what was behind the door, but I was no longer thinking clearly. To oppose Marilyn almost felt like opposing my mother and I decided I couldn't endure much more anger.

The guest room was delightfully and soothingly quiet. I slipped open the window and felt the cool breeze, dropped my clothes on the floor and let the refreshing air slide over my skin. Tossing back the sheets I laid down on the huge bed; it was alien for me to sleep by myself. No cats, dogs or steady breathing of another body. I was totally alone and felt a deep dark emptiness within. Finally, blessed sleep did come. My soul could rest and my body would regain strength and composure.

Chapter 30

MONDAY MORNING

Forty-five years of waking up early didn't stop because I was in Yucaipa. Like clockwork my eyes opened and I felt refreshed to start a new day. This of course meant it was 4:30 a.m. by the clocks on Rocky Mountain Time. I got up, dressed and tiptoed down the hall into the kitchen and put on a fresh pot of coffee.

I slipped into the dark, living room. It was tranquil there and Brad was asleep on the sofa in the family room at the other end of the house. I sat in the upholstered chair by Noel's ocean painting. We all painted and Mom proudly hung our paintings in her home. Noel did mostly landscapes, I more illustrative western-art and Marilyn had exquisite copies of the old masters. Mom had Marilyn paint what Mom wanted, probably providing her with a little commission.

Our art work told its own story if one contemplated the paintings. It was *Poor Marilyn* who got formal art lessons and painted regularly as a teenager. She even sold miniatures at a nearby mission. Noel's art training came from high school, and even though I had a few community classes here and there, I was self-taught. Noel and I continued to paint, but Marilyn gave it up and only did the few copies Mom wanted.

I looked at Noel's ocean scene. She really had a way with water and the transparency of a wave. It actually looked wet and was coming playfully to the viewer. She was so proud of this particular painting and had given it, unframed, to our parents as a Christmas present. The bafflement is that Mom found a frame she liked, but it was too large for the painting. Rather than have Dad cut down the frame, an easy project, she had the painting restretched and another artist paint some sand at the bottom. Why would she do that? I really don't know, nor do I know what happened to that piece after the estate was settled.

After about thirty minutes of sitting in the living room, acquiring some solace and inner peace, Marilyn came in and sat again in the overstuffed chair opposite mine. She was totally silent, yet I could feel her stare through the darkness. There was no greeting at all, no good morning, no thank you for the coffee, no "go to hell in a hand-basket," one of Mom's favorite phrases. Just nothing but the loud silence of hatred vibrating around her. I had already decided to calmly tell her exactly how I felt. I hadn't seen her display anything but hostility for two days. I knew that anger was often a normal reaction in the case of death, but being on the receiving end felt all wrong.

I spoke quietly not to wake Brad. "Marilyn, you have really hurt my feelings and the feelings of other people here around you. You aren't the only one grieving. We are all grieving. I came to help you and you have treated me like dog shit. You told me last night to leave with Brad. I have an open ticket, I don't have to leave, I planned to help you. You have insulted me at every turn and I don't get it. You have been hostile and mean and then you turn saccharine sweet while sticking knives in everyone." I paused a minute then continued hoping she was listening. "Noel knows antiques better than any of us and you didn't ask her to help with appraisals. Brad knows cars and you didn't talk to him. You have been collecting this information about Mom's possessions for weeks, maybe months while she languished in the hospital…"

Marilyn's voice came from her mouth but had a different tone than I ever heard her use before. It came right out of a horror movie growling and clawing towards me with an almost demonic edge to it. In all honesty I don't remember the words but I know it started with her usual baiting sentence.

Before she got on a roll I stood up putting my palm in the air as to silence her. "I'm not sparring with you, I am not arguing with you. I'm not playing games anymore, and I'm not afraid anymore." I put my coffee cup on the end table. "I just wanted to let you know how I feel. I'm going to take a shower now and we can talk more when I get out. I need you to open the garage so I can get a shovel and dig up a few of Mom's iris out of the garden. I want to plant them in Montana so I will always have something she loved."

I started walking down the hall when the screeching began rolling behind me.

"You can't have a shovel! I'm not opening the garage! What about your tables?"

"Call Bekins." I retorted from the hall.

"I won't."

As I turned to enter the bathroom I whispered, almost to myself, "Then you can go to hell."

Those words, "I won't," were the last I ever heard my sister speak. When I got out of the shower she was gone.

Chapter 31

ABANDONED

*All the world is a stage and men and
women
Are merely players
They have exits and entrances
And one man in his time plays many parts.*
– William Shakespeare, *As You Like It*

I've always been a creature of routine. When you spend your whole adult life working, your body becomes accustomed to some things and for me it is the morning shower. I have been accused of doing absolutions while in there and that may be true. The shower is my retreat my place of prayer, and my fortification for each new day.

After drying I wrapped my wet hair in a turban, put on reasonably clean clothes and headed for the kitchen and another cup of caffeine. Brad was in the kitchen struggling to awaken after his second night on the uncomfortable sofa. He had a mug in his hand and looked at me groggily. "What's going on? Aunt Marilyn just woke me up and said she had to go. She wished me luck or something and said goodbye. Hey, I was in a deep sleep somewhere on a beach holding my girlfriend. Is there another emergency?"

I glanced at the clock on the stove, 6:30 a.m. in California. "No emergency, Son. It appears I gave her too much truth in too short of a time for her to digest, my mistake."

I went and opened another can of cat food for Waylon, put it in his bowl and filled a smaller one with milk. I patted his head and gently rubbed his ears. I must admit that once more I was bewildered by Marilyn's reaction, but then I shouldn't have been as the preceding days had been one disquieting event after another lined up like boxcars.

Brad and I were left abandoned at Mom's house, about seven miles from the nearest town. Marilyn had taken off for parts unknown. At least she had warned us she wouldn't take us to the airport. Good Lord, Marilyn was behaving more and more like our mother of the past. If there was something unpleasant, by their exclusive definitions of unpleasant, something they didn't want to deal with, they just got in the car, rammed down the accelerator and spun off. Déjà-vu. Hearing a simple truth, which she could not deal with, Marilyn had sped off down the road – just run baby run! If the apple doesn't fall far from the tree, where does that leave me?

Brad and I stood numbly looking at each other. We were stuck with no transportation. He had flight reservations at the airport an hour's drive from where we were. Once again we went to the phone books and started contacting every transportation company we could find. The cheapest service was $50 cash and between us we counted a little less than $20. We didn't know at the time that a taxi would take a credit card and didn't think to ask.

To compound matters, the keys to Grandma's car, along with the garage door opener, had left with Marilyn. The realization hit us both simultaneously that on top of everything else, Marilyn didn't trust us. "Look, Son, we are in a pickle here. We've got to get the hell out of this house and out of this town in a hurry. I'm calling your Aunt Noel, it is the only way." I picked up the phone and dialed Noel's number in Orange County. It rang longer than it should have and I could tell by the way she eventually answered that she was in bad shape. Her voice was shaky and weak at the other end. I explained the situation and she told me Cyndie wasn't home, then she paused a minute, put it all together and told us she would be right up, a drive of a few hours.

After calling Noel, Brad and I went and packed up our backpacks, which didn't take long. I still wanted some of Mom's iris so I rummaged around the kitchen tool drawer again and found something with which to dig. There was no way to tell colors as the iris were just beginning to bud. I also wanted to assure that the plants would live so I cut the side sprouts of about five little plants. Back in the house I found some plastic bags, wrapped the roots in a wet paper towel and put them on the top of my pack being careful not to break the corms.

Brad and I muddled about the house, cleaning up the dishes and making the beds. After a while we heard Noel's little truck drive in. Her face was flushed and her brace had been strapped on hurriedly. Obviously, she had dressed quickly and arrived in record time to rescue the personae non gratae. She started frantically wiping down the counters, tables and door knobs with a damp towel. I could tell she was angry.

"I don't trust her. I don't trust her!" she repeated. "She is going to call the cops and accuse you of stealing something."

Brad's eyes widened and he looked dubiously at his aunt. I couldn't even make eye contact with him for fear of laughing. Was she paranoid too? Was the total loss of reasoning inherent to the family? Finally, after rubbing down everything she could, she looked at both of us satisfactorily. "Let's get the hell out of here."

It was only a few months later that I appreciated fully what Noel did for Brad and I. We were accused of taking things from my parent's home. The defense was our prophetic Noel who simply stated to the lawyer, "Hey, they both had backpacks. Just how much do you think they got in them?" The accusations stopped. If there were any charges, they were not pursued in the slightest as there simply were no grounds.

The events surrounding Mom's death came crashing into my mind like a bad car wreck as we propelled at dizzying speed toward the freeway and the Ontario Airport. I felt sickened with the smells of exhaust, diesel and the oppressive air. When we finally departed the insanity of the freeway and pulled into the parking lot near the front entrance of the airport, I felt relieved.

Brad unfolded himself from the back bench of the little truck and looked as if our planet was occupied by aliens. I looked at him and he was shouting within, without making a sound. His face revealed it all, not only had the earth shattering event of his grandmother's death taken its toll, but the freakish behavior of women he once admired and trusted further compounded his confusion. He was about to break and I could see it. The young man I was leaning on so heavily the last few days was feeling weak in the knees and desperately needed to distance himself. I decided not to go inside with him.

We embraced each other, then we pushed away each saying I love you. He didn't turn around or wave as he left. I stood staring as he shouldered his pack, threw his shoulders back and walked straight for the airport doors.

My sensitive stomach wretched. I looked around the parking lot wondering where I could throw up. I took some long, deep yoga breaths and managed to get hold of myself while hanging onto the door of Noel's little truck breathing in the polluted air of southern California.

"Are you OK?"

"I think so. Give me another minute and then we can go."

We too were running out of conversation. Still taking purposeful breaths I hiked up my left knee into her truck, reached over her and grabbed the steering column to pull the rest of me in.

Chapter 32

SECRETS

As Noel pulled onto the freeway and the green in my face receded, she looked at me sideways. "Do you ever tell anyone about our childhood?"

"Only the good parts."

"Me neither." In a lower voice, she continued, "I did tell Julie when she went to live there for a while to keep a close eye on her little girl and not to leave her alone with Granny."

"I know. Julie never believed anything you told her, so she checked with me. I was always a little pissed off she never believed you. What was with that?" I didn't wait for Noel to answer. "I told her you were giving her valid advice. Didn't she figure out why none of our kids visited the grandparents without us until they were at least seven or eight? I've never told my kids, and both husbands very little."

"It's like a stigma," Noel said quietly.

"Well, hell yes! You certainly aren't writing down on an application that you were a battered child. People think of the battered child syndrome and assume you are carrying on the tradition or are all fucked up because of it. There are no accurate statistics out there for people like us who actually went on to lead some kind of normal lives. Everyone assumes you beat, yell and belittle your own kids. Tell them you went to shrinks and it sends their eyebrows up to the ceiling. You might as well slap a big yellow caution sign across your forehead. Hey! I'm a teacher. How do you think people would perceive me if they knew the home I came out of? What would they think if they knew you and I spent years in counseling to get over the hurdles?"

Noel smiled, "We did get over the hurdles didn't we?"

"Not without some pretty banged up knees. Look at Marilyn, for God's sake. She claims she doesn't even remember most of her childhood. Shoot, she used to call me her "memory" and I'm five years younger. You know that's normal, a lot of kids suffering trauma don't remember it. What is funny is now psychologists are trying to figure out what percentage don't remember. That's a hoot! How can you figure out who doesn't remember when they can't remember? Do I report her to the Convenient Amnesia Anonymous Group?"

"You're too funny," Noel commented while she peered on ahead in the traffic. I was launched into my lecture mode. Well, I had read about the subject and have been in counseling more than once.

I flashed back to 1986 with quite a different kind of conversation with Marilyn. I had been down to visit family and we were waiting for the train to take me back. I loved the train station in downtown LA with its beautiful murals, arches and mosaics. We were laughing and talking about some ancient event when Marilyn took my hand gently and looked in my face. I could see past the color of her eyes and into her pained soul.

"Kat," she said quietly, "I don't remember our childhood. You are my memory."

I didn't know then how to respond. I was amazed by her statement. I knew people could suppress memories and distort them, but it never occurred to me that someone could suppress decades of their life with just flashes and glimmers.

I honestly understood not remembering horrific days and I could accept that, but to also suppress the good times and the fun times was more difficult to wrap my head around. It wasn't an auto accident or head trauma that caused her amnesia, it was self-preservation; it's called traumatic amnesia. Marilyn really didn't remember our childhood. Not the tragedy of lost boys from another country, but the entire childhood that lives within each of us. Marilyn had lost great memories of playing on Dad's boat, Christmas lights going bad and the dog pulling over the tree. She lost playing in the sand at the beach, or the tipi Dad put up in our backyard every summer.

I decided then that this needed to be remedied, so in my own way over the years I told her her own stories. I made a point of never telling her the traumatic truth of bodies slamming against the walls, but rather told her of beach parties and coloring Easter eggs and Halloween pranks. Marilyn would always laugh, call me on the phone and say, "You are my memory." I'd smile, always with a bit of melancholy in my heart, that someone could lose the sweet side of their youth. Lose the hard candy melting in our mouth, our baker grandfather making roses of icing on our tongues and us lining up in front of a mirror, tongues sticking out, looking at the little precarious pink buds then giggling as we ate them.

I told her about my nightmares and how she brought me through them by making all the beautiful little doll dresses, how she made me look forward to morning. I told her often that I loved her and how much she meant to me and I didn't tell her what a snob she was at times.

Marilyn's best friend had died as a young adolescent. It was unexpected and totally traumatic for her. The young girl had a cerebral hemorrhage in her sleep and was gone without a sound. I know it left a terrible hole in Marilyn's life, as the girl lived down the block and they saw each other daily. Was that when Marilyn lost her memory? I don't know. I just know over the years, she would tell me quietly, "You are my memory."

I've been fortunate to have a good memory. My husband and a girlfriend both used to accuse me of "selective memory" and both of them were under the impression I remembered only the "good things." What they failed to realize was I only "talked" about the good things. I chose never to share the bad and sad things. I didn't suppress the memories, I just decided early in my life that I couldn't hold onto the horrors or they would drown me like a rock tied to my leg. I couldn't hold onto sorrow or self-pity and still move on. So, I just placed all the crap in a box in the back of my mind.

Actually, to be more honest, I visualized taking my sorrows, and putting them in a little baby blanket. I would wrap the problems up in the blanket and give them to Jesus. This is true. I imagined I walked up to Jesus and laid them at his feet, then I'd move on as he smiled at me. Now, I wasn't a religious fanatic in any way, that is just how I dealt with things. If they were too ugly for me to handle, I just visualized bundling them up and taking them to God in prayer. That was my reality then and my reality now. I believe I stumbled out of an insane situation as a whole and healed person, a healing, however, that has taken decades.

My mind came back to Noel and her question. "I'm just strung out and looking for a reason to giggle. Quite frankly, I'm feeling rather numb. Oh, by the way, I told Marilyn I wanted her to give the coin collection back to you."

"Did you really?"

"Yeah, and that I wanted Dad's gun. Mom put both up in the recessed hall light fixture." I giggled as I spoke at the thought of my mother and the myriad of little hiding places she had throughout her house. Then she would call me up in Montana like I was the back-up memory for her too, and tell me where she put things.

Good grief, I was Marilyn's memory and mother's confessor.

The tires of Noel's truck made a rhythmic sound on the pavement as we drove for a while in silence. She reminisced about finding the Chinese coin under the Ginkgo tree in our neighbor's yard in LA.

The Ginkgo tree was huge, one of the first imported to California from China. It stood at the side lot between the Matthew and Piligian homes. People actually used to come around just to see it.

The Matthews, planning their estate, had landscaped with rare trees before they built. Whatever befell them, they converted their triple garage into a home and it remained that way on the back of their overgrown lot. Mrs. Matthews was a small woman and quite the recluse. She wasn't well, crippled with arthritis, and always said she was sad she only had one child, long grown up and gone. She told us she heard our mom screaming at us and felt badly, but there was nothing she could do. I'm sure that was true, it was the 1950s, a historical time for lying and deception, both in homes and in our country. To this day I hate the '50s and the poodle skirts, it was all so phony and pink.

"Noel, I wonder why Mom kept your coin collection. Did you ever ask for it back?"

"Oh yeah. I wasn't trustworthy you know," and she got a little sarcastic smile. "Not after the huge fight over the piggy banks." She looked over at me and I felt a little nervous thinking she should be looking at the road.

Oh God, yes. That was an ugly scene and I remember it like

yesterday. Noel and I had two huge, ceramic piggy banks from Mexico. Hers was baby blue with huge Mexican flowers painted in bright colors with little white, curlycue lines swirling about. Mine was slightly smaller and we sat them side by side on our little gray bookcase. Dad always brought us silver dollars from his "hunting" trips (later I wondered what he was hunting because most forests don't have silver dollar trees). Friends also gave us different coins. Then Noel found the real Chinese coin.

We collected bottles from people up and down our block and earned the penny deposits back. We both had quite the little coin collections. Sometimes we would earn money working for the neighbors or selling lemons from our backyard tree. Not much money, but our little banks did jingle with change when we shook them, as we often would. Both of us also, on rare occasions, would stick a table knife into the coin slot, turn the bank upside and see what we could slide out for penny gum or something small. Only the small coins, dimes and nickels, would slide down the knife. We weren't successful at getting the larger coins out. The fat, piggy banks were our coin storage facility. At the time the bottoms were sealed with clay, not with cork or rubber as you see today. Basically, you had to break the pig to get your coins if you didn't know our "trick."

Noel, around fifteen years old at the time, figured she must have had about twenty silver dollars. She actually went to our mother and requested permission to break the seal and get to her loot. It was quite an event when Mom came into our room, took a small hammer and opened the bottom plug. The contents spilled out on Noel's bed, but immediately everyone could see there were only a few silver dollars there. Noel's face turned pale from bewilderment. Both of us stared at the small pile of coins and a few folded paper dollars. Where were all the coins?

My mother's reaction was to stand up, double up her fists and fly into an instant, uncontrollable tirade. She went from zero to 60 mph in about as long as it takes to read this. Yelling at the top of her lungs, she reached toward Noel, her face contorted and red, screaming that Noel was a thief and a liar. She started pummeling Noel's head and chest with her fists screaming, "Liar! Liar! Liar!"

Noel put up her arms in defense trying to fend off the fast furling blows. She didn't fight back but placed her arms over her head and face protecting herself while protesting, "I didn't steal it! I didn't steal it!" Mother paid no attention to her pleas, but continued bashing her again and again.

My response was to start yelling too, but I was yelling at Mom to stop beating on my sister's head. Even if Noel had taken the money, and she hadn't, it was hers to take anyway. As usual, none of this made sense in my young mind then, nor does it today. Not only were Noel and I numb from the loss of the money, we were at a loss that our mother didn't believe we were innocent. Noel's credibility was stripped away again and again with each assaultive blow. I may have been screaming, but as usual, I was also paralyzed by fear as I my sister was beaten.

Mom finally exhausted herself and left. Relieved to have it all over, Noel and I sat in our room, arms around each other. The money was gone, tragically, but thankfully so was our mother. We both knew neither of us had taken the coins. The list of suspects was very short.

It was decades later that our mother showed Noel her coin collection. There, amongst it all was the missing silver of long ago, even the Chinese coin. How she got it and why she kept it is only a guess.

We reached Noel's and Cyndie's house. I reached over to Noel again as she parked in her daughter's driveway. "We did good, Sis. We broke the chain. We treated our kids really nice."

Chapter 33

THE FINAL BATTLE

Where, after all
Do universal human rights begin?
In small places, close to home — so close and
so small
That they cannot be seen on any map of the
world...
Unless these rights have meaning there,
They have little meaning anywhere.
– Eleanor Roosevelt

There were far too many battles at home to list. There was a final, physical battle between my sisters and Mother, however. It wasn't the end of punishments or verbal abuse, but the beginning of a new method of assault.

Noel was sixteen or seventeen when the last altercation took place. There never was a justifiable reason for the beatings, not that physical violence on another can ever be justified. Noel was on her way to escape our home to our aunt's ranch in Ramona. She went there frequently, mainly to visit our dad's sweet sister who had some inclination what was going on in our home.

Marilyn was a freshman in college. Both girls had adult bodies and were definitely not little girls anymore. Marilyn was in her room studying when my mother and Noel started arguing loudly in the doorway between the kitchen and dining room. Their voices rose rapidly to a giant screaming roar. I came out of my bedroom to see what was going on and stood against the opposite wall.

To my horror I arrived just in time to see Mom shove Noel from the kitchen against the dining room door, pounding her with her fists and yelling close to her face. Mom rarely used profanities, but a collection of insults and labels plastered the air. Noel wasn't fighting back but raised her arms as usual in defense, covering and protecting her face. She dodged under the blows trying to minimize the contacts. Fueled by adrenalin, Mother was putting her whole weight and body into this particular flailing-fist beating. Noel was moving along the wall trying to escape the blows while my mother was in full launch mode, punching her repeatedly.

I froze, leaned into the wall and started gasping for air, collapsed down to my knees, as if I was the one being hit. I felt powerless as I witnessed the terrible scene in front of me. Up until now, we never struck our mother back. Never! And we never called her names. We just didn't.

This particular day Mom lost all control, mercilessly hitting Noel repeatedly. She grabbed Noel's hair, twisting it in her fingers and slammed Noel's head against the wall. Suddenly, out of her room Marilyn came flying around the corner. She was coming so fast I don't think her feet touched the ground as she barreled toward our mother. Her left hand was in a tight fist as she streaked toward the two entangled bodies. Mom was so engaged in her brutality and Noel in protecting herself that neither of them saw Marilyn hurling at them like a white tornado. Marilyn's whole body gathered speed and seemingly flew through the air. She opened her hand slapping my mother hard and fast across her face. "Stop this! Stop it now!"

I'm sure Marilyn got Mom a couple more times. She hit her with years of pent up frustrations and anger unleashed. Marilyn hit our mother with such force, will and determination that Mom was stopped stock-still in her tracks. Mom had never been hit. The shock of it all caused her arms to go limp. She turned, walked through the kitchen and out the back door where she sat stunned and silent on the back stoop. Her favorite daughter, the gifted one, had just risen up against her.

Our lives radically changed that day. Mom stopped beating us completely and almost forever, she never hit us again like that. Within a little over a year, both Noel and Marilyn were married and out of the house leaving only me.

That was the last battle. Mom didn't hit me for another forty-five years. That one wasn't bad. She still pushed me now and then, but in 2000 she smacked me because I had interrupted her while she was watching her cat Waylon. I was fifty-six years old and just stared at her in silent disbelief.

Chapter 34

INTERTWINED

Think of a French braid and maybe you will understand a dysfunctional family better: Each member is woven in with the next and the next, until all are wound together twisting and turning. Sometimes you can see the strands on the top, while others are hidden beneath another. In a family, we reflect differently and are viewed differently, depending on where we are in relationship to the braid. Who we are next to at one point is not who we will be close to later. The difference in my family was that two major hanks of hair escaped the braid leaving just one, and that was Marilyn.

When our own children were small, Noel and I, around the same time, moved from southern California and out from the influence and pressure of the family. Those literal, physical moves of bag, baggage, kids and dogs, afforded us the opportunity to learn and grow without being twisted into the main family's unhealthy dynamics. Moving away was our saving grace, although we didn't see it clearly as such for forty years. We fell out from under the weight of the constant criticism, demeaning comments and twisted, sociopathic behavior. I'm not saying it still didn't affect us, it did, but it affected us so much less that we were able to grow. The freedom of being away let us choose our own paths and move out of the "forest" taking our children with us. Outside the forest we could start to count the trees.

Noel, much like the character of Will in *Good Will Hunting*, became a person with tenacity. She found her own worth and developed a deep understanding of how our family functioned — or didn't. She wasn't tactful though, a trait that could be viewed as a two-edged sword. In Noel's quest for truth and honesty she could be abrasive in her comments, not only calling a spade a spade, but she would point out that it was a rusty, worn and an inferior chipped spade. In short, Noel was and continues to be the original "tell it like it is" woman. This without a doubt offended many, especially those who really didn't want to know the truth. Those members of the family who wished to stay in Fantasyland dancing with Tinker Bell forever were put off by Noel, including some of her own children.

What was tragic for Noel was that she always told the truth no matter how unpleasant. She didn't lie to her children about their father's infidelity, or her mother's; she laid all the ugliness out on the table for everyone to see. Ugly can take up a lot of space. So she was shunned from many gatherings after her children left home.

I, for one, appreciated her honesty. I wouldn't have chosen the same venues she did for making some of her statements, however, I appreciated her straightforward approach. I admired her strength to be able to do it. When Noel told her kids something they didn't want to hear or accept, they would call me for confirmation of the story. If they didn't like the way the message was delivered or the package was wrapped, I would then have to confirm what she told them was true.

I, too, had a great deal to learn about living and raising children with the goal of creating some reasonable form of normality. I'm still working on that project and probably will be until my dying day. Attempting to be a good little wife, I majored in home economics after nursing didn't work out. My first class was child growth and development. I found that libraries could help me with books, programs and peers to talk to. I also learned by observation.

In my second year of college, I had a bit of a meltdown and was referred to free psychiatric counseling. Naively, I still didn't see any problems until I was encouraged to join a group therapy project where I started seeing my life and choices more clearly. The biggest help of all was to learn I wasn't alone and had not suffered the worst treatment. I learned that what I thought was "normal" wasn't even close. For two years, like a small seedling growing, I managed to create a nurturing environment for myself, barely speaking to my mother and communicating mainly with my dad. I busied myself with college and managed to stay away from their home the larger part of that time without hurting their feelings.

My main form of communication became the written word. I tried to wrap the spades in a soft "blue cloud cloth" as Langston Hughes would write in his poem the "Dream Keeper": *Away from the too-rough fingers of the world.*

Marilyn wasn't so fortunate. She stayed in southern California and became more entrenched in a lifestyle woven of lies and deceit until it was hard to tell where one strand left and another began. Her relationships with everyone were tenuous at best, with multiple marriages and boyfriends, frequently overlapping. Like my mother she had few close friends.

Noel and I moved to the public sector where both of us, forced by economic hardship, became employed outside our homes. We also became active in our respective communities with church and scouting. I taught preschool, Sunday school and was a Scout leader. Noel was involved in similar activities. These environments allowed us to observe the actions of other parents, adults and friends. It was a nurturing time for both of us and, of course, we never broke the code of silence or told anyone of our backgrounds.

No, we didn't reveal the black dark secrets and we didn't talk to each other. We were war buddies who didn't talk about the battles. It wasn't until our children left home that we actually discussed our own childhoods. We had gone to visit Marilyn in Los Angeles, taking the Greyhound together from northern California. I remember clearly after our arrival, sitting in Marilyn's little backyard oasis, the wild parakeets chirping merrily away in the eucalyptus trees surrounding her enclosure.

The conversation came up calmly and without emotion. It was

imperative that we communicate about our mother, our lives and our plans for Mom's future. She was still the powerful matriarch of the family, but aging alone and wilting daily. The time was overdue for us to sit down and talk frankly, honestly and openly without hostility. This was the one and only time that *Poor Marilyn* actually acknowledged we were battered children. Statistically that would have been correct because one-third of victims never recall or refuse to recall their abuse. So there we were, a lovely environment, the three of us facing one another about our shared childhood over a cup of tea.

As we talked it became evident that some of our nightmares were actual events, how at times the three of us had huddled in fear when someone came to the house one night when we were alone. We only knew our reactions to things not the who or why. Mom always denied leaving us alone, but we all knew that wasn't true.

That day the three of us, for the only time in our adult lives and for less than an hour, agreed on two things: One was we were battered children and the other was that we needed to do something about Mom. With that said, we also agreed to talk about it further in the future, but that didn't come to fruition.

What Noel and I did not realize that afternoon in LA, nor did we start getting clues for another few years, was that Marilyn was already sliding down into the black abyss of mental illness. We couldn't help her. We couldn't reach out and grab hold as she made her slide twisting and turning into the maelstrom of functional insanity.

Chapter 35

COLD

Noel and her daughter Cyndie were currently living together in a lovely two-story townhouse in Orange County. Both were talented women in arts and crafts and their combined decorating abilities turned their home into a Better Homes & Gardens poster for all to see. Noel was the queen of the bargain shoppers; she had to be for so many years out of necessity and later just seemed to fall into outstanding deals. People called her when they wanted to get rid of something and sometimes the thrift shops would give her a call before putting something on the floor. I still say she could decorate a boxcar if she had to and folks would be envious of her. It was always entertaining to me when people thought she was wealthy because of her furniture. Between the two women their home was a trophy.

The lot was postage size by Montana standards, but worked well between Noel's physical disability and Cyndie's busy life style. We entered through the garage into a small garden filled with bougainvillea, sweet smelling flowers, and a small gravel rock way around a statue of St. Francis of Assisi. This was, after all, March in southern California and a refreshing break in the weather. As we entered I looked about the visual potpourri. Noel chirped, "Nothing over three dollars," then she removed her back brace with a sigh of relief.

We both sank deeply into the comfortable chairs in her living room. Could all this have happened in three days? The frantic rides to airports across five states, strange hospitals, death and then a walk in the twilight zone? The whole trip so far had seemed like an out-of-body experience with a complete sense of unreality about it.

I got Noel an ashtray and a Coke from the fully stocked refrigerator. "Did you see any of this coming?"

She pulled back the tab on her Coke releasing the carbonation with a fizz. "Yes, yes I did somewhat, but not to this extent. I noticed a few weeks ago that some of the nick-nacks around Mom's house were missing. You know, she never rearranged things in twenty years so you could spot something moved or changed right away. That copper bell I gave her from India sat on the same spot for fifteen years." Noel took a sip of her soda and continued, "I didn't ask why the stuff was moved or where. I just thought Marilyn was washing them or something. You know though, I have to tell you, I told Mother not to go to that particular convalescent hospital."

Both Noel and I were smoking together, what better excuse? My mother had died and my older sister was acting like Lucrezia Borgia. I rationalized that I could stop smoking tomorrow, while lighting one up inhaling deeply. "So why did she?"

"I don't know, maybe because I told her not to. She always was strong willed, but this bordered on the ridiculous; she'd cut off her nose to spite her face. I've been in so many of these hospitals around here I'm somewhat of an expert on the quality of care. Cyndie said she even tried to stop her from being moved so early from Community Hospital. Marilyn had already arranged for the transportation."

"You know Kat, they gave Mom the wrong antibiotic for MRSA. I asked her to show me her incision and when she pulled back her hospital gown and showed me her hip, I had to stand back a bit. It stunk! The wound actually smelled like rotting flesh — old meat." Noel's nose curled up in recollection of her own description. "There were red blisters on her infection as well as pus. It was disgusting, about the size of your fingernail and all squishy." She reached for another cigarette and I realized she was actually chain smoking. "They didn't tell Mom she had an infection until Saturday. It was too late then! I couldn't get anyone to listen to me and I might as well have been screaming at a rock. Marilyn was just moving ahead like a ship in the fog with absolutely no clue as to what she was doing. She seemed deaf to anything that we told her. She'd call her nurse friend in San Francisco every time we told her something and her friend would tell her the same thing. She told me this herself. Then she would move in the opposite direction.

Noel and I were trying to unravel a chain of events without a full picture. What had happened to Marilyn that caused her radical and hostile personality changes? I related to Noel how close Marilyn and I had been for years, but a little over a year ago I had to pull back from her in self-preservation. Her phone calls to me became angry and hostile and over things that seemed so unimportant. Noel just shook her head as she listened. "Do you think it was the pain pills she was taking before her last back surgery?"

We then talked about all the people we had known to have had different reactions to medications. I told her about my friend who actually began shaking and crying uncontrollably at work, only to discover it was not a mental breakdown, but a reaction to her medications. I told her that almost everything coming out of a pharmacy scares me. All I wanted to do was take vitamins and eat blueberries the rest of my life. Noel laughed.

I told her the tone of Marilyn's phone calls had changed about eighteen months ago including those to her nieces and they had talked about it with each other. She had also written me a few letters criticizing things I had said or done. I hadn't taken any of it too seriously until last summer when she left me for four days confessing that she could no longer stand to be around our mother.

We talked on and on until we noticed the sunlight was dimming and we really were coming to no conclusions about anything. We were hungry, I wanted a beer and then there were the cigarettes. I would have given it all up but Noel struggled out of her chair, re-braced herself and we drove off to the corner store.

We weren't gone thirty minutes, coming back to a flashing red message light on her phone. Someone had called and we thought perhaps it could have been Cyndie or even Marilyn. It was the funeral home, they wanted us to call right away. I wondered how they got this phone number. What now, we thought? We immediately returned the call with the number dashed rapidly on a napkin. We got a recording, their staff had gone for the day and there was only the emergency answering service. I left a message that we were returning their call, having no clue as to why they wanted to contact us. It was Marilyn who they needed to contact, and I'm sure they had all her information.

By this time Noel and I genuinely were getting concerned about Marilyn's whereabouts. She hadn't contacted anyone since leaving Brad and I early that morning in Yucaipa. I knew she had an appointment at the funeral home about nine o'clock that morning. Had she not shown up? Was that what the call was about?

Our concerned emotions for Marilyn changed from angry to sympathetic for all she had been through. It wasn't a far reach to think and verbalize that she might harm herself. We knew she had been suicidal on previous occasions in her life, and that she was feeling responsible for our mother's death. I too had fought and won over the dark prospect of self-destruction and understood the black abyss one could fall into without seeing a way out.

One time Marilyn got so depressed that Noel had to go over to her house, force her to shower, clean up and eat. She had been in such a state for days that she had totally neglected herself. Marilyn's depressed states were tragic and for a while I thought she was over them completely. At that time she was dating a psychiatrist and actually doing a little volunteer work on a suicide hotline.

Our concern for her welfare deepened and we started calling all the numbers we had to locate her. We hit paydirt on our call to Julie, but the conversation was stilted and halting as if someone else was sitting at her dining table listening. It sounded like we were on speaker phones. We expressed how concerned we were about Marilyn. No one seemed to know where she was and we didn't know if she had been in a wreck or, heaven forbid, harmed herself. I told Julie there had been a call from the funeral home and we didn't even know if Marilyn had shown up for her appointment that morning.

Julie, rather casually as if an afterthought said, "Oh, it might have to do with the fact that the funeral home needs all three signatures from you guys to cremate Grandma."

I nearly sputtered into the phone. "Three signatures? That is ludicrous! Grandma's arrangements were prepaid! They had her signature!"

That was when Julie's cover slipped exposing her deception that she was either with her Aunt Marilyn or had talked with her during the day. She started back peddling in her conversation realizing her error at an alarming yet comical speed. I thought, listening to Julie back pedal, "give them enough rope and they'll hang themselves." I momentarily enjoyed her discomfort. She claimed she didn't know that the signatures were needed for sure, exaggerating the *know* part, but then *though*t, emphasizing the word, that might be the problem.

We just thanked Julie and hung up relieved Marilyn wasn't lying on a morgue slab herself. We thought we would let the matter drop. Noel was in too much pain to care about much else.

Noel and I struggled upstairs and I made a little pallet between her bed and an oversized birdcage. I could have slept on a rock. It reminded me of the days I spent in the Sierra Nevada Mountains packing in with my horse. This floor was carpeted, though, and a bit warmer. In the Sierras I would have had a shot of whiskey to take the ache out of my bones before I rolled into my sleeping bag. Noel's huge German Shepherd saw a spare spot on the floor and laid down with his back to mine, that was my last recollection that night.

Before my plane left Ontario the next morning, I stopped in an airport shop and picked up a little 6 x 8 inch spiral notebook.

I flipped open the first page, reached in my teacher purse for the collection of pens, selected one and started scribbling furiously.

First, I jotted down sequentially the events of the previous days. I wrote down the words I used and those I received. I documented times and who was there. Writing was my way to make sense of things and I didn't want to forget a detail that I might need later.

Then, rather than dwell on all my mother's problems I made a list, not of the bad things, but all the positive things that had happened in our lives. Glaring errors always seem to wipe out the ten or fifteen really good things a person has done. It isn't the blessings humans tend to count, but the perceived sins against them. For some reason, the people I knew up to this point had always emphasized what was wrong and rarely what was right. I wanted to remember my mother for her good qualities and she had more than a few.

Chapter 36

THE GOOD THINGS

The past was like a story, in which one thing led to another, and the world was not a boundless mystery, but a finite thing that could be comprehended

...

– Ken Follett *Pillars of the Earth*

Is the cup half full or half empty? I love that question. Recently I heard someone say it is easier to walk with a half-full cup of coffee than with a full one. There are multiple ways to see every situation. My daddy told me there were three sides to every story: His side, her side and somewhere in the middle, the truth. There really are more than three sometimes and it is hard to unravel everything in one's life, especially if that life has been a quagmire of truths, lies and perceptions.

My childhood home was not always doom and gloom. There were those days when the sun broke through the clouds and lit up our world. There is a collection of wonderful, even beautiful attributes about both my parents. Mom read and taught me to read the most wonderful stories. She gave voice to different characters in such a way they would come alive and bound off the pages. If it were a scary tale she would dramatically draw out her delivery, shake a bit and use a lower voice. If the characters were animals or children she would raise her pitch with her Scottish lilt making us smile. I could listen to her for hours, curled up at her knees while she read to us in the evenings, sitting in her favorite rocking chair. She was simply gifted and enchanting as she read.

I said earlier, in her later years she read novels to the blind on a local radio station and there was one particularly funny time when she was reading Ken Follett's *Pillars of the Earth* on air. I had read the book earlier and kept telling her to read ahead, that there were laws about some things going out on the airwaves. Now, for some reason I never talked to my mother about sex, and she was not taking my advice to read ahead in the book. Finally I said, "Mom, there are explicit sexual descriptions in the book. You can't read them on the air!"

We both laughed later when she said she was having to do a little "editing" as she was reading aloud.

I believe she did try to create a sense of fun for her children, but like having friends, really didn't know how. One of her great endeavors was puppet making, an activity we all participated in for a very long time. We made puppets from scratch on our tile counters in the kitchen at home after the chores were done. The bodies were of balsa wood with hook-and-eye joints, the heads we fashioned with paper mâché giving them a variety of personalities. They took hours and hours to make, painting little details on their faces and sewing the costumes. Mom had a second hand White sewing machine and she taught us all how to use it. We'd make the outfits out of scraps from our own clothes.

Dad got involved and built us a professional puppet stage out of thick plywood that seemed to fill our bedroom. He painted the facade with designs and then hung a little red velvet curtain that we could open on a wire.

It was really fun when we invited all the neighbor kids in and would have a "show" for them. Mom's Scottish cousins told me later that had been their favorite activity with her as kids in the Highlands. Mom would write plays and they would all be the performers.

She taught us handcrafts. When I was seven she patiently taught me to embroider. We would sit on the sofa side by side in the afternoons, both with embroidery hoops and threaded needles. Step by step, stitch by stitch she taught me the running stitch, then the back stitch, and later, the satin. The blank flour-sack cloths became alive with color and designs as we worked. The gift of learning to embroider actually pulled me out of one of my own depressed episodes years later, so thank you Mom.

When a young neighbor got cancer my mother visited her every day until the young woman died and then she took in the neighbor's daughter until her father could find a housekeeper.

In high school Mom sponsored my club when no one else would. She even gave me a surprise sixteenth birthday party, including pizza. She kept trying, and since I was her third daughter, perhaps she was getting a little better at it. She and I went to plays and musicals at the Greek Theater together. We shared the same taste and expanded both our worlds when we saw the Grand Kabuki from Japan.

I wrote about the good things in my tablet. I believe now that she, too, suffered depression at times and it just wasn't diagnosed back then. There would be such long periods of time when she didn't clean and we literally had maggots in our sinks, our clothes would mold waiting to be ironed and ants marched over the laundry waiting to be washed. By the time I was eleven or twelve and my sisters a little older, we just divided up the chores and the rule was, "if you want something done, do it yourself."

As Mom got older she made me beautiful things like the crazy quilt pillow. She crocheted vests and afghans and knitted shawls for me. She asked me to give her my one and only doll to restore. She went to a great deal of trouble and expense having it restrung, a new wig put on with new shoes and then making it exquisite new clothes. I think we were both beaming when she returned it to me. Both my parents were supportive and kind about my divorce and backed me all the way. Then, as a new teacher in Montana and not being able to make ends meet, she sent me $100 every month. That little boost made all the difference in the world. Mom couldn't say she was sorry, but she showed it the best way she possibly could and for that I am grateful. We were great friends in the end.

Chapter 37

BELOW ZERO

The coldest I have been personally is nineteen degrees below zero Fahrenheit, which would be about minus twenty-five degrees Celsius. I have friends who have been out in temperatures lower than that but that was my personal best.

The first thing that happens after leaving a warm building is your nose hairs freeze instantaneously. You get the feeling that there are small boulders pressing between your septum and the outside of your nose. You don't bother blowing because you know that no paper product made will dislodge those boulders nor do you have the capacity to blow. You could pick them out, but society frowns on that and something in your quickly freezing brain tells you that picking might not rid you of that sensation. The next sensation, even if you are dressed for the part, is that your front teeth hurt. There is real pain and the only remedy is to slam your mouth shut to prevent any more frozen air coming in. Hopefully, you have a face mask of some sort and quickly understand why photos of residents in Siberia always appear to be so grim. I had a true Russian Ushanka hat my mother had brought me from one of her trips along with a face cover.

I have experienced cold, but nothing like the emotional frigidly that followed me from California. Two days passed before Marilyn was able to return to the mortuary and sign the needed autopsy permission forms. None of us knew then, except for what Julie had said, that our signatures were required. I was home in Montana before the mortuary finally located me and called. They instructed how they would fax the paper work to me which I would sign, have notarized and then fax it back. What I had to explain to them was that they had contacted rural Montana and no one around had a fax machine. At the time of my mother's death we did not have high speed Internet.

I explained to the mortuary that my husband was seriously ill. Tests were being run the next day at a hospital in Idaho and I requested they fax the forms there where I could fax them back. I didn't dare close my eyes for a minute because all I could see was my mother laying cold on a shelf somewhere while the family was playing games with each other. Marilyn could have let me know while I was still in California.

When I got home from the hospital the next day, I wrote my son Vince in Australia telling about his grandmother's passing, everyone's odd behavior and that his stepfather was gravely ill. It was a difficult letter to write. I had given him a quick call about his grandmother, but now I had to tell him about the trust and also the clause which stated if you opposed it you were out. What an amazing clause. How could that be allowable in a court of law?

That was another revealing lesson and I learned: there is a huge difference between a will and a trust. One main difference is a trust does not go through a probate court and subsequently there is no watchdog nor legal recourse for beneficiaries. The key word here is *trust,* or as it worked out in my case, the lack of. The executor of a trust can interpret the entire thing as they want and twist and turn an estate like a corkscrew. They have full power and answer to no one. A will, on the other hand, has to be followed according to the law.

I can't warn people strongly enough to seek legal help. The homemade computer manufactured will is also a "grave error," and all puns are fully intended. Whatever the cost of a legally drawn will by a reputable lawyer it is worth every penny. Mom thought she was saving us all money, but she fell into one of her often quoted proverbs of being "penny wise and pound foolish."

My headstrong mother didn't want a court involved in her business. As a result, her business was not conducted according to her wishes, far from it, even though that became the mantra Marilyn said and wrote repeatedly. "I'm honoring Mother's wishes."

Noel did seek a lawyer's advice and was told there was nothing they could do other than act as our intermediary. They did write Marilyn's attorney and request a copy of the trust. That action was a declaration of open warfare. The letters, phone calls and emails started flying down the highways, byways and cyberspace. Accusations abounded with every pot calling each kettle black. There were some facts though, one being that Marilyn was not complying with California state law by not being forthcoming with a copy of the trust.

Her lawyer wrote to say she was "grieving" and unable to make copies. Personally, I felt she was waiting for the whiteout to dry. While she was "grieving" she was living in my mother's house. While she was "grieving" she was writing bundles of mean and hateful letters to her sisters and gleaning the house like an expert. Marilyn wrote me that she didn't have enough money to pay the bills and I needed to continue paying the house payment as I had faithfully done since borrowing money from Mom years before, but I was to make these payments to her. She wrote saying she didn't want any more "discussions" and hung up the phone on absolutely every attempt at conversation.

We still had no accounting and no idea what was going on while Marilyn was "grieving." She had plenty of money as she had access to all the bank accounts that she knew of.

Chapter 38

APRIL

By the first of April it became apparent that the joke was on us and our lawyers. No copies of anything had been sent, offers of negotiation were denied and doors closed firmly on Noel and I. Marilyn, we found out later, was busy writing checks to herself and making donations to different groups that we never heard of.

April 4th was the day of Mom's memorial. I thought April Fools' Day might have been a better day. Our cousin who was a minister wanted to officiate, but Marilyn chose a man whose last name was Faux. Ironic isn't it? Faux is the French word meaning false, untrue and counterfeit. Marilyn herself did not inform me of the service but another cousin did, and a few days later Noel let me know. About a week after that I got a letter from Marilyn with instructions where I should send any eulogy I wished to be read. That I did, requesting Julie to deliver it. I sent a copy to Mr. Faux, Marilyn and Julie.

Marilyn gave Cyndie family photos and Cyndie made a beautiful collage of our mother's life including my parent's wedding photo. The old sepia-toned pictures were all cut and trimmed, glued one on top of another with little pieces of flowers and lace. It was a beautiful creation displayed at the service, however, no one told Cyndie that the pictures were originals, handed over to her to be destroyed. Three years later I found the display in Cyndie's garage and was able to salvage a few. It wasn't her fault, she didn't know, and absolutely felt terrible when I told her.

I felt the memorial was just another grandiose performance,

the charade of charades. It was a farewell to the many performances of Isobel's life. Marilyn choreographed a memoir to a pedestal of hypocrisy, and I was content not to participate in the symbolic canonization of my mother.

Several cousins wrote me later about the service and how lovely it was. Mr. Faux read an edited version of the eulogy I wrote. The cousins wasted no time, as did a few others, kindly sending me copies of my mother's memorial leaflets.

Fascinating how funerals always have so much food. Where did that tradition come from? One of my Montana neighbors said he never missed a funeral because of the "good eats." All the cousins commented on how lovely the potluck was at the house, and that friends and family had plenty to eat with everyone contributing.

Marilyn also wrote both Noel and I about the funeral including copies of the invoices for the catering service, flowers and a variety of musicians including a bagpiper. She had paid and tipped everyone out of Mom's account, however, there were no receipts for that. She printed beautiful memorial cards and inserted business cards for one of the nieces. Her party cost approximately $1,500 which "was a deal" as she explained in her letter. I couldn't help wondering why there were costs that included tiki torches, deodorant, and platters. This was a potluck. The people brought the food and there were plenty of platters at my mother's house. No one recalled seeing tiki torches anywhere.

Once the service was over it was my greatest hope that the family could put down their swords and heal. We had an estate to deal with and slowly I was coming to the realization it was much larger than I had imagined. That is when I learned that a "tax appraisal" is quite different from a "market appraisal." Mom's large home sat on five acres of prime property in San Bernardino County.

No one in the family wanted the house or land which saddened me, but if it was to sell then it was logical that Julie, now a real estate broker, should sell it. Less than six days after that suggestion I received a terse email from her saying everything would now be forwarded to Marilyn. The warning lights started flashing again.

Marilyn's poison pen letters continued with the hardest-hitting aimed for specific holidays, Mother's Day and birthdays. She had taken up semi-permanent residency in the home and hadn't put it on the market. I didn't have a problem with that at first, but eventually I did. When I said that Noel and I were picking up the bills I didn't actually mean we were paying them. Marilyn was paying everything out of our mother's savings accounts and sent us what appeared to be excellent accountings; we were to split the left-overs three-ways. Theoretically, we paid one-third each for everything.

While Marilyn was "grieving" we paid her attorney, we paid her utilities and her gasoline. We paid her groceries and we paid for the postage and paper to mail us insulting letters. We were buried in little receipts and copies of receipts and bills. We paid for the packaging that started to come and we paid for poor Waylon.

Waylon Jennings, the cat mother loved and Marilyn hated, wasn't long for this world after Mom died. Marilyn told the family that a nice lady was "walking down the road and needed a barn cat," so she gave Waylon to her. The truth was Waylon was stuffed into a cardboard cat-carrier and so terrified that he apparently clawed and tore his way through before she could get him to the car. There was a receipt for the next plastic carrier that Marilyn put Waylon in to take him the vets. I figured out the scene from the receipts and the vet bills which Marilyn had included in her accountings. She had told me the cat was boarded for a day — but the bill clearly stated — euthanized.

Amazing how Marilyn relayed the story to family even describing the barn where Waylon was, along with the other cats residing there. I should have, could have, taken him back to Montana with me. Had I known this would be his fate, I would have. Sometimes I think Marilyn would have been quite happy to euthanize both Noel and I, given the opportunity.

Chapter 39

MAY

May is a glorious month in Montana. The snow has melted, the hills are splattered with color and the green is so fresh it appears edible. May gives us hope and a feeling of euphoria; we feel invincible having once again survived a Montana winter. Because it was May and the lilacs were blooming, I could stand the onslaught of vicious letters. One thing about a letter, it is a one-sided conversation, a monologue with no back and forth. Unless you choose to answer. My husband advised me wisely not to answer her and I didn't.

Instead, we developed a humor of our own. It was a bit of a walk from the mailbox by the road to the house and as we entered we would yell, "incoming," as if we were in a foxhole being shelled.

Marilyn sent so many bills and accounts that she would bind them in blue folders, with purple dividers and Celtic design stamps on the pages. Inside I found the deep, conniving, and dark work of a Machiavelli. I was accused of everything imaginable and unimaginable. I had to be the most self-centered, mean, belly crawling individual that ever inched her way across earth.

Boxes with Mom's stuff began arriving and we added to our "incoming" joke the new slogan, "get the garbage bags." Some boxes I actually put on rubber gloves to go through. Marilyn literally mailed the accumulation of everything no one would want from someone's home. She dumped entire bathroom drawers and shipped the contents, complete with nail fragments, rusted bobbie pins, curly gray hairs and old rubber bands. More than half of the boxes shipped went to the dump. There were half used, dried tubes of toothpaste, Bayer aspirin bottles partially opened and a collection of old thermometers still containing mercury. I kept the old blue package of Red Cross bandages thinking they might be of interest to the local museum. She even mailed Dad's WW II compact suction snakebite kit. It was unused, the antiseptic long evaporated. Even the best of the hoarders wouldn't have wanted what was mailed to me, but Marilyn's records showed multiple boxes shipped, one or two every few days and we couldn't deny that we received things from our mother's estate.

Then came the pink, twin-size, flannel sheets. I couldn't figure that one out because my mother didn't use flannel and pink was definitely not her color. They weren't hers and Marilyn was well aware that I didn't own twin beds.Thank goodness we were spared the foodstuff leftovers, but not the old throw-away items from the kitchen like the faded, fake, plastic fruit. That one made us laugh and laugh as I put them on my head and danced like Carmen Miranda before tossing them in the trash.

Between the boxes of trivial garbage came the crafted missiles to inflict pain. Some were legal things, but mostly bills and accusations. It also became our habit to crack a beer before opening a box or letter.

In May I realized that Marilyn's promise to me to be fair to Noel and give her due share was false. The resounding sound of "No!" heard throughout my mother's illness and ensuing death now were projected to sister Noel. She was in need of medical care and Marilyn wouldn't help financially so Cyndie and I took up the bills and paid them.

May was when I fully realized that Marilyn's mantra of "Mother's wishes" was a piece of shit. I think I figured that out while I was planting my garden. If I heard, "I'm honoring Mother's wishes" one more time I might just throw up. And where was my granddaughter's money? I was clearly made executrix of it, but the funds were never given to me.

May was when Marilyn sent Brad a four-page, single-spaced letter telling him that his grandmother made a "mistake" promising him the '67 Dodge and that she didn't know the value of it. This was untrue. Brad and I, along with a dozen or more men sticking their heads through the window had told her the value of the car. But, as Marilyn wrote in her letter to Brad, he could "buy" the car. She actually sold the car to none other than Brian Carper, the man who took Mom on her last ride to the hospital, the man who had parked the car in the garage, and told us it was worth more than appraised. Marilyn, we were told, gave him a great deal.

May was when I got nasty cards from a niece saying how disrespectful I was to her grandmother and "cruel" to her Aunt Marilyn for taking so much from her and leaving her to do all the work. She wanted me to drop the lawsuit against *Poor Marilyn*, a lawsuit that didn't exist and of which there were no grounds. Her letter was one-sided with no defense and no questioning. She could have called or inquired, but by then she had joined the other side believing everything she was told and questioning nothing.

I didn't answer any of the letters and I didn't tell them that, in addition to everything else, Marilyn received all of the life insurance.

May was when I fully realized that honoring Mother's wishes was a poor excuse for manipulating and stealing from the family. May was the month my heart broke. I had not only lost my mother, but a sister, two nieces and a nephew. Everyone was gone. All resemblance to a family that was loved and supportive was gone, up in smoke and a pack of lies.

Chapter 40

SUMMERTIME

Doesn't everyone love the summer? School is out, teachers get a rest and the kids go swimming. Up here the boats are cleaned out, lawnmowers started up and the snow blowers put away. The first of June I pick fresh asparagus, the snow peas wind up the trellis and begin to produce. Summer is great in Montana where we all relish and drink it in.

June somehow found Marilyn refreshed down there in southern California still parked in my parent's home. She must have gone to the dollar store or someplace similar and bought dozens of little red velvet bags about one inch by two inches. In those she individually packed and mailed me Mother's junk trinkets. Hand painted ceramic name tags, a trove of silly things that I threw out, and in one, my mother's wedding rings.

In June, Marilyn wrote she couldn't find Betsy, my father's .38 Special police revolver I had requested. Her attorney wrote me that my granddaughter Fiona's money was in good hands, but that her parents needed to petition the court to have it put in her existing closed account in California. This was an entire falsehood. The attorney, who I suspected Marilyn was involved with, was now an active player in the deception. We didn't need to petition the court, the funds could simply be deposited. There was never an acknowledgement that I was her executrix.

There was some humor, but the kind that hit the pocket book. Marilyn had the most illogical fencing installed on the Yucaipa property explaining it could be marketed as "horse property" and thus increasing its value. That joke cost me several thousand dollars. Apparently, the girl never fenced a thing. When you fence an animal in you put up a fence all the way around, it is the same for a kid, dog or horse. Marilyn had a five-foot, chain-link fence installed on the back of my parent's property from point A to point B, a straight line, enclosing nothing and connecting to nothing! Furthermore she failed to cross the long disputed easement the other neighbor was using. What could have been a $10 job up here in the mountains cost over $3,000 in San Bernardino.

In June, Vince in Australia with a new family, received a four-page, single-spaced letter from Marilyn explaining why he was cut out of the trust. It started with his crime at the age of eighteen of not buying her a Navy peacoat and ended up by his failure to send baby pictures of his daughter. Marilyn told him his grandparents would have been so ashamed of him. Nothing of course was further from the truth, but it hurt nonetheless, and shredded any ties that Vince may have felt for his family here in the states. It affected his own self-esteem, and laid guilt for a few immature decisions as a teenager. She clearly had forgotten her own youth or what it was to have some emotions.

Vince withdrew into his shell taking his battered feelings with him. Her sword-strikes against him were fatal. There were no discussions, no phone calls, no defense, just prosecuting attorney, judge and executioner all rolled into one.

I kept getting letters from Marilyn also asking when I was coming down to get the tables. When I attempted to call and make arrangements with her she would hang up the phone, and when I wrote her with potential dates she would answer that she couldn't then because she was involved with her granddaughter. No – I can't do that. No – I won't be available. No – I'm not feeling well. No. No. No. All in writing.

In June I purchased a large plastic bin and started putting all her letters in it. I shoved it under my bed and referred to it as the "tub of lies." It filled up quickly.

Chapter 41

AUGUST

Toward the end of August I received a letter from Marilyn, in which I was given the "privilege" at last of receiving two dates to return to California and meet with her. She wrote that I could come to the house and retrieve the two small tables I wanted and that she would be available only on the given days. Neither day was on a weekend, and I was starting school, attending meetings and putting my classroom together for a new flock of students. In addition, my husband's health was declining slowly like sand slipping through an hourglass and Marilyn knew this.

Those two major factors afforded me the legitimate excuse not to go. They were impossible dates contrived to be the least convenient or practical. I responded that I would try and get someone to go to the house on her dates and do the packing for me. The same day I got her letter, I also received one from her attorney Mr. Sanders. In his letter he accused me of bullying Marilyn. I considered the possibility then that it was Marilyn who was typing letters on Mr. Sanders' stationary. This didn't seem like an accusation a real attorney would make, and besides, my contact with Marilyn was so limited.

After spending countless hours calling movers and shipping firms, I managed to find a wonderful individual in Yucaipa who agreed to go to my mother's house on the prescribed date and time and pack the items for me. Not only would he do that, he also promised to ship them to Montana. For under $300 I was able to get all the little items my father promised his grandsons, in addition to the two small tables. I avoided the wrath and tirades of another ugly face-to-face, heart-pounding scene with Marilyn. I saved airfare as well as time and considered it an exceptionally good deal and smiled at the coup.

Chapter 42

FALL

The larch needles turned golden and the maple tree out front was bright red. The fall winds came early as storms crawled across the graying sky dumping a mosaic of colored leaves onto the sodden ground. The night air got chilly and we started our home-fire burning routine again.

The poison pen letters continued to arrive with occasional surprise boxes containing bizarre items, routinely now heading for the trash. My father's Navajo baskets did arrive along with three old woolen blankets Marilyn said she found in the garage and "I was in luck." She didn't know how lucky I was. Had she watched Antiques Road Show I would never have gotten them. She returned to me every gift I had ever given Mom from the time I was seven and included the prank gifts I also had given to Dad. Worn card decks and battered games were mailed up to me as the silly list went on and on endlessly.

Marilyn, who had one time admitted losing $25,000 of her brother-in-law's estate, was now captain of one valued over a million dollars. Noel and I were basically clueless as to the real financial worth of our mother and still are. Some of that information came out more than a year later. We were like mushrooms in the dark, not knowing the bills being accrued nor what in the end we would pay, including Marilyn's lawyer. We supported Marilyn in style for over six months.

By fall Marilyn had gleaned the house of the major large items.

Her favored niece got Mother's silverware and silver chaffing dishes and she walked away with arms piled high. She received the throne chair, which was a gift from the Hancock family that was supposed to go to Vince.

Noel and I finally received a copy of the trust. It appeared to be an amateur, counterfeit of the original. The first part had been typed out on Mom's old Remington, but the list of gifts was in my mother's European style of handwriting, but was not our mother's. There were major handwriting differences in the copies we received and any clerical worker could spot the changes in ink, and the larger cursive was more spread out than Mom's. The handwriting on the additions was not the normal writing style of an aging individual making changes. We could also see that the new writing was done with a heavier hand and a different pen. In short, we were provided copies of an obviously forged document. It didn't take a handwriting specialist to see these discrepancies. What confirmed the forgery was the new handwriting giving Slither my great grandfather's powder horn and my father's spurs.

But don't forget the "guillotine clause." Contest anything, oppose anything and you are out completely. Noel and I were both silenced with our legal hands tied behind our backs. Marilyn, who was out of control, was in complete control of everything, bank accounts, homes and the distribution of wealth. There was no help for the rest of us.

I started requesting records to verify everything I had been told. Sixteen months after Mom's death I finally received the hospital forms for that black Thursday when she was last admitted. I read it slowly. It said that she had diarrhea for ten days and was generally weak. That conflicted with what Marilyn had said earlier, that Mom had been so constipated her stool had to be dug out. It went on to say that she had a possible clot and then listed allergies to medications I had never heard of. Her temperature on the form was unreadable, but it went on to say she felt fuzzy in the head and that her daughter said her memory was "different." I kept reading that she was pale and also not urinating. Not peeing! I thought, for God's sake how long had she not been peeing? The form was difficult to read and I followed with my fingers each hastily written section. On the lower left of the admittance form was a section titled Suspected Abuse. That section was signed and noted that the PD (Police Department) had been notified. Both were circled yes.

I double checked and looked again and again. Was that correct? How can I explain the emotion that came over me? I was shredded and numb from over a year of stress. I thought I had become anesthetized to the lies and non-stop harassment. I fell back on what I knew best, my criminal law experience. I never thought I would have to shift into this gear with my own family. I picked up the phone and with a determined jaw called the office of the San Bernardino District Attorney.

The first person I spoke to was courteous and kind, "How old was your mother?"

"Eighty-seven," I replied

"And when did you get this form?"

"It was sixteen months ago or so that it happened. I just got the form."

"Hold on, please."

The seconds, minutes and hours ticked by. It was the usual bureaucratic thing. The copies of the hospital admittance form had to be sent with a cover letter and an investigation launched. I was given the name of an overburdened, but nice man in Adult Protective Services. I also was given the name of a compassionate woman who was an ombudsman.

Ombudsman? What is that? It was explained that an ombudsman is a government person who would act as a mediator regarding my mother's case. They would assist me, and if she had been living, they would have assisted her through the bureaucratic maze to get some help. Help for Mom was way too late, but perhaps I could get her justice. Even after a year, multiple calls and four written letters, I had not received a copy of her autopsy.

In October, a year and a half after my mother's death, I was still emailing, calling and writing San Bernardino's legal offices. Now I had other worries. Marilyn wasn't giving Noel any money, just dribbling out a pittance now and then. It was the ultimate control, and continued abuse from the grave as far as I was concerned. Noel may have had physical handicaps, but her mental faculties were fine, in fact they were acute. She didn't need this harassment. Marilyn bought, with Noel's money, a home in the remote area of northern California. It actually was further away from medical help or any excuse of a town than I was in Montana, and five hundred miles from Los Angeles. Marilyn refused Noel any money on a regular basis, but doled it out in an almost whimsical manner through a bank thirty-five miles from Noel's new house in the fields.

Noel did move into the sight unseen home in need of repairs. Cyndie and I were both trying to help her in spite of the distance factor. Noel's monthly income was meager and there were times her groceries were too. Now the way the trust was written, "if" anything happened to Noel, if she died out there, the rest of her inheritance would be split between Marilyn and me. Poor Noel could have laid on the floor of her house for weeks and no one would have known and perhaps that was the plan.

Nothing was going to surprise or shock me from now on. Again and again I wrote and called San Bernardino County with no response. Then I started contacting Shasta County to protect Noel and get her some assistance. There was no response from either county.

Time passed slowly and the months of frustration, exhaustion and bewilderment seemed to collide all at once. Tears started streaming down my face just as my husband came into the room. Gently, he put his arm around my shoulder. "Let it go, Kat. They aren't going to do anything. They just look at her as one less old person to deal with."

"She could have lived." I started to sob and was enveloped into his blue denim cowboy shirt. He was a great comfort and after all, nothing more could be done.

My niece Cyndie said there wasn't anything anyone would do about my mother's death. She said in the medical field it would be considered an "allowable death." Law enforcement was overwhelmed and wouldn't investigate a cold case of an eighty-seven year old's death. It seemed to me that her earthly departure had been accelerated.

My husband, a Navy Corpsman for thirteen years, reiterated that nothing would be done about her death. She was too old. I know this is difficult to accept, especially in the 21st century in the United States but it remains sadly true. Approximately 1 in 10 Americans aged 60+ have experienced some form of elder abuse. Some estimates range as high as 5 million elders abused each year. One study estimated that only 1 in 14 cases of abuse are reported to authorities.

It took almost two years to close the estate. Everything was convoluted in the greatest way possible. ReMax wanted to show the house and they had a potential buyer, but had such run-ins with Marilyn, that they contacted me in Montana. Could they possibly deal with me, was their question. I was flattered but had to inform them that it was a trust and only Marilyn could authorize anything. The house was finally sold by, or possibly to, Brian Carper's wife, the realtor. I never really knew. She was the one to whom I gave my Amish painting

Dad's gun was never found and Marilyn's attorney finally wrote that a police report had been made regarding its theft. When I contacted the Yucaipa police department, they had no record of such a report nor of my sister.

Noel's missing silver dollar collection was "found" and would be returned to her, but not without Marilyn twice writing me asking if I wanted it. Why would I want it? It was Noel's. It also wasn't the original collection, which were real silver; newer coins had been substituted that had little or no value.

Marilyn was now referring to her attorney as "Tim," and Tim wrote me saying the Pre-Columbian artifacts had indeed been donated to the Los Angeles Museum of History. The Museum was very courteous in their reply to my letter and even contacted other facilities, however, they never received the artifacts.

It appeared Marilyn had been lying to us for a long time. UCLA had no record of her graduating and actually she barely attended. She had been an employee there, but got involved with a professor and was terminated. Golly, I thought, I had bragged about her for years as having graduated with a 4.0 grade average. How embarrassing. I hope I don't have to go back and explain that to anyone.

Chapter 43

BIRTHDAY GREETINGS

At the end of February, Marilyn sent me what I now refer to as the nineteen-page *I Hate You Letter*. I am sure she intended that it arrive on my birthday. Marilyn didn't just write me another offensive letter. This one she obviously had labored over for weeks and possibly months. It was a masterpiece of charges, blame and denunciations. I was accused of being a thief and a criminal along with other sins. The letter arrived in a 12 x 18 envelope curled up like a serpent in my rural mailbox.

I thought Marilyn had already exhausted all the insults she could find in an entire Thesaurus. This letter Marilyn actually had bound as a manuscript in a dark blue embossed folder with a purple preface sheet. She had stamped intricate pseudo-Celtic designs on the face sheet, as if it was a royal proclamation from the Queen. How quaint, she actually chose different designs for each section of her letter.

The booklet began with my name, minus the traditional salutation. It began with the obvious: *"This is a long letter, but reading it won't require a fraction of the time you've spent talking and writing about me in the past couple of years."* Oh good grief, my head began to spin. I got up and poured myself a shot of whiskey. The letter was just more paranoia and a creation of fiction, however, it was believed by the author. How would she know I talked to anyone? No one was speaking to anyone else with the exception of Noel and no one was speaking to her either. And writing? That part was true. I did write her at first and then occasionally wrote to her lawyer, always keeping things on a business level.

Marilyn's letter to me continued with magnificent denials of everything she had done. She hadn't cheated, lied or ignored me, then went on to state how aggressive I was, her mind mirroring her own reflective actions. What kind of disease was I dealing with? She listed all the things I had done wrong since the age of three, but that she had loved me my whole life. Now I could have laughed, but there was a serious tone to this. Did Queen Elizabeth tell Mary Queen of Scots she loved her before having her head removed? I think not.

It was clear that Marilyn had been harboring all kinds of emotions no one was fully aware of until our mother's death. Her sense of reality was so totally eschewed. Her letter was difficult to read and my hands began to shake. She accused me of *"unleashing an evil force against her."* Marilyn was clearly stumbling around, lost in her own darkened mind. It must be hell in there, walls of mirrors projecting back your own actions. *"You dismissed all my efforts to be a good sister just at a time I could have used your help. Your behavior appears most perfidious."*

I had to look up the word *perfidious* in the dictionary. It means deliberately treacherous.

The poor girl flipped facts and actions so craftily. She went on to write that she hadn't abandoned Brad and I in Yucaipa, but rather fled to *"loving arms"* because we were so cold, materialistic and aggressive. Well, she fled with at least $14,000 cash stuffed in her handbag. She then went on that it was a *"supposed roll of hundred dollar bills"* and she was *"protecting the trust."*

In her demented thought process, Marilyn had raised the bar of deception and deceit to an art form. It was complete and hardly refutable unless someone sat down and actually believed the other party. I've heard it said that sociopaths so believe themselves that they can actually pass a lie detector test. The playing field was switched and no one noticed the new position. Marilyn had become the Queen of Hearts in Alice and Wonderland. Off with their heads!

My husband stood up quietly, got a beer, lit a cigarette and read my face. "This one must be a doozy," one of our favorite lines from a Kurt Vonnegut story.

"Yes, this one is a doozy," I said refilling my glass. How many pages does it take to shred someone to pieces and tear their known world apart? One black dot on a piece of white cloth? One page with three words that just say, "I hate you?" This letter went on like the never-ending story, single-spaced. It was a rap sheet belonging to someone else, the fictionalized phantom evil sister, divided into three parts.

Part II said, "Please try to consider the impact on your soul." Wow, written by one claiming openly to be an atheist.

At the end of her booklet she included a letter, also sent to Noel. Actually, Noel never received it and that was OK with both of us. She might have felt left out because Noel's was only four pages long. I did call Noel right away and apologized for my behavior sixty years ago. I was sorry I was scared of the dark and woke her to turn the light on so I could go to the bathroom. The two of us started to laugh until tears were running down both our faces. I thanked her for the comedy relief and we began to see the whole situation with some humor.

The husband's advice was good. I hadn't written Marilyn or spoken with her in over a year. When it became obvious her mind was derailing, he suggested pulling back and that was the wise thing to do. She wanted a fight but I was not striking back, fighting takes a minimum of two.

At this point I still had not told my husband the gory details of our lives. The code of silence was still incredibly strong and often strange to understand for both the insiders and those viewing us. It is my observation that many survivors also tend to be enablers. We just want everyone to be happy and to be accepted; we go to great extremes to fit into normal situations.

Two years after my August visit with my mother, the August

Marilyn couldn't stand being with her for a day, she took her little group of followers to Scotland for a vacation. She not only took her husband, son and my nieces but also their children. Nice. I hope they enjoyed themselves on the trip their mother and I paid for. It must have been quite the little tour group. My cousins in Scotland weren't all that comfortable with them and wrote me later. They had met them at a park and decided then not to have them to their homes. They were old and got away with it nicely, but they were totally aware of what they were doing.

When Marilyn returned to California, they chartered another plane with detailed explanation of where Father's remains had been dropped. They managed to get Mother's ashes distributed approximately fifty miles south of the target zone. Julie wrote me how beautiful it was that her grandparents were now together. I didn't respond. I reasoned it best to leave her with that lovely illusion. I knew those Sierra Mountains well.

Chapter 44

THE LAST BOX

The last box arrived two years later on my birthday. I honestly hadn't expected any more. The house had been sold, material goods distributed and the radioactive clouds seemed to be settling down. The only one of Noel's children I heard from was Cyndie. I was a rascal and sent Marilyn a postcard during the winter that had two lines, not nineteen pages. I'm sorry now I did it, but I did. I used a dark black sharpie and wrote LIAR! across the front and then below, "I'll never speak to you again." I was hoping her postman, neighbors and husband would all see it before it was delivered to her hands. I had to let some feelings out.

The last box was delivered up my dirt road one late afternoon by UPS. I brought it inside, set it on the kitchen counter and got out one of the steak knives to cut through the tape.

As I folded back the lid, the contents were immediately recognizable from the photos my cousin had sent me of Mom's memorial. Inside the square box, without any of Marilyn's usual packing material, sat the blue urn that had held my mother's ashes, amazingly, unbroken.

Instantly, repulsed at the idea that my mother's remains had actually been in this urn, I recoiled in horror and gasped. What more could this vicious woman do to me? I felt the color drain completely from my face and I wanted to drop to the floor. To compound and further infect the wounds she continued to open, Marilyn had placed alongside the urn Mom's treasured, antique vanity set, also without any packing material. The tortoise-shell back of the hand mirror had cracked against the urn. I can only think her intention was that I would open a box of broken chards much like our broken family, smeared with the leftover ashes of my mother's body. What a birthday gift!

The mirror was mercifully intact but the frame was tarnished and dented. I stood shaking my head back and forth. By now curiosity had brought my husband shuffling into the kitchen. His health had continued to decline and his chest was so thin he looked like a shirt hung on a hanger. He looked at me, peered at the urn and simply picked it up and without a word, took it out to his old brown truck. He left the vanity on the counter.

Coming back in the house he made a bee line for the refrigerator and a beer then lit another cigarette. Exhaling slowly he said, "Well, she left some of your mother's ashes for you." Then with his bizarre humor he started to laugh, "I guess that's the end of your book babe — not much left is there?" He quickly got kind again when he saw the look on my face and asked if I wanted him to take it to the dump with the tons of other crap from Mom's house.

No! I couldn't take my mother's handful of remains to the dump. That would never do. I couldn't have the urn in the house and I certainly couldn't see it bouncing around the old truck. The urn was beautiful and someone, not knowing the history might really love it. I sent him back out with his mission to drive to Idaho and the Goodwill! Yes, — with the smidgen of ashes left inside. I couldn't touch them and I'm sure everyone would understand.

The vanity set I carried gently upstairs to the loft and packed it away in another box Dad had given Mom when they were young, in love and full of dreams. All of it was shoved into the back of my linen cupboards.

The next day I woke and unexpectedly felt lifted, euphoric and buoyant. It was a beautiful breathtaking morning in Montana. As the sun slid up to welcome the day I stood facing my forest covered mountains. Spreading my arms out and reaching up as a Native American had taught me, I greeted life and nature, breathing in slowly the cool pure air of peace and love.

The words of Martin Luther King rang through my head.

Free at Last – Great God Almighty, I'm free at last.

EPILOGUE

Six years later my life was quite different from when my mother died. I lost my husband to lung cancer just after Mom's estate closed. Noel flipped her house in the field, made a profit, and now lives in a small town in Washington. Brad took up cross-country long-haul trucking and I chat with him frequently on the phone. Cyndie works with lawyers researching malpractice cases.

Six years, almost to the day after my mother's death, over $11,000 of hers was found in a Missouri bank. It was on the "found money" website. Mom had, in her infinite wisdom, sent it there two weeks before her surgery. Fiona, my granddaughter was named as beneficiary. I had to get out the old hoops and start jumping again, but this time I had a strategy. As executrix, Marilyn had to still be notified and the first thing I did was send her formal notification with a return receipt requested. I now laugh when I think about it. Her return receipt came the same day as Attorney Tim's letter. I was standing out on my road, picking up the mail and burst out laughing, both were sitting in the black mailbox side by side. I could see her in my mind, driving madly across LA, knees under the steering wheel while putting on her lipstick in the rear view mirror, just to meet Tim.

I was many steps ahead of her this time for I had already spoken several times with the trust manager in Missouri and told him our story. Following his advice I sent out these notifications. When Marilyn contacted him he told her that Fiona had a closed account in California, and that they would make the direct deposit there, by-passing her.

It was refreshing to deal with honest and compassionate people whose intent was to do the right thing.

Tim's letter also brought a chuckle. It was the same old thing, slightly admonishing me that I should have "had Fiona's parents' petition the California Superior Court where Fiona had resided." Silly man, he had been informed multiple times that she lived in Australia.

I can smile and wonder where else my foxy mother hid money and just who was she hiding it from?

Way too frequently we pick up a paper or watch a news clip of a new crime. The criminal is arrested and suddenly family and neighbors are all saying, "There was never any indication…" or, "I find it unbelievable. I've known them twenty years and they were so nice." And the usual, "Oh my gosh! It is such a shock." These are the comments when the sociopath next door is discovered. These are the characteristics of a "good sociopath." They are charmers, "such a nice person," that each of us at some time may have fallen into their web.

Our story isn't unique, but it is one that needs to be told for a variety of reasons, not for a pity party, for goodness sake. Get over it! My objective is to educate the reader about several things. One is mental illness. I will never know exactly when my sister Marilyn went from a compassionate little girl to a bitter and basically crazy old woman. Atrophy is a slow process. Our abusive childhood undoubtedly played a huge role, however, there were two survivors. That too is fascinating on several levels. It is estimated that one-third of abused individuals will deny the abuse even when there is irrefutable evidence. That makes prosecution of perpetrators and healing of victims extremely difficult. How can you heal when you are denying the wounds?

It is difficult to estimate how many survivors there are because of the code of silence and the people who go on to lead normal lives who don't end up abusers, alcoholics, or in prison. I was aware from the age of seven there was something wrong with my mother. At sixteen I started a notebook called, *"Ideas."* When I saw something about child raising or craft ideas for children I cut it out and put it in my notebook. I knew then I would become a different kind of person. It was a long and bumpy road and I'm still learning.

The stigma of battering in our society is definitely real. For those who do speak out, estimates are that 10% of battered children have what is referred to as a false or distorted memory. They are a group of silent "walking wounded." If you asked an audience of people to stand if they were battered, I can assure you a good percentage, even if they had been, would not stand. I myself would have think about it.

Today there are help groups for adult survivors, some of which are even online. I'm not going to them. I don't want someone else to call me in the night telling me tearfully about their nightmares. Writing this book I have had to lower myself into the dark abyss again and it is painful.

I truly am moving on.

My hope is through this story others will say, "Oh – I'm not alone and there is help if I want it. I have to decide. I have to make the first step."

Take care of each other. Take care of your aged. Take care of your wills. Seek professional advice if you are in a bog or down in the depths. Get someone to help you. It wasn't your fault.

It is a Simple Rule:
Love One Another

Isobel Graham's autopsy indicated her death was the result of multiple complications following hip surgery, including pulmonary thromboembolisms in both lungs. She had been diagnosed with MRSA, which severely weakened her body and immune system and she had "c-diff," which caused renal failure. The autopsy included that "some matters would be best discussed with an attorney."

The seventy-year-old collection of family photos has never been seen again despite multiple requests from lawyers, family members and friends. Only Marilyn knows their whereabouts.

www.ingramcontent.com/pod-product-compliance
Lightning Source LLC
Chambersburg PA
CBHW051646040426
42446CB00009B/1001